EDUCATIONAL

ADVANCED LEVEL

Revise A2

History

Modern British and European

Author

Michael Scaife

Contents

Specification lists   5

AS/A2 Level History courses   10

Different types of questions in A2 examinations   12

Exam technique   14

Four steps to successful revision   16

Chapter 1 The development of democracy in Britain, 1832–1992

1.1 Reform of the electoral system   17

1.2 The Reform Acts of 1832 and 1867   18

1.3 Politics and parties 1868–1918   20

1.4 Politics in the 1920s   23

1.5 Political parties and government, 1931–92   24

1.6 The influence of the trade unions and the media   26

Sample question and model answer   29

Practice examination questions   31

Chapter 2 Poor Law to Welfare State 1830–1948

2.1 From laissez faire to Welfare State   32

2.2 The Poor Law   33

2.3 Public health, housing and factory legislation   37

2.4 Education   40

Sample question and model answer   43

Practice examination questions   45

Chapter 3 Britain and Ireland 1798–1921

3.1 Irish nationalism   46

3.2 Support for the Union   49

3.3 British policies towards Ireland   51

3.4 The Irish economy   52

Sample question and model answer   54

Practice examination questions   54

Chapter 4 German nationalism 1815–1919

4.1 The origins and development of German nationalism to 1860   55

4.2 Economic nationalism   57

4.3 Bismarck   57

4.4 German nationalism and the German Empire, 1871–1919   59

Sample question and model answer   62

Practice examination questions   63

Chapter 5 Economic modernisation in Germany, c.1880 – c.1980

5.1 The German economy 1880–1914   64

5.2 The First World War and its aftermath   65

5.3 The German economy under the Nazis   66

5.4 Post-war Germany   68

Sample question and model answer   71

Practice examination questions   74

Chapter 6 Dictatorship in Russia 1855–1956

6.1 The tsarist autocracy 1855–1917   75

6.2 The Revolutions of 1917   78

6.3 The Communist dictatorship   79

6.4 The growth of opposition   81

6.5 The Russian economy   84

Sample question and model answer   86

Practice examination questions   88

Chapter 7 Autocracy and reform in Germany and Russia

7.1 Tsarist Russia and imperial Germany   89

7.2 Opposition and reform before 1914   90

7.3 The overthrow of the imperial regimes   92

7.4 The Soviet Union and Nazi Germany   93

Contents

7.5 Opposition to the Communist and Nazi dictatorships   95

Sample question and model answer   97

Practice examination questions   100

Chapter 8 Historical investigations: 19th-century Britain

8.1 Chartism   101

8.2 Gladstone and Disraeli 1846–80   105

Sample question and model answer   110

Practice examination questions   112

Chapter 9 Historical investigations: 20th-century Britain

9.1 The decline of the Liberal Party, c.1900–1929   114

9.2 Appeasement: Anglo–German relations 1918–39   118

9.3 British politics 1918–51   123

Sample question and model answer   125

Practice examination questions   127

Chapter 10 Historical investigations: Lenin and Stalin

10.1 Lenin 1903–24   129

10.2 The Soviet Union under Stalin, 1924–41   133

Sample question and model answer   136

Practice examination questions   137

Chapter 11 Historical investigations: Bismarck and Hitler

11.1 Bismarck and the unification of Germany   138

11.2 Hitler and the Nazi state 1933–39   141

11.3 Hitler and the origins of the Second World War   144

Sample question and model answer   148

Practice examination questions   150

Practice examination answers   152

Index   160

AQA History

MODULE	SPECIFICATION TOPIC	CHAPTER REFERENCE	STUDIED IN CLASS	REVISED	PRACTICE QUESTIONS
Module 4 (M4) European/ World History	Germany, Russia and the Soviet Union in the 19th and 20th centuries	7.1–7.5, 10.2, 11.2			
	Russia and the USSR, 1881–1985	6.5, 10.2			
	Germany, c1880–c1980	5.1–5.4, 11.2			
Module 5 (M5) British History	Britain 1841–1914 See also AS chap 1.4 and chap 4	8.1, 8.2			
	Britain 1918–1951	9.1–9.3			
Module 6 (M6W) Written paper option	Hitler and the origins of the Second World War, 1933–41	11.3			
	Great Britain and appeasement in the 1930s	9.2			

Examination analysis

The specification comprises three unit tests. For each of Units 4 and 5 candidates choose one alternative. For Unit 6 candidates either present a Personal Study or take a written paper on one of the set topics.

Unit 4	Candidates answer two questions on their chosen alternative: one compulsory source–based question one essay question from a choice of three	1 hr 30 min test	15%
Unit 5	Candidates answer two questions on their chosen alternative: one compulsory source–based question one essay question from a choice of six	1 hr 30 min test	15%
Unit 6	Written paper option: one compulsory three–part question.	1 hr 30 min test	20%

For the source–based questions in Module 4 up to four sources are provided, approximately 400 words in total. Three questions are set on them, testing the evaluation of evidence and understanding of change and continuity over a period of at least 100 years. In Module 5 two or three sources are provided, approximately 400 words in total. Two questions are set, focusing on historical interpretations and perspectives. In both modules sources may be either primary or secondary or a mixture of the two. In Module 6 (written option) three or four extracts, approximately 300 words in total, are provided. The extracts and the questions focus on interpretation of events or issues which have generated historical debate.

Synoptic assessment is carried out through Units 4 and 5. In Unit 4 the third sub–question of the source–based question and the essay questions are synoptic in nature. In Unit 5 the second sub–question of the source–based question and the essay questions are synoptic in nature. This means that 22% of the total marks (10% from Unit 4 and 12% from Unit 5) are allocated to synoptic assessment.

For Unit 6 (Personal Study option) you will have to submit a study of approximately 3000 words analysing a historical issue or problem. This may based on the work you have studied in Units 1, 2, 4 or 5 or on a comparable topic. You will be guided and supervised in this by your teacher.

OCR History

MODULE	SPECIFICATION TOPIC	CHAPTER REFERENCE	STUDIED IN CLASS	REVISED	PRACTICE QUESTIONS
Module 4 (M4) *Historical Investigations*	Gladstone and Disraeli 1846–80	8.2			
	Bismarck and the unification of Germany 1858–71	11.1			
	Lenin and the establishment of Bolshevik power 1903–24	10.1			
	Chamberlain and Anglo–German relations 1918–39	9.2			
Module 5 (M5) *Themes in History*	Poor Law to Welfare State 1834–1948	2.1–2.4			
	Development of democracy in Britain 1868–1992	1.1, 1.3–1.6			
	Britain and Ireland 1798–1921	3.1–3.4			
	The challenge of German nationalism 1815–1919	4.1–4.4, 5.1			
	Russian dictatorship 1855–1956	6.1–6.4			
Module 6 (M6) *Independent investigation*					

Examination analysis

The specification comprises three unit tests. For Units 4 and 5 candidates choose one of the options listed and answer one question on it.

Unit 4	Candidates answer two questions on their chosen alternative: one compulsory source-based question one essay question from a choice of two	*1 hr 30 min test*	*15%*
Unit 5	Two essay questions from a choice of three on each option	*1 hr 30 min test*	*20%*
Unit 6	offers two alternatives: Coursework option: an extended essay of about 2500 words, or Open book examination	*1 hr 30 min test*	*15%*

For the source-based questions in Unit 4 four sources are provided totalling 500–600 words. At least three of the four are extracts from the writings of modern historians. Two sub-questions are set, one testing understanding of why historians interpret the same evidence differently and one requiring an application of all the sources to an issue of historical interpretation.

Synoptic assessment is carried out through Unit 5 and carries 20% of the marks.

For Unit 6 candidates undertake an historical investigation of their own. OCR publishes in advance a list of essay questions from which candidates select one to answer in the context of an historical issue or debate of their own choice. This is then assessed either through a coursework essay or an extended essay written in an open book examination. For the coursework option candidates may devise their own question.

Edexcel History

MODULE	SPECIFICATION TOPIC	CHAPTER REFERENCE	STUDIED IN CLASS	REVISED	PRACTICE QUESTIONS
Module 4 (M4) (Examination option)	The age of Lord Liverpool, 1815–27	See AS chap. 7.1			
	France 1815–30	See AS chap. 7.1			
	The age of Peel, 1832–46	See AS chap. 1.4			
	Securing the state: Bismarck and Germany, 1871–90	See AS chap. 10.3			
	Fascist Italy, 1924–39	See AS chap. 11			
	From peace to appeasement: British foreign policy between the wars	9.2			
	Expansion and aggression: German foreign policy, 1933–39	11.3			
Module 5 (M5) (Examination option)	Representation and Democracy in Britain, 1830–1931	1.1–1.4, 1.6			
	The state and the poor in Britain, c.1830–1939	2.1, 2.2			
Module 6 (M6)	Radicalism and the British State: the Chartist experience, 1838–50	8.1			
	Decline of the Liberal Party, c. 1900–29	9.1			
	Hitler and the Nazi State: power and control, 1933–39	11.2			
	The Soviet Union after Lenin, 1924–41	10.2			

Examination analysis

The specification comprises three unit tests. For each externally examined unit test you choose one option.

Unit 4	offers two alternatives:		
	examination option: one essay question from a choice of two	1 hr 30 min test	15%
	or individual assignment		15%
Unit 5	offers two alternatives:		
	examination option: one three-part source-based question	1 hr 15 min test	15%
	or coursework assignment		15%
Unit 6	one two-part source-based question	1 hr 45 min test	20%

For Unit 5 questions two or three sources are provided, 250–300 words in total. Sources are mainly primary but one will be secondary. Three sub-questions are set, focusing on the process of change over a period of at least 100 years.

Synoptic assessment is carried out through Unit 6. For this unit candidates will be provided with 5 or 6 sources which will be both contemporary to the period studied and secondary; the sources will total 750–800 words. The questions focus on a key area of historical debate.

For the Individual Assignment option in Unit 4 candidates investigate a topic of their own choosing. The assignment is written under supervision in 4 hours. For the coursework option in Unit 5 candidates study a historical topic covering at 100 years, focusing on the process of change. The required length is 2000–2500 words.

WJEC History

MODULE	SPECIFICATION TOPIC	CHAPTER REFERENCE	STUDIED IN CLASS	REVISED	PRACTICE QUESTIONS
Module 4 (M4) Period study	Wales and England, c.1880–1914	See AS chap 4			
	Wales and England, 1939–1980	See AS chap 6			
	Europe, 1852–1917	10.1, also AS chap 7.2			
Module 5 (M5) In-depth study	Coursework or externally set assignment				
Module 6 (M6)	Wales and England, c.1815–1914	1.1–1.3, 2.1–2.4			
	Europe, 1815–1917	6.1, 6.2			
	Europe, 1878–1980	6.1–6.4			
	Reform and protest in Wales and England, c. 1830–48	8.1, also AS chap 1.3			
	Britain and Europe, c.1929–1939	9.2			
	Nazi Germany, c.1933–45	11.2			

Examination analysis

The specification comprises three unit tests. For each unit test you choose one of the options listed above.

Unit 4	Two essay questions from a choice of three for each period.	1 hr 30 min test	15%
Unit 5	offers two alternatives: individual assignment (coursework) or externally set assignment (open book examination)	3 hr test	15%
Unit 6	Candidates answer two essay questions: one (from a choice of two) on the period study one (from a choice of two) on the in-depth study	1hr 40 min test	20%

Both options in Unit 5 require investigation of a problem or issue arising from your in-depth study. The coursework option requires you to produce an assignment of 3000–4000 words. The externally set option requires you to write, under supervised conditions, an assignment of at least 1000 words on a Board nominated problem or issue.

Synoptic assessment is carried out through Unit 6. The questions on the period study will focus on change over a period of at least 100 years. The questions on the in-depth study focus on historical interpretations; candidates will be provided with two extracts for analysis and evaluation.

NICCEA History

MODULE	SPECIFICATION TOPIC	CHAPTER REFERENCE	STUDIED IN CLASS	REVISED	PRACTICE QUESTIONS
Module 4 (M4) European History	Unification of Germany, 1848–71	4.1–4.3, 11.1			
	Causes of the Second World War, 1918–41	9.2, 11.3			
Module 5 (M5) Change over time	Nationalism and Unionism in Ireland 1800–1900	3.1, 3.2, 3.4			
Module 6 (M6) British/Irish History	Politics and Society in Victorian England 1868–1894	8.2			
	The Partition of Ireland 1900–1925	3.1			

Examination analysis

The specification comprises three unit tests. For each unit test you choose one option. In addition to the options listed above there are options in Module 5 on Liberalism and Nationalism in Europe 1814–1914 and the clash of ideologies in Europe 1900–2000.

Unit 4	External examination	1hr 30 min test	15%
Unit 5	External examination	1hr test	20%
Unit 6	External examination, including use of sources	1 hr 30 min test	15%

Synoptic assessment is carried out through Unit 5 by requiring candidates to undertake a thematic study over a period of 100 years.

AS/A2 Level History courses

AS and A2

All History A Level courses being studied from September 2000 are in two parts, with three separate modules in each part. Students first study the AS (Advanced Subsidiary) course. Some will then go on to study the second part of the A Level course, called A2. Advanced Subsidiary is assessed at the standard expected halfway through an A Level course: i.e. between GCSE and Advanced GCE. This means that the new AS and A2 courses are designed so that difficulty steadily increases:

- AS History builds from GCSE History
- A2 History builds from AS History

How will you be tested?

Assessment units

For AS History, you will be tested by three assessment units. For the full A Level in History, you will take a further three units. AS History forms 50% of the assessment weighting for the full A Level.

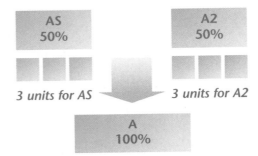

Each unit can normally be taken in either January or June. Alternatively, you can study the whole course before taking any of the unit tests. There is a lot of flexibility about when exams can be taken and the diagram below shows just some of the ways that the assessment units may be taken for AS and A Level History.

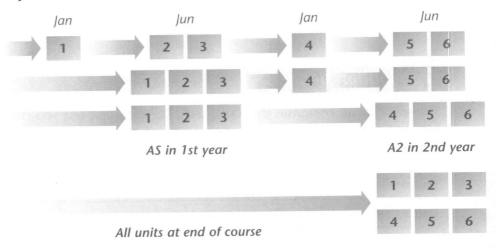

If you are disappointed with a module result, you can resit each module once. You will need to be very careful about when you take up a resit opportunity because you will have only one chance to improve your mark. The higher mark counts.

A2 and Synoptic assessment

After having studied AS History, you may wish to continue studying History to A Level. For this you will need to take three further units of History at A2. Similar assessment arrangements apply except that some units, those that draw together different parts of the course in a synoptic assessment, have to be assessed at the end of the course.

Coursework

Coursework is an option at A2 Level in all specifications except NICCEA. If your course includes coursework, follow closely the advice of your teacher and make sure you allow yourself plenty of time to complete the assignment, especially if you have to submit coursework in other subjects. OCR and WJEC offer as an alternative an open book examination. Again, it is important to allow plenty of time to carry out the preparatory investigation.

Key skills

It is important that you develop your key skills throughout your AS and A2 courses. These are important skills that you need whatever you do beyond AS and A Levels. To gain the key skills qualification, which is equivalent to an AS level, you will need to collect evidence together in a portfolio to show that you have attained Level 3 in Communication, Application of number and Information technology. You will also need to take a formal testing in each key skill. You will have many opportunities during AS and A2 History to develop your key skills in Communication and Information technology.

It is a worthwhile qualification, as it demonstrates your ability to put your ideas across to other people, collect data and use up-to-date technology in your work.

What skills will I need?

For A Level History, you will be tested by *assessment objectives*: these are the skills and abilities that you should have acquired by studying the course. The assessment objectives for A Level History are shown below.

Historical knowledge and understanding

- recall, select and deploy historical knowledge accurately, and communicate knowledge and understanding of history in a clear and effective manner

Historical explanations

- present historical explanations showing understanding of appropriate concepts and arrive at substantiated judgements

Historical interpretation

In relation to historical context:
- interpret, evaluate and use a range of source material and
- explain and evaluate interpretations of historical events and topics studied.

Assessment of your work will also take into account the quality of your written communication, including clarity of expression, structure of arguments, presentation of ideas, spelling, grammar and punctuation. This will not be awarded separate marks but will be assessed as part of the first assessment objective.

Different types of questions in A2 examinations

In A2 History examinations, different types of question are used to assess your abilities and skills. Unit tests mainly use either source–based questions or essay questions.

Source-based questions

The types of question you may encounter are:

- Explanation of references in the sources in the context of your knowledge of the issue.

  Here is an example:

  Explain what is meant by the term 'second industrial revolution' in relation to the development of the German economy, c.1880–c.1920.

  Assessment and Qualifications Alliance specimen question

- Comparison between two sources. At A2 Level questions usually focus on comparison of views and interpretations rather than factual content.

  Here are two examples:

  How far does Source C challenge Taylor's interpretation in Source B of Bismarck's aims in 1870?
  OCR specimen question

  How far do these two sources differ in their explanations of the decline in support for the Liberal Party?
  Assessment and Qualifications Alliance specimen question

- Evaluation of the reliability or usefulness of one or two of the sources.

  Use all the information available to you – the content of the source, the information given to you about it by the examiners, comparison with the other sources, your own knowledge – to decide what use a historian could make of it.

  Here are two examples:

  Study Source A. How valid is the interpretation offered by A. J. P. Taylor on Hitler's foreign policy?
  Assessment and Qualifications Alliance specimen question

  Using Sources A to D, explain why the wisdom of the policy of appeasement has caused disagreement among historians.
  OCR specimen question

- Use of sources and own knowledge to construct an account of continuity and change over time.

  Here is an example:

  Use these sources to outline how the electorate changed in the years 1832–1928.
  Edexcel specimen question

- Use of sources as evidence to answer a broader question, e.g. to construct a discussion or evaluate a judgement.

  This type of question usually requires you to use your own knowledge as well as the sources.   Make sure you refer to both: failure to do so is one of the commonest mistakes made by candidates.

  Here is an example:

  'The cult of personality and terror consolidated Stalin's absolute grip on power within Russia.' Using your own knowledge and the evidence of all five sources, explain how far you would agree with this interpretation of Soviet politics in the 1930s.
  Edexcel specimen question

Essay questions

At A2 Level two main types of essay question are set.

• **Questions focusing on causation.** These may require an analysis of the causes of an historical event or process, or may suggest a cause for discussion. In either case, you should aim to consider a range of causes and to make a judgement about their relative importance. If the question suggests a cause, make sure you give it proper consideration as well as discussing other causes which you may decide are more important.

Here are three examples, formulated in different ways but all about causation.

Why did Poland become the occasion for the outbreak of war in 1939?

OCR specimen question

How important a factor was the weakness of British defences in influencing the British government to adopt a policy of appeasement in the years 1935–38?

Edexcel specimen question

'Hitler's single aim in foreign policy was to expand in the East.' How far do you agree with this view?.

Edexcel specimen question

• **Questions requiring you to make or evaluate a judgement.** Often such questions take the form of a quotation, which you are required to discuss.

Here are some examples:

'A tragic dress–rehearsal for 1917.' Is this a valid assessment of the 1905 revolution?

WJEC specimen question

Consider the arguments for and against the claim that Stalin depended on the dictatorship already established by Lenin.

OCR specimen question

Thematic questions

All specifications include a requirement to study a theme over a period of at least 100 years. Questions focus on understanding of continuity, change, trends and turning points. You are not expected to demonstrate detailed knowledge of the whole of the period but you will need to know the main developments and turning points. It is important to ensure that you draw material for your answer from the whole of the period.

Synoptic questions

Synoptic assessment concerns your understanding of the connections between the essential characteristics of historical study. It accounts for 20% of the total marks for Advanced GCE.

Synoptic questions test your knowledge and understanding, your ability to explain and evaluate interpretations of historical events and issues and your capacity to present historical explanations and arrive at substantiated judgements. A variety of question types is used but all require you to address an issue, formulate an argument and reach a substantiated judgement. You are also required to make connections between historical perspectives relevant to the question set. For example, a question on social reform in the 19th and 20th centuries might consider both political factors (political parties responding to electoral reform) and changes in the climate of opinion (state intervention instead of laissez faire). Questions will focus either on causation or assessment of historical judgements and interpretations. It is essential to adopt an analytical approach and to consider alternative causes or interpretations.

Exam technique

A2 History builds on, and progresses from, the knowledge, understanding and skills established by AS History. Your AS History course will have developed your understanding of historical concepts, your skills in interpreting and evaluating source material and your ability to explain your knowledge and understanding of history. The A2 course develops these skills further and at the same time extends and deepens your historical knowledge.

It is important to remember that History is not a subject which can be learnt from a single text. This study guide will provide you with the essential knowledge and ideas you need to understand the topics you study but you will need to build on this by the wider reading suggested by your teacher.

What are examiners looking for?

History examiners indicate the length of answer expected by the mark allocation and the type of answer expected by key words in the questions.

See note at bottom of p.15.

The mark allocation tells you two things: how much time to devote to each part of the question or paper and the relative difficulty of the question. Questions allocated higher marks are not only to be answered at greater length but are more testing. In source-based questions, a question which asks you to use all the sources and your own knowledge to evaluate a historical judgement is more testing than one which asks you to compare two sources, and would earn more marks. But at A2 Level even questions with a lower mark tariff make intellectual demands which should not be underestimated.

Key words point you to the type of question. The most common types of question are those, which require an analysis of cause and consequence, and those, which require an assessment or judgement.

Explain, Examine, In what ways?

These instructions call for a piece of analytical writing. Be sure to focus on the issues required by the question, e.g. aims, factors, policies, results, interpretations.

Why?

This asks for an analysis of causes. Make sure you do not leave out important causes and that you consider long-term causes as well as short–term ones. A good answer will consider the relative importance of causes and how they are linked together.

Compare

If you are asked to compare two sources, look for similarities and differences. Be sure to reach a conclusion resulting from the comparison. In essay questions which call for comparison (e.g. between two statesmen, two policies, two interpretations) make sure you give equal attention to each and that you reach a balanced conclusion.

Assess, Evaluate, How far? To what extent?

These instructions require you to make a judgement. The examiners expect you to set out the main arguments on opposite sides and balance them in your conclusion. For example, you might assess the success of a statesman by explaining his successes and then his failures. Or you might evaluate an interpretation by explaining the grounds for agreeing with and then examining alternative interpretations. Most questions which begin with the word 'how' (e.g. 'how valid', 'how serious', 'how successful', 'how important') are of this type. Another way of setting this type of question is to offer you a judgement for assessment and ask why you agree or disagree. This type of question, in its various forms, is far the most common at A2 Level.

Some dos and don'ts

Dos

Do answer the question

- No credit can be given for good History that is irrelevant to the question

Do be sure to refer to source material if the question requires it

- You will lose marks if you ignore this. You will also lose marks if you answer entirely from the sources if the question asks you to use your own knowledge as well.

Do spend some time planning your answers

- This is especially important for questions requiring extended writing. It will ensure that your argument is coherent and that you avoid omissions.

Do use the mark allocation to guide how much you write

- A question allocated 20 marks out of 30 or 60 out of 90 requires a piece of extended writing.

Do pay attention to correct spelling, grammar and punctuation

- Quality of written communication is taken into account in all assessment units.

Do write legibly

- An examiner cannot give marks if the answer cannot be read.

Don'ts

Don't produce undirected narrative

- Most questions require you to use your knowledge to follow the instructions given in the key words of the question.

Don't introduce irrelevant material

- You will get no credit for it.

Note

The different Boards use marking systems which allocate between 25 and 60 marks to similar questions. In this book 30 marks have been allocated to both essay questions and source-based questions to indicate their equivalence. In the course-based questions marks have been allocated to sub-questions in the same proportions as in specimen questions produced by the boards.

Four steps to successful revision

Step 1: Understand

- Study the topic to be learned slowly. Make sure you understand the logic or important concepts.
- Mark up the text if necessary – underline, highlight and make notes.
- Re-read each paragraph slowly.

GO TO STEP 2

Step 2: Summarise

- Now make your own revision note summary:
  What is the main idea, theme or concept to be learned?
  What are the main points? How does the logic develop?
  Ask questions: Why? How? What next?
- Use bullet points, mind maps, patterned notes.
- Link ideas with mnemonics, mind maps, crazy stories.
- Note the title and date of the revision notes
  (e.g. History: Lenin, 3rd March).
- Organise your notes carefully and keep them in a file.

This is now in **short-term memory**. You will forget 80% of it if you do not go to Step 3.
GO TO STEP 3, but first take a 10 minute break.

Step 3: Memorise

- Take 25 minute learning 'bites' with 5 minute breaks
- After each 5 minute break test yourself:
  Cover the original revision note summary
  Write down the main points
  Speak out loud (record on tape)
  Tell someone else
  Repeat many times.

The material is well on its way to **long-term memory**.
You will forget 40% if you do not do step 4. **GO TO STEP 4**

Step 4: Track/Review

- Create a Revision Diary (one A4 page per day)
- Make a revision plan for the topic, e.g. 1 day later, 1 week later, 1 month later.
- Record your revision in your Revision Diary, e.g.
  History: Lenin, 3rd March 25 minutes
  History: Lenin, 5th March 15 minutes
  History: Lenin, 3rd April 15 minutes
  ... and then at monthly intervals.

Chapter 1

The development of democracy in Britain, 1832–1992

The following topics are covered in this chapter:

- *Reform of the electoral system*
- *The Reform Acts of 1832 and 1867*
- *Politics and parties, 1868–1918*
- *Politics in the 1920s*
- *Political parties and government, 1931–92*
- *The influence of the trade unions and the media*

1.1 Reform of the electoral system

After studying this section you should be able to:

- *outline the development of the electoral system since the early 19th century*

LEARNING SUMMARY

Parliamentary Reform

EDEXCEL	M5
OCR	M5 (synoptic)
WJEC	M6 (synoptic)

In the early 19th century Britain had a parliamentary system of government, but it was not democratic. In England and Wales before 1832, there were 435 000 voters out of a population of 14 million. In the counties only 40-shilling freeholders could vote. In the boroughs the franchise varied but the number of voters was very small. There were 92 county MPs and 417 borough MPs. Fifty-six boroughs had fewer than 40 voters. The electorate in Scotland, which had 45 MPs and Ireland, which had 100, was tiny. Parliamentary democracy developed through a series of changes in the electoral system.

This meant the middle classes but not the working classes.

The Great Reform Act (1832) increased the number of voters to over 700 000. In the counties £10 copyholders and £50 leaseholders were given the vote. In the boroughs the old qualifications were replaced by a uniform £10 householder qualification. Eighty-six small boroughs in England and Wales lost one or both MPs. Sixty-five seats were re-allocated to larger counties, 65 to newly created boroughs, eight to Scotland, five to Ireland.

This extended the vote to working-class men in the boroughs.

The Second Reform Act (1867) added £12 ratepayers (£14 in Scotland) to the county franchise, but the major change was in the boroughs, where the vote was given to all male householders and £10 lodgers. The electorate increased to nearly 2.5 million out of a population of 30 million. Fifty-two borough seats were abolished. Twenty-five were re-allocated to counties, 19 to existing or newly created boroughs, six to Scotland. An important feature was that Birmingham, Leeds, Liverpool and Manchester became three-member boroughs.

The Secret Ballot Act (1872) ended the system of voting in public and reduced bribery and intimidation in elections.

The Corrupt Practices Act (1883) laid down limits for election expenses and prescribed penalties for bribery and corruption in elections.

This extended the vote to working-class men in the counties.

The Reform and Redistribution Acts (1884–5) introduced a uniform franchise for counties and boroughs – male householders and £10 lodgers. The electorate was increased to 5.7 million but about 40 per cent of men were still excluded by this definition. There was a major redistribution of seats, resulting in single-member constituencies except in big cities.

The Parliament Act (1911) limited the powers of the House of Lords and reduced the maximum interval between general elections from seven years to five. In the same year payment for MPs was introduced.

The Representation of the People Act (1918) gave the vote to all men over 21

> This meant a mass electorate, including women for the first time.

and women over 30. The electorate was now over 21 million. There was a redistribution of seats to achieve equality of size between constituencies.

The Equal Franchise Act (1928) gave the vote to women over 21.

The Representation of the People Act (1948) abolished plural voting (the right of people with property in two constituencies to vote in both). Seats were redistributed in accordance with the recommendations of the Boundary Commission set up in 1944. Boundary changes have been made at intervals since then.

The Representation of the People Act (1969) lowered the voting age to 18.

1.2 The Reform Acts of 1832 and 1867

After studying this section you should be able to:

- explain the structure of British politics in the early 19th century
- assess how far this structure was change by the Great Reform Act
- explain why the Second Reform Act was passed in 1867

LEARNING SUMMARY

The British political system in 1830

| EDEXCEL | M5 |
| WJEC | M6 (synoptic) |

Political power in the early 19th century was largely in the hands of the landowning class. They dominated parliament. The heads of the most important landowning families formed the House of Lords. The landed aristocracy controlled the election of many of the 658 MPs in the House of Commons. In the counties, with open voting and widespread bribery, voters followed the wishes of the great landowners. Many of the boroughs had only a handful of voters and were controlled by patrons, who were usually local landowners. Most boroughs were in the agricultural south.

> These were known as pocket boroughs.

The landed aristocracy also dominated the government. All but four members of Grey's cabinet in 1830 were in the House of Lords. Through the patronage system the government controlled the House of Commons. No government resigned as a result of losing a vote in the Commons between 1783 and 1830.

Key points from AS

- **Causes and terms of the Reform Act**
  Revise AS pages 19–20
- **The Chartist movement**
  Revise AS page 22

The two political parties – **Whigs** and **Tories** – were really rival factions within the ruling class. They had no political organisation outside parliament. They did not set out rival programmes at elections. There was no party discipline in the modern sense. Many MPs regarded themselves as independent.

The political system reflected the social structure of 18th-century Britain. By 1830 social changes resulting from the industrial revolution, above all the rise of the industrial middle class, brought pressure for change. The demand for reform came from both the middle class and the working class, particularly in the years 1815–21 and again in 1830–32. It was led by the radicals, who derived their ideas from the American and French revolutions. In the Reform Crisis of 1830–32, radicals, middle classes and working classes came together in Thomas Attwood's Birmingham Political Union.

> Many large industrial towns, such as Birmingham and Manchester, were unrepresented.

> Note that the Whigs intended reform to preserve privilege by extending it to the middle classes.

By 1830 the Whig leaders had reached the conclusion that limited reform was necessary. Giving the middle classes a share in political power was not only justified by their growing economic power but would make it possible to deny the claims of the working classes, which the Whig aristocrats viewed with as much horror as the Tories.

> William Pitt the Younger entered Parliament at 21.

The Tories, however, opposed reform. They argued that the existing system worked well: why change it? They claimed that nomination boroughs allowed promising young men to enter parliament at an early age and that all the important 'interests' in the country – landowners, merchants, the professions – were represented. The industrial middle class countered that industry was grossly under-represented and the landed interest over-represented. Of course the landed classes wanted to retain their privileged position and the Tories had no wish to change a system that worked to their advantage.

> **KEY POINT**
> The split in the Tory party over catholic emancipation in 1829 allowed the Whigs into office and thus led to the Reform Crisis.

The effects of the Great Reform Act

EDEXCEL   M5
WJEC   M6 (synoptic)

The main effect of the changes in the franchise was to give the vote to the **middle classes** in the boroughs. The redistribution of seats gave greater representation to the industrial north and midlands. Thus, as the Whigs intended, the Act restored the balance of the constitution by giving proper representation to a class which had previously been under-represented.

> **KEY POINT**
> The Reform Act maintained the principle that political influence should be confined to those who had a 'stake in the country', i.e. property.

In practice the political domination of the landed classes was little affected. Electorates were still tiny and open voting and bribery continued. Consequently voters, especially in the counties, still followed the lead of the local landowners. The agricultural south was still over-represented. Most MPs were still from the landed classes, though a few businessmen and industrialists joined them. Governments therefore were still overwhelmingly aristocratic.

The Act was important in the development of the political parties. For the first time registers of voters had to be drawn up. The parties therefore set up registration committees to ensure that as many as possible of their supporters were registered. These formed the basis for local party organisations. At the same time the establishment of the Tory Carlton Club and the Whig Reform Club marked the beginnings of central party organisation.

At the national level the parties became more responsive to the needs of the new electorate. The Whig reforms of the 1830s followed the example of the Reform Act itself in responding to pressures for reform. Peel's Tamworth Manifesto of 1835 had the clear aim of adapting the Tory Party to the needs of the new electorate – hence the adoption of the name 'Conservative Party'. Perhaps the outstanding example of the importance of the shifting political balance between the landed classes and the industrial middle class was the repeal of the Corn Laws in 1846. The Corn Laws were introduced in 1815 to protect agriculture. The campaign of the **Anti-Corn Law League** from 1839 was spearheaded by two industrialists, Cobden and Bright, both of whom became MPs. They argued that the Corn Laws not only caused high bread prices but hindered the growth of the economy and particularly the manufacturing sector.

> **KEY POINT**
> The repeal of the Corn Laws led to a realignment of the political parties. The Peelites, who supported the repeal, eventually joined the Whigs to form the Liberal Party.

See Chapter 8.1 for a fuller discussion of Chartism.

The **working classes** were disappointed by the Reform Act. They had played an important part in the agitation for reform in 1831–32, but the Reform Act denied them any share in political power. This resulted in the rise of the **Chartist movement** in the years 1838–48. The aim of the Chartists was to establish a democratic parliament, which they hoped would then address working-class grievances. The demands of the Charter, particularly the demand for universal male suffrage, were unacceptable to both the landed and the industrial middle classes.

> The Chartists failed to achieve any of their objectives in their own time, but by 1918 all the points of the Charter except the demand for annual parliaments had been met.

KEY POINT

The Second Reform Act, 1867

| EDEXCEL | M5 |
| WJEC | M6 (synoptic) |

Key points from AS

- **The Second Reform Act, 1867**
  Revise AS pages 30–31

He said in 1864, 'Every man ... is entitled to come within the pale of the constitution'.

The Liberals were known as the 'Adullamites'.

See also page 107.

Pressure for further reform developed in the 1860s:

- The formation of New Model Trade Unions from 1851 onwards was a sign of the growing capacity for organisation of the skilled working class.
- The Radicals had never ceased to press for further reform and their voice became stronger under the leadership of John Bright, who made a series of great speeches on the subject in 1858–9.
- They gained an important ally in 1864 when Gladstone declared himself in favour of reform. He had been particularly impressed by the support of the Lancashire cotton workers for the North in the American Civil War.
- The death of Palmerston in 1865 removed a major obstacle to reform.
- His successor, Russell, favoured reform and along with Gladstone introduced a Reform Bill in 1865. This Bill was defeated by a combination of the Conservatives and a section of the Liberals led by Robert Lowe, who believed that the working classes were too ignorant to be entrusted with the vote.
- Pressure from outside parliament was mounting. There were mass meetings and a disturbance in London when a meeting planned for Hyde Park was banned.
- The incoming Conservative government, led by Derby and Disraeli, introduced another Reform Bill. Disraeli thought reform was inevitable and therefore wanted the Conservatives to get the credit.

1.3 Politics and parties 1868–1918

After studying this section you should be able to:

- explain how the expansion of the electorate affected both Houses of Parliament and the political parties
- assess the importance of the women's suffrage movement and other pressure groups in the development of democracy

LEARNING SUMMARY

The House of Commons

EDEXCEL	M5
OCR	M5 (synoptic)
WJEC	M6 (synoptic)

The Reform Acts of 1867 and 1884 more than trebled the size of the electorate. From 1885 two-thirds of adult men were able to vote. The great majority of the new electors were working class: the 1867 Act gave the vote to urban workers, the 1884 Act to agricultural labourers and industrial workers in the many smaller industrial towns and villages. In 1868, however, elections were still conducted by open voting and were marked by bribery, corruption and intimidation. The Secret Ballot Act (1872) and the Corrupt Practices Act (1883) were important in changing the character of elections and allowing the new voters to exercise their votes independently.

The growth in the size of the electorate made it necessary for political leaders to devote much more effort to gaining support in the country through election campaigns. Gladstone's victory in 1868 was achieved partly by a vigorous campaign in which he spoke all over the country, and his Midlothian Campaign was equally important in the 1880 election.

The social composition of the House of Commons, however, changed comparatively little. Since MPs were not paid, they were drawn almost entirely from the middle and upper classes. It was only with the emergence of the Labour Party at the beginning of the 20th century that there was a small group of MPs from working-class backgrounds. They depended at first on trade unions for financial support but in 1911 payment for MPs was introduced.

One of the first was Keir Hardie.

The political parties

EDEXCEL M5
OCR M5 (synoptic)

From 1867 Birmingham had three MPs but electors had only two votes, so they had to be distributed carefully.

The changes in the electoral system led to changes in the organisation of the parties. In Birmingham, Joseph Chamberlain set up a network of ward organisations, partly to make the most effective use of Liberal votes. From this developed the National Liberal Federation, which provided help for constituency parties in fighting elections. The Conservatives set up the National Union of Conservative Associations in 1867, following this in 1870 with the appointment of a National Agent (J.E. Gorst) and the establishment of Conservative Central Office.

Electoral changes forced both parties to seek support from all classes. The Liberal Party gained support across the social range from Whig aristocrats to working-class radicals. A few trade unionists were elected as Lib-Labs. The importance the Conservatives attached to winning working-class support is shown by the setting up of Conservative working men's associations and clubs. In the 1880s Lord Randolph Churchill founded the Primrose League, which had two million members by 1912. Some historians would claim that Disraeli created the modern Conservative Party by associating it with 'Tory democracy', a phrase actually coined after his death by Lord Randolph Churchill. The growth of working-class Conservatism was an important feature of late Victorian politics.

Especially in Lancashire.

The electoral reforms also gave rise to two new parties. One was the Irish Nationalist Party, which won over 80 seats in every election from 1885 to 1910 and held the balance of power, with crucial effects, after the 1885 and 1910 elections.

Key points from AS

• **Formation of the Labour Party**
Revise AS pages 59–60

Its first Secretary was Ramsay MacDonald.

The other was the Labour Party. The granting of the vote to working-class men suggested the possibility of a separate party to represent the interests of labour. The leaders of the New Unions which developed from the 1880s advocated political action to improve social conditions by legislation and government intervention. The formation of the Independent Labour Party by Keir Hardie in 1893 was an important step but the key development came in 1900 when the Labour Representation Committee was set up, with representatives from the trade unions, the ILP, the Fabian Society and the Social Democratic Federation. This became the Labour Party in 1906.

> The organisation of the political parties changed in response to the widening of the franchise.
>
> **KEY POINT**

The development of a more democratic electoral system also led to the formation of extra-parliamentary pressure groups. The Fabian Society and the SDF were two such groups, but there were also temperance societies (particularly influential among nonconformist Liberals), peace societies, and women's suffrage societies. Joseph Chamberlain's Tariff Reform campaign, which he started in 1903, may also be regarded as a pressure group.

The Women's Suffrage Movement

EDEXCEL	M5
OCR	M5 (synoptic)
WJEC	M6 (synoptic)

Key points from AS

- **Votes for Women**
  Revise AS pages 57–58

Most Liberals favoured votes for women but some feared that women were more likely to vote Conservative.

It also made it difficult for the government to agree without seeming weak.

The extension of votes to working-class men in 1867 and 1884 raised the question of allowing women to vote. John Stuart Mill proposed this in the debates on the 1867 Reform Act. Suffrage societies were formed in many areas in the 1870s and 1880s. The National Union of Women's Suffrage Societies (founded 1897) and the Women's Social and Political Union (1903) formed powerful pressure groups.

The election of the Liberals in 1906 gave hope to both groups and the WSPU drew a great deal of attention to the issue by its increasingly militant tactics. There were, however, powerful forces working against the women. Ideas about the role of women in the family and the community which today would be regarded as prejudice were deep-rooted and sincerely held. The issue was tied up with the question of granting the vote to the 40 per cent of men who still could not vote. The militancy of the WSPU convinced some men that women were not fit to have the vote. Asquith, the Liberal Prime Minister, stalled as long as he could and the issue had still not been resolved in 1914.

> The pre-war suffrage movements failed to achieve their object, but in 1918, in recognition of the contribution they had made to the war effort, women over the age of 30 were given the vote. But at the same time it was given to men over 21.
>
> **KEY POINT**

The House of Lords

EDEXCEL	M5
OCR	M5 (synoptic)
WJEC	M6 (synoptic)

Key points from AS

- **The 1909 budget and the struggle with the Lords**
  Revise AS pages 54–55

The Conservatives encouraged them to do so, hence the nickname 'Mr Balfour's poodle'.

The maximum interval was previously seven years.

You should be able to explain the significance of these dates.

Until 1911 the House of Lords had the power to veto bills passed by the House of Commons. The widening of the franchise in 1867 and 1884 meant that a House elected by over 60 per cent of the adult male population could be overruled by a hereditary House. This was particularly galling to Liberals since the House of Lords had a permanent Conservative majority, which was strengthened by the defection of Whig aristocrats from the Liberal Party in opposition to the First Home Rule Bill in 1886. In 1893 the Lords rejected the Second Home Rule Bill and between 1906 and 1908 they rejected several Liberal bills, despite the huge majority won by the Liberals in 1906.

The issue came to a head over Lloyd George's 1909 budget. After two general elections in 1910, the powers of the Lords were curtailed by the **Parliament Act** of 1911. They were not allowed to reject a money bill and could only delay other bills for two years. This meant that the will of the elected House would ultimately prevail. To counter the argument that this would allow governments to force through measures for which they had no electoral support, the interval between general elections was reduced to five years.

1868–74	Gladstone's first ministry
1874–80	Disraeli's second ministry
1880–85	Gladstone's second ministry
1886	Liberal Party split over Home Rule
1900	Formation of Labour Representation Committee
1906	Liberal election victory
1911	Parliament Act
1916	Lloyd George replaces Asquith – split in Liberal Party

KEY DATES

1.4 Politics in the 1920s

After studying this section you should be able to:

- *outline the development of the political parties in the 1920s*

The decline of the Liberals and the rise of Labour

| EDEXCEL | M5 |
| OCR | M5 (synoptic) |

For a fuller discussion of the decline of the Liberals see Chapter 9.1.

The First World War led to a re-shaping of the party system. In 1915 Asquith formed a coalition but he was widely regarded as the wrong man to lead the country in a war. In 1916, he was overthrown and replaced by Lloyd George. The bitterness this caused ensured that the Liberal Party would never again hold office, though many historians would argue that this was only one, and perhaps not the most fundamental reason for the decline of the Liberals. At the end of the war, Lloyd George was re-elected as Prime Minister with the support of the Conservatives and the Coalition Liberals. By 1922 the Conservatives felt they had no more use for him and he was overthrown. There was then a short period of three-party politics, but by 1924 it was becoming apparent that Labour was replacing the Liberals as the alternative to the Conservatives.

Key points from AS

- **The Labour Governments 1924 and 1929–31**
  Revise AS pages 67–68

In the 1929 election Labour won 288 seats, the conservatives 260 and the Liberals 59, so no party held an overall majority.

The divisions among the Liberals facilitated the rise of Labour, but perhaps it would have happened anyway as a result of the enfranchisement of the working classes. At the end of the war the Representation of the People Act produced a genuine mass electorate. In 1922 Labour became the official opposition and in 1924, after an election which gave no party a majority, Ramsay MacDonald formed the first Labour government. It depended on Liberal support and lasted for less than a year, but it demonstrated that Labour was now the alternative to the Conservatives. The formation of a second Labour ministry in 1929 – again a minority government but this time with the largest number of seats in a hung parliament – underlined this.

He also made good use of the new medium of radio.

These developments in the Liberal and Labour parties obviously benefited the Conservatives. They were the dominant partners in Lloyd George's coalition government and then held office themselves until 1929 except for the brief interlude of the first Labour ministry. But this might not have happened if the Conservatives themselves had not adjusted to the new era of the mass electorate. They had a solid basis of upper- and middle-class support, and by the 1920s had clearly become the party of business. Their leaders, Bonar Law and Baldwin, were both industrialists rather than landowners. They also attracted substantial support from the working classes, building on the foundations laid by the Conservative working men's associations and the Primrose League. Baldwin took pains to present himself as an 'ordinary' man. Under his leadership the Conservatives rejected the notion of class war and accepted the need for government to engage in social reform and management of the economy.

Between 1830 and 1931 the electorate had been expanded from a small minority of men to include all adults of both sexes, and government by the landowning classes had therefore given way to democracy.

The parties had to develop national and local organisations and draw up programmes to win the support of the electors.

KEY POINT

You should be able to explain the significance of these dates.

1918–22	Lloyd George coalition
1924	First Labour ministry
1924–29	Baldwin's Conservative government
1926	General Strike
1929–31	Second Labour ministry

KEY DATES

1.5 Political parties and government, 1931–92

After studying this section you should be able to:

- *outline the changing fortunes of the three main political parties between 1931 and 1992*

LEARNING SUMMARY

Labour

OCR ▷ MS (synoptic)

> Most Labour MPs regarded MacDonald as a traitor, especially after this catastrophic election result.

Key points from AS

- **The second Labour ministry, 1929–31**
  Revise AS pages 67–68
- **The Labour Governments, 1945–51**
  Revise AS pages 76–79

The Great Depression cut across the development of the party system. In 1931 the second Labour ministry, faced by a financial crisis, collapsed. MacDonald then accepted office as Prime Minister of a National Government, with Baldwin as his deputy. The idea was that a coalition was necessary to deal with the crisis but the great majority of Labour MPs strongly disapproved. Thus the national Government, though technically a coalition, was Conservative-dominated. The electorate, however, approved: the 1931 election gave the National Government an overwhelming victory and Labour was reduced to 52 MPs. It still had one-third of the votes, however, and gradually rebuilt its strength. The Second World War brought a suspension of normal politics with the formation of the wartime coalition. The inclusion of a number of Labour ministers in this was important in preparing Labour for office.

Attlee and Gaitskell

The 1945 election not only marked a reversion to normal party politics but produced a sweeping victory for Labour under Attlee – the first time it had won an overall majority. The result demonstrated that electors blamed the Conservatives, who had dominated the National Governments, for the social evils of the 1930s, especially unemployment, as well as for foreign policy failures. Labour offered a more wholehearted commitment to social reform – full employment, a housing drive and a National Health Service.

Labour's hope that, with a mass electorate with a majority of working-class voters, it was now the natural party of government was, however, to be dashed. It gained widespread credit for establishing the **Welfare State**, but its belief in government planning of the economy, of which nationalisation was part, was less popular. Nationalisation of key sectors of the economy was accepted, though the results did not arouse great enthusiasm among either workers in the nationalised industries or consumers. But by 1951 electors were questioning both the need for further nationalisation and the competence of the government in managing the economy. Controls and austerity were increasingly unpopular.

Labour's defeat in 1951 opened a debate in the party which continued for the rest of the century. The left believed that Labour should commit itself to a wholeheartedly socialist programme of nationalisation, state control of the economy and redistributive taxation – essentially waging a class war. To this was added from the late 1950s nuclear disarmament. The more moderate wing of the party argued that electoral success would only come by making Labour attractive to middle-class voters as well as traditional Labour supporters. These divisions helped to keep Labour out of power from 1951 to 1964. Gaitskell, leader from 1955 to 1963, failed to persuade the party to water down its commitment to further nationalisation.

Wilson and after

He promised to do so through 'the white heat of technology'.

In 1964 Labour regained office under Harold Wilson, who promised to provide managerial efficiency in modernising the British economy. A key element in this was the reform of industrial relations, but opposition from the trade unions forced the government to abandon its plans. This, along with the devaluation of the pound in 1967, left electors feeling that Labour was no more able to solve Britain's economic problems than the Conservatives. Labour lost the election of 1970.

Edward Heath's Conservative government (1970–74) had equal difficulty in tackling the problems of the economy and industrial relations. Not surprisingly, the two elections of 1974 showed that the electorate had no real confidence in either party. Labour returned to office in February 1974 without a majority. It gained a small majority in a second general election in October but lost it again in by-elections. It was overtaken by an economic crisis resulting from a combination of Britain's poor economic record and the 1973–4 oil crisis.

> **KEY POINT**
> Labour's claim that its links with the trade unions would enable it to handle them more successfully than the Conservatives was undermined by a series of strikes (the 'winter of discontent') in 1978–9.

Labour was decisively defeated in 1979. The left, which believed that Labour had been defeated because it had not been socialist enough, gained control of the party. Michael Foot, who was elected leader in 1980, led it to a disastrous defeat in the 1983 election. Some Labour right wingers defected and formed the Social Democratic Party. Neil Kinnock, who replaced Foot in 1983, drove out the militant extremists and strove to return Labour to the centre ground.

> **KEY POINT**
> By 1992 Labour had regained public confidence sufficiently to cut the Conservative majority to 21, though it was disappointed not to have won the election.

The Conservatives

OCR   M5 (synoptic)

Consensus politics: the two parties agreed on the main social and economic policies

Hence the charge that the period 1951–64 was 'thirteen wasted years'.

Key points from AS

- **The Conservatives, 1951–64**
  Revise AS pages 80–81

Economic policy which aimed to control inflation by controlling the money supply.

After their unexpected defeat in 1945, the Conservatives rebuilt their organisation and developed the idea of 'One Nation' Conservatism, which accepted the welfare state. They also accepted most of Labour's nationalisation measures and the commitment to full employment. The 1950s and 1960s were therefore a period of **consensus politics**. The Conservatives won three successive elections in 1951, 1955 and 1959 because they appeared to offer greater unity and competence than Labour, which was divided by the issue of nuclear disarmament. By 1964, however, Britain's sluggish economic performance cast doubt on the government's competence at the same time as it was hit by the Profumo scandal and a squabble over the succession to Macmillan.

The Conservatives returned to power in 1970 under Heath, who was elected leader by a process more in keeping with a democratic party than that which had produced Douglas-Home in 1963. Heath was troubled, and eventually brought down, by the problem of the trade unions – a problem that also played a major part in bringing down the Labour governments which preceded and followed.

Following their defeat in 1974 the Conservatives looked for a new leader and new policies. With the election of Mrs Thatcher as leader in 1975 and as Prime Minister in 1979, they adopted monetarism as their economic policy. Government spending was cut, nationalised industries were privatised and trade union law was reformed. These policies, known as **Thatcherism**, combined with Mrs Thatcher's handling of the Falklands crisis, the popular sale of council houses and the turmoil in the Labour party, enabled the Conservatives to win the 1983 and 1987 elections. Mrs Thatcher's increasingly authoritarian attitude towards her colleagues and her refusal to back down over the highly unpopular poll tax led to her overthrow in 1990. She was succeeded by John Major, who, contrary to expectations, won the general election in 1992 but found himself saddled with a party increasingly divided over Europe.

> The 1979 election marked a turning point in post-war politics. Thatcherism represented the end of the consensus that had characterised the policies of the two parties in the previous 30 years.
>
> **KEY POINT**

The Liberals

OCR ▸ M5, (synoptic)

The Liberals never recovered from the split between Asquith and Lloyd George. They came together sufficiently during the 1920s to gain 59 seats in 1929, but were again divided by the formation of the National Government. Half of the Liberals elected in 1931 supported the National Government. The independent Liberals were reduced to 33 MPs. In post-war elections the electoral system meant that they were 'squeezed' between the two main parties and were reduced to six MPs by 1951. Lacking the support of either business or the trade unions, they were at a considerable financial disadvantage. The number of Liberal MPs did not reflect the number of votes they gained even when their fortunes were at their lowest ebb. Not surprisingly, one of their main demands was proportional representation. In 1974 the Liberal's share of the vote increased to 19 per cent, but they still gained only 14 seats.

> Liberal candidates often came second in individual constituencies.

> Proportional representation: electoral system which allocates seats to parties in proportion to the number of votes gained. Neither of the other parties was interested.

In the 1980s the Liberals formed an alliance with the SDP, which had split away from Labour in 1981. The Liberal-SDP Alliance won 23 seats in 1983, 22 in 1987 and, as the Liberal Democrats, 20 in 1992.

> You should be able to explain the significance of each of these dates.

1931	Formation of National Government (MacDonald)	
1940–45	Churchill's wartime coalition	
1945	Election: Labour victory	
1951–64	Conservative ministries under Churchill, Eden and Macmillan	**KEY DATES**
1964	Election victory for Labour led by Wilson	
1970	Election: Wilson defeated by Heath	
1974–79	Labour ministries (Wilson and Callaghan)	
1979	Election: Mrs Thatcher becomes Prime Minister	

1.6 The influence of the trade unions and the media

After studying this section you should be able to:

LEARNING SUMMARY

- outline the changing role of the trade unions in political life
- assess the effects of the growth of mass media on British democracy

The trade unions

EDEXCEL ▸ M5
OCR ▸ M5

The political influence of the trade unions in the 19th century was limited. The New Model unions were mainly concerned to improve their members' wages and

Key points from AS

• **Trade unions**
Revise AS pages 58–59
• **The General Strike**
Revise AS pages 66–67

See above, page 21.

Syndicats is French for trade unions; syndicalism meant using direct action, i.e. strikes and even violence to seize power.

At party conferences the big unions had 'block votes' based on their membership.

conditions of work and to provide insurance against sickness and unemployment. Their main political interest was in combating legal threats to their activities. Since many of their members gained the vote in 1867, both Gladstone and Disraeli enacted legislation in their interest. A few trade unionists were elected as Lib-Lab MPs from the 1870s onwards.

The leaders of the 'New Unions' formed in the 1890s were more politically minded, arguing that political action was necessary to improve social conditions. As a result the trade unions played a key role in the formation of the Labour Party. The Taff Vale Case (1901) convinced many previously sceptical union leaders that it was in their interests to have a political party to represent labour. The success of the infant Labour Party in persuading the Liberals to pass the Trade Disputes Act (1906) and the Trade Union Act (1913) seemed to confirm this. The link between Labour and the unions was strengthened by the decision of the mineworkers in 1909 to give their support to the party.

The formation of a political party to represent labour and trade union interests did not prevent serious industrial trouble breaking out. There was a series of strikes in 1910–12 and further industrial trouble in 1920–21. Both sets of disputes led to violence and confrontation with the government. Some trade unionists were attracted by syndicalism and argued that workers should use the strike weapon for political ends. When the miners, the transport workers and the railwaymen made an informal agreement to support each other, there seemed a danger that they could bring the country to a standstill. In 1921 this Triple Alliance broke down but in 1926, when the miners were faced with further wage cuts and longer hours, the other unions supported them in the General Strike. Baldwin's Conservative government saw this as a threat to the democratically elected government and organised counter-measures. The TUC itself belatedly realised that the General Strike could lead to revolution and backed down. Many of its leaders had never wanted a general strike in the first place.

The failure of the General Strike weakened the trade union movement. In any case in an era of high unemployment trade union activity was difficult to sustain. Moreover, although the support of trade unionists enabled Labour to emerge as the largest party in the 1929 election, the collapse of the second Labour ministry in 1931 left both the party and the trade unions weakened throughout the 1930s.

With the election of Labour in 1945 the trade union movement at last had a government sympathetic to its aims and ideas. For much of the next 30 years the unions were at the height of their power. Under the constitution of the Labour Party they played the key role in formulating party policy. MPs sponsored by trade unions ensured that their views were heard in the Commons. Whichever party was in power, gaining their co-operation seemed to be essential for successful management of the economy. At the same time their activities seemed increasingly, especially to Conservatives, to be one of the causes of Britain's economic decline. Thus the Conservative victory in 1979 can be ascribed partly to the series of strikes known as the 'winter of discontent' in 1978–9.

> Mrs Thatcher abandoned the practice of consulting the unions over economic policy and curbed their activities by enacting new trade union laws.
>
> **KEY POINT**

The media

EDEXCEL — M5
OCR — M5 (synoptic)

Most importantly *The Times*.

In the mid-19th century newspaper readership was confined to the educated middle class. There was no national press but most provincial towns had their own newspapers. The London papers were naturally the ones which had most influence but they concentrated mainly on factual reporting, e.g. detailed accounts of parliamentary proceedings.

The extension of the franchise, the expansion of elementary education and the growth of a popular press went hand in hand. The 1867 Reform Act was followed by the 1870 Education Act, which made elementary education available to all. Consequently most children attained a basic standard of literacy. This development lay behind the foundation of the *Daily Mail* by Alfred Harmsworth, later Lord Northcliffe, in 1896. This was the first mass-circulation newspaper and soon reached a readership of over a million – mainly lower middle class rather than working class. It was written in a style to appeal to people with limited education and it aimed to capture attention by turning the news into stories or even making news by looking for 'scoops'. It also encouraged popular prejudices which it believed would help to sell the paper – for example, fostering hostility to the French and the Boers in the 1890s and to the Germans in the years before 1914. It was soon followed by others, notably the *Daily Express* (1900), the *Daily Mirror* (1904) and the *Daily Herald* (1912). The popular press became the main means by which the voters enfranchised in 1867 and 1884 gained their political knowledge and often their political opinions.

Some provincial newspapers, especially the *Manchester Guardian*, were important for their influence on middle-class voters.

The role of the popular press as opinion formers became perhaps even more important with the creation of a mass electorate in 1918 and has remained important ever since, as shown by the claim of *The Sun* to have won the 1992 election for the Conservatives. Two important points should be noted. First, the majority of the mass-circulation newspapers throughout the 20th century supported the Conservatives. Second, their circulation gave their proprietors the potential to exercise great political influence and some, e.g. Beaverbrook, exercised it to the full.

Proprietor of the *Daily Express*.

The extension of the vote to a mass electorate in 1918 almost coincided with the rise of a new medium of mass communication, radio. In 1922 the British Broadcasting Company was formed and in 1926 it became a public corporation, the BBC. By 1939, 90 per cent of households had a 'wireless'. The BBC became an important source of news and politicians soon realised that radio provided a direct means of communication with voters in their own homes. Baldwin proved particularly adept at using it, while Lloyd George and Ramsay MacDonald, who were accustomed to addressing large meetings, were less able to adapt their style. Churchill's use of radio to boost national morale during the Second World War was masterly. In the 1950s the rapid spread of television produced an even more powerful vehicle of mass communication. The first major politician to make effective use of it was Macmillan. From the 1960s the ability to perform effectively on television was a vital attribute for the successful politician. By the end of the period, questions were being raised about whether parliament was being devalued by the attention politicians gave to television.

> The rise of the mass media was essential for the development of democracy but also gave the media great power.

KEY POINT

Sample question and model answer

Study Sources A to C and answer questions (a), (b) and (c) which follow.

Source A

From a speech by Thomas Macaulay in the debate in the House of Commons on the Reform Bill, 1831.

'I hold it to be clearly necessary that in a country like this the right of suffrage should depend on a financial qualification. Every argument which would persuade me to oppose universal suffrage, persuades me to support the measure which is now before us. I oppose universal suffrage because I think it would produce a destructive revolution. I support this measure because I am sure it is our best security against revolution.'

Source B

From a speech by Lord Derby at the time of the Second Reform Act, 1867.

'No doubt we are making a great experiment and "taking a leap in the dark", but I have the greatest confidence in the sound sense of my fellow-countrymen and I entertain a strong hope that the extended franchise which we are now conferring on them will be the means of placing the institutions of this country on a firmer basis.'

Source C

From *England 1914–45*, by A.J.P. Taylor, 1965.

The existing householder franchise dating from 1885, though often called democratic, gave the vote only to three adult males out of five, and of course women did not have the vote. The pre-war register was flagrantly out of date. A new one, on the same basis, could not include the millions of men in the services. Yet it would be monstrously unjust to leave them out. And if men serving their country were to be enfranchised, why not women in the services also? … The Representation of the People Act, which became law in June 1918, marked the victory of the Radical principle 'one man, one vote'. It added more votes to the register than all its predecessors put together. It settled in principle the question of votes for women, which had caused so much turmoil before the war. Yet it went through almost without fuss. War smoothed the way for democracy.

(a) Study Sources A, B and C. What do these sources reveal about the reasons for the widening of the franchise in the period 1832–1928? [4]

> This question focuses on understanding of the sources.

(a) In 1832 and 1867 it was based not on belief in democracy but the need to strengthen the political system. Macaulay (source A) wanted to avert revolutionary change by linking the vote to financial status, i.e. the middle class. Derby (source B) wanted to strengthen the 'institutions of the country', though this involved a 'leap in the dark', i.e. votes for working-class male householders. By 1918 the democratic principle for men was accepted – under the pressure of war – and this made it impossible to refuse the vote to women (source C).

(b) Use your own knowledge. Choose any ONE Parliamentary Reform Act of the 19th century which you consider to have been a turning point in the development of parliamentary representation in Britain. Explain its significance as a turning point. [10]

> Compare 'before and after'. Develop the points in further detail.

(b) Choose 1867 Reform Act – a turning point because it gave the vote to all male householders in the boroughs, i.e. working-class men. Extension of the franchise to working-class men in counties (1884) was the logical consequence. Then it was only a matter of time before the vote was given to all men, householders or not. The 1867 Act also gave the vote to £10 lodgers in the boroughs and £12 leaseholders in the counties. Thus it doubled the electorate to 2.5 million. Four large towns were given three

MPs; as electors only had two votes, local party organisations became important – a significant political development.

(c) Study Sources A, B and C and use your own knowledge. Examine the view that extension of the franchise in the period 1832–1928 came about only when political leaders overcame their fear of its consequences. [16]

This is an outline answer, to which you should add more detail.

Note that references to sources are woven into the argument.

Refer to reform riots.

(c) Following the French Revolution there was widespread fear of democracy among the upper classes. At the same time Radicals demanded universal male suffrage. Throughout the period advocates of democracy faced a large body of opinion, mainly upper and middle class, which mistrusted it.

Whether the franchise could safely be extended was an issue in 1832 and 1867 but thereafter other reasons were more important. In 1832 source A argues it is safe to embark on limited reform, but not universal franchise. But there was another question: Would it be safe *not* to widen the franchise? Macaulay believed reform would avert the threat of revolution. But there were also other reasons for reform, especially the growing economic power of the industrial middle classes, which made it wise to harness their support to the political system. Reform offered political advantages for the Whigs.

1832 showed that, contrary to Tory fears, the franchise could be safely widened, but the political classes were still worried about giving the vote to the working classes. Many, e.g. Adullamites, distrusted democracy. Even Derby, whose ministry was responsible for the 1867 Act, called it 'a leap in the dark' (source B). But Gladstone had come out in favour of working-class franchise. Many believed that it was inevitable and desirable as a way of strengthening public support for the political system. Other factors were concern about the danger of not extending the franchise and Disraeli's wish to gain political advantage from reform.

Hyde Park riots showed strength of demand for reform.

After 1867, safety became less of an issue, though many, especially Tories and members of the aristocracy, were still reluctant to open the door to universal franchise. The 1884 Act was the logical consequence of what had been accepted in 1867. Conservative opposition arose primarily from fears of possible effects on their electoral fortunes, and the price for their acceptance of it was a Redistribution Act. But the franchise was still restricted: women and 40 per cent of men were excluded (source C). And there was still a residual link to the notion of 'a stake in the country' in the male householder qualification.

E.g. Gladstone's great speaking campaigns, appealing directly to voters.

Fears that extension of the franchise would lead to revolutionary change were not borne out by political developments in the late 19th century, though it did lead to changes in the style of politics. The Conservatives succeeded in winning working-class support (their longest period of dominance since the 1832 Act followed the 1884 Act). A working-class party (the Labour Party) was slow to emerge. Though mistrust of democracy remained a consideration, the biggest issue after 1900 was not whether further extension of the franchise was safe but whether it was fair to deny the vote to women (and to the 40 per cent of men who were still without it). This issue of principle came up against deeply ingrained habits of thought as well as considerations of political advantage (which party would women vote for?). The suffragettes also posed for the Liberal governments the question that had faced the governments in 1832 and 1867

Sample question and model answer (continued)

Conclusion.

– whether to give in to pressure. The war clinched the matter – not just because of the contribution of women but, as source C shows, because it also made it impossible to maintain the existing restriction on male franchise. Even so, women were not given the vote until the age of 30 – because it was feared that otherwise they would outnumber men. This inequality could not be sustained and was righted in 1928.

Reasons for successive Reform Acts were complex. In 1832 and 1867 opponents genuinely feared the consequences of democracy. After 1867 opponents of democracy were fighting a rearguard action. The principle of the working-class franchise had been conceded. Fear of democracy was replaced by political calculation about the consequences of particular proposals and hostility to change in the role of women in society.

Practice examination questions

1 Examine the forces which (a) promoted and (b) hindered the process of parliamentary reform in the period 1832–1928.

[30]

2 Examine the reasons for the changing fortunes of the Liberal and Labour parties in the period 1868–1992.

[30]

3 Examine the reasons for the changing influence of trade unions in British politics during the period 1868–1992.

[30]

4 How far has the influence of the media in British politics changed during the period 1868–1992?

[30]

Chapter 2

Poor Law to Welfare State 1830–1948
The following topics are covered in this chapter:

- From laissez faire to Welfare State
- The Poor Law
- Public health, housing and factory legislation
- Education

2.1 From laissez faire to Welfare State

After studying this section you should be able to:

- understand how views about responsibility for the poor changed during the period

LEARNING SUMMARY

Changing attitudes

EDEXCEL	MS
OCR	MS (synoptic)
WJEC	M6 (synoptic)

The economic theory of laissez faire was based on the work of Adam Smith.

In the 19th century laissez faire was the predominant philosophy about social and economic questions. Government interference in the economy was believed to be ineffective and even harmful, as well as possibly costly. It was also held that intervention to help the poor was bad for their character because it undermined their self-reliance and encouraged idleness: the aim of social legislation should be to encourage independence through self-help. Similarly restriction of hours of labour was not only contrary to laissez faire ideas but also an interference in the 'liberty' of the workman.

The industrial revolution and the growth of towns which accompanied it, however, presented society with a whole set of new problems. Two groups of people drew attention to these problems.

The prime aim of the Evangelicals was to spread the gospel to the working classes.

- The humanitarian movement aimed to improve conditions for the working class. Many humanitarians came from the Evangelical movement in the Church of England.

The leading utilitarian was Jeremy Bentham.

- The utilitarians, although they advocated laissez faire, also placed great emphasis on efficiency. For this reason they sometimes took the lead in social reform, even though this meant government intervention. For example, since sickness was a major cause of poverty, efficient administration of the Poor Law required government action on public health. Their belief in efficiency also led them to instigate commissions of enquiry which produced much of the evidence on which social reform was based.

Thus during the 19th century the state gradually took an increasing role in social reform. Progress was, however, often slow because of the belief in laissez faire and the opposition of vested interests.

Around 1900 the climate of opinion began to shift towards a more positive view of the role of the state. There were a number of reasons for this.

- The social surveys of Booth and Rowntree revealed that nearly 30 per cent of the population was living in poverty.
- The extension of the vote to the working classes made social reform an increasingly important political issue.
- The formation of the Labour Party presented a challenge to the existing parties, especially the Liberals.
- The ideas of middle-class intellectuals such as the economist J.A. Hobson, the sociologist L.T. Hobhouse and the members of the Fabian Society had an important influence, particularly among left-wing Liberals. This was seen in the rise of the New Liberals with their collectivist ideas, as opposed to the individualism of Gladstonian liberals.

Sometimes described as a 'social service state' – see below, p.35.

The reforms of the Liberal governments of 1905–15 were a significant step from laissez faire towards a welfare state. They were based on the principle that the state had a duty to ensure a minimum standard for its citizens but they fell short of a comprehensive system of social security. The Conservatives opposed many of the Liberal reforms but in the inter-war years, under the leadership of Baldwin, they accepted the new role of the state in social welfare and even consolidated some of the Liberal reforms. By 1939 Britain had moved a long way towards a welfare state but it was left to Labour after 1945 to build on these foundations. The post-war welfare state differed from pre-war social security arrangements in that it was based on the principle of 'universality'. Pre-war social services were primarily for the working class; the post-war welfare state catered for the entire population.

> In the 20th century the role of the state in dealing with social problems increased dramatically, culminating in the Welfare State.

KEY POINT

2.2 The Poor Law

After studying this section you should be able to:

LEARNING SUMMARY

- *explain the origins and working of the Poor Law Amendment Act*
- *explain how and why state intervention to help the poor developed before and after the First World War*
- *show how these developments culminated in the Welfare State*
- *compare Victorian and 20th-century provision for the poor*

Provision for the poor in 1830

EDEXCEL	M5
OCR	M5 (synoptic)
WJEC	M6 (synoptic)

Key points from AS

- **The Poor Law Amendment Act, 1834**
  Revise AS page 21

A system devised by the Berkshire magistrates in 1795.

- Each parish was responsible for its own poor. To this end a parish rate was levied by the Overseers of the Poor.
- The poor were classified into the impotent poor (the sick, the old and children), the able-bodied poor (the unemployed) and the idle poor (those who refused to work).
- In many parishes workhouses were set up to provide for the poor but this was by no means universal.
- In much of southern England the Speenhamland System had been adopted after 1795. This meant that outdoor relief (money payments) was given to poor labourers whose wages were inadequate. The payments depended on the size of the labourer's family and the price of bread.

By 1830 the old Poor Law was under fire for three main reasons:

- the total cost of poor relief in 1830 was estimated at £8 million
- outdoor relief under the Speenhamland system was alleged to encourage idleness, since labourers knew their wages would be supplemented. (It also encouraged employers to pay less than a living wage, which meant that other ratepayers were in effect subsidising them)
- there was much variation between parishes, which offended utilitarians with their passion for efficiency.

A utilitarian, **Edwin Chadwick**, was the most influential member of a commission which was appointed in 1832 to investigate the Poor Law. It recommended a complete overhaul of the Poor Law, based on three principles:

- encouraging the poor to look for work and not to rely on the Poor Law
- value for money – cheap, efficient and uniform administration
- central supervision of the system.

These principles were embodied in the Poor Law Amendment Act of 1834. The central feature was the **workhouse**. Outdoor relief could still be given to the sick and aged in some cases but otherwise poor relief would only be provided in workhouses. Parishes were to be grouped into Poor Law Unions and a central Board of Commissioners, with Chadwick as its secretary, was to supervise the system. The underlying view seemed to be that poverty was an avoidable misfortune and that the poor needed to be discouraged from seeking relief. Hence workhouses were to be run on the principle of 'less eligibility', which also had the convenient result of making them cheaper to run.

> Life in the workhouses would be 'less eligible', i.e. less attractive, than the condition of the poorest labourer outside it.

The operation of the Poor Law

EDEXCEL	M5
OCR	M5 (synoptic)
WJEC	M6 (synoptic)

The New Poor Law was popular with ratepayers (largely middle class) because the overall national cost of poor relief was immediately cut by 40 per cent. By 1838, 90 per cent of the parishes of England and Wales had been grouped into Unions and workhouses were rapidly established.

It was highly unpopular with the working classes and played a part in the rise of the Chartist movement. It seemed that poverty was being treated as a crime and there was undoubtedly a punitive element in the workhouse regime. Husbands, wives and children were kept separate. Meals had to be eaten in silence and the food was poor. The work was hard – tasks such as stone breaking and bone grinding were similar to those in prison.

> Hence the nickname 'Poor Law Bastilles'.

> **KEY POINT**
> The Poor Law Amendment Act achieved its aims of cutting costs and deterring the poor. Fear of the workhouse was ingrained in working-class attitudes for the remainder of the century.

But there was a cost. Class divisions were sharpened, as shown by the growth of an anti-Poor Law movement in the north, which merged into the Chartist movement at the end of the 1830s. And in the south, where wages of agricultural labourers remained pitifully low, there was great hardship.

The New Poor Law never operated fully in the way Chadwick had envisaged. It proved too expensive for each Union to provide separate workhouses for able-bodied men, women, children, and the sick and aged. In industrial areas, cyclical unemployment made it impossible to abolish outdoor relief, since there were sometimes too many out of work at the same time to accommodate them in workhouses. This failure to take account of the nature of unemployment in industrial areas was one of the great weaknesses of the Act, which had been framed primarily to cope with conditions in the agricultural south.

> Alternate periods of high demand and slack demand. The latter led to mass unemployment in industrial areas.

The harshness of the New Poor Law was somewhat mitigated by reforms from the 1840s. In 1842 separation of husbands and wives and of parents and children was ended. In 1847 the Poor Law Commission was replaced by the Poor Law Board. Poor Law schools were set up. Poor Law infirmaries gradually improved. Outbreaks of dangerous diseases between 1863 and 1865 led to parliamentary debates which resulted in the provision of better medical care.

> **KEY POINT**
> In spite of these improvements, working-class families who fell on bad times would endure considerable hardship rather than go into the workhouse.

The Edwardian Age

EDEXCEL	M5
OCR	M5 (synoptic)
WJEC	M6 (synoptic)

> Booth estimated in 1889 that 30.7 per cent of the inhabitants of London were living 'in poverty'.

Key points from AS

• **The Liberal reforms**
  Revise AS pages 53–54

Public opinion about the treatment of the poor began to change in the late 19th century. The surveys of Charles Booth in London and Seebohm Rowntree in York undermined the Victorian belief that poverty was caused by laziness or weakness of character. In York families of men in full employment were close to the starvation level. In times of depression workers were simply unable to find work. It was impossible for the poor to save for old age: in London 45 per cent of old people were in serious poverty.

There were other reasons, too, why the problem of poverty was a subject of public debate by 1900.

• The long depression from 1873 to 1896, followed by further years of high unemployment in 1904–5, underlined the point that poverty was often the result of economic circumstances beyond the control of the worker.
• The unemployment which resulted from the depression put the Poor Law system, dependent on finance from the rates, under increasing pressure.
• The example of Germany, where social insurance schemes had been introduced in the 1880s, pointed to an alternative approach.

The outcome of this debate was a developing public opinion in favour of state intervention to help the poor. The Liberal governments of 1905–14 took the first important steps towards a welfare state:

• free school meals and medical attention were provided for poor children
• labour exchanges were set up to help the unemployed find jobs
• the Trade Boards Act aimed to establish minimum wages in low-paid 'sweated' industries
• old age pensions were provided at 70 for those with an income below £21 per annum
• the National Insurance Act (1911) tackled two of the main causes of poverty, sickness and unemployment, by providing insurance schemes funded by contributions from the worker, the employer and the state.

The situation in 1914: the 'social service' state

The Liberal reforms marked a shift away from the individualism of the 19th century to an acceptance of the need for state intervention to tackle poverty. Nevertheless state intervention was still limited. Old-age pensions were small and went only to the very poorest old people. National Insurance did not provide medical attention for the worker's wife or children and sick pay was limited to 13 weeks. Insurance against unemployment covered only certain trades where the demand for labour fluctuated most and provided benefit for only 15 weeks in any 12 months. Even these limited reforms were questioned by many people, who feared they would remove incentives for the poor to look for work and save for old age.

> The main ones were building, shipbuilding and engineering.

The Poor Law was left untouched. A Royal Commission on the Poor Law, which sat between 1905 and 1909, failed to reach agreement and published both a Majority and a Minority Report. Neither was acted on. This meant that when benefits under the National Insurance scheme were exhausted, the workhouse remained as the last resort for the sick or unemployed. Similarly those not covered by unemployment insurance, such as agricultural labourers, were still required to turn to the workhouse in extremity.

> **KEY POINT**
>
> The Liberals set up what has been described as a social service state – one which tried to ensure certain minimum standards but no more. It was not a welfare state.

Between the wars

EDEXCEL M5
OCR M5 (synoptic)

The shift towards state intervention begun by the Liberals continued in the inter-war period, though somewhat unevenly because of high unemployment.

- The Unemployment Insurance Act (1920) extended the 1911 scheme to most workers earning less than £250 a year except agricultural labourers and domestic servants. This covered 60 per cent of the labour force. Agricultural labourers were brought into the scheme in 1936.
- The biggest problem, in view of the high unemployment of the inter-war years, was what to do when the 15 weeks covered by unemployment insurance ran out. In 1921 Lloyd George accepted the principle that the state would continue for another 15 weeks to pay 'uncovenanted' benefit, i.e. benefit to which the worker had not contributed by insurance. There were several changes in the way this was administered. By the 1927 Unemployment Insurance Act benefits would continue indefinitely provided the worker could show that he was genuinely seeking work. In 1931 the benefit was cut by 10 per cent and subjected to means testing. In 1934 it was replaced by unemployment assistance paid by the Unemployment Assistance Board. This was also means tested and caused much bitterness.
- Old-age pensions were increased to 10 shillings a week in 1919. In 1925 a contributory pension scheme was introduced by Neville Chamberlain. The pension was payable from age 65 and pensions were provided for widows and orphans. For those not covered by the scheme the old non-contributory pension at age 70 continued.
- The Poor Law was abolished by the Local Government Act of 1929, also the work of Neville Chamberlain. The local authorities (county and county borough councils) took over the workhouses, most of which now functioned mainly as hospitals or old people's homes. They were required to set up Public Assistance Committees to be responsible for care of the poor, though most of this work was transferred to the Unemployment Assistance Board in 1934.

Nothing, however, was done to extend the health insurance scheme established in 1911. Moreover, the benefits could do no more than mitigate the effects of high and prolonged unemployment in what became known as the depressed areas.

> This was the 'dole'.

> The Means Test took account of all family income, so unemployed men could be dependent on the wages of their wives or unmarried children.

> The depressed areas were the older industrial areas in the north-east, north-west, Wales and Scotland, where large numbers of men were unemployed for years.

The establishment of the Welfare State

EDEXCEL M5
OCR M5 (synoptic)

Key points from AS

- **The Welfare State**
  Revise AS pages 76–77

> The work of Aneurin Bevan.

The Second World War provided the spur to a further step forward. The wish to construct a better society after the war resulted in the publication of the **Beveridge Report** in 1942. This set out plans to overcome the five 'giant evils' of want, disease, ignorance, squalor and idleness and provided the basis for the establishment of the Welfare State by the post-war Labour government. The main features were as follows.

- Child allowances (introduced by the wartime coalition government).
- The National Health Service provided free medical care for the entire population. Hospitals, which were previously provided by charities or local authorities, were nationalised.
- A new National Insurance scheme, covering all adults, provided sickness and unemployment benefits, old age pensions at 60 for women and 65 for men, widows' and orphans' pensions, maternity allowances and death grants.
- The National Assistance Act provided assistance for those not covered by the National Insurance scheme, e.g. old people already drawing pensions who were not entitled to pensions under the new scheme, unmarried mothers and handicapped people. Local authorities were also required to provide homes and welfare services for the elderly and the handicapped.
- The National Industrial Injuries Insurance Act.

Labour set up a welfare state based on the principle of 'universality': the services provided by the state should be provided for rich and poor alike, since services provided for the poor alone would be second rate.

You should be able to explain the significance of each of these dates.

1834	Poor Law Amendment Act
1909	Old Age Pensions Act
1911	National Insurance Act
1929	Abolition of the Poor Law by the Local Government Act
1948	National Health Service

2.3 Public health, housing and factory legislation

After studying this section you should be able to:

- *explain the development of public health legislation from 1848 to 1875*
- *explain how the provision of housing for the working classes was improved by government action*
- *explain the origins and development of factory legislation*

Chadwick and public health

OCR	M5 (synoptic)
WJEC	M6 (synoptic)

There were no planning laws, so builders tried to cram in as many houses as possible.

In 1842 Chadwick published his *Report on the Sanitary Condition of the Labouring Population of Great Britain*. It revealed a series of problems arising mainly from the rapid growth of industrial towns.

- Overcrowding and bad housing.
- Lack of sanitation: working-class houses relied on outside privies connected to cesspits.
- Lack of pure water: only the rich had water piped to their house – everybody else had to rely on stand-pipes or pumps in the street. The water often came from polluted rivers.
- Health hazards arising from overcrowded burial grounds.
- Serious outbreaks of infectious diseases, e.g. the cholera outbreak of 1831–2 which caused 30 000 deaths in England, Wales and Scotland.

The result was a rising death rate (20 per cent higher in 1849 than in 1831).

Make a summary of Chadwick's aims and achievements.

Chadwick's interest in public health arose from his position as Secretary to the Poor Law Commission. He argued that sickness caused people to become paupers and that therefore it would in the long run save money to tackle the problem. One of the reasons for the state of affairs he described was that measures to tackle public health problems depended on local initiative. Many towns had set up Improvement Committees but their powers and efficiency varied enormously. He therefore proposed a centralised national system to improve public health, rather like the New Poor Law. He found less support for this, however, than for the reform of the Poor Law because, while the latter was designed to save money, the provision of adequate sanitation and water supplies was likely to be expensive.

John Snow, who discovered the link between cholera and impure water, was also important in bringing about this Act.

The **Public Health Act** of 1848 was therefore a compromise. It created a General Board of Health, headed by Chadwick, with powers to set up local Boards of Health in areas where the death rate was high or there was a local petition for one. Progress was slow, however: by 1854 only just over 10 per cent of the population was covered by local boards, many of which were slow to act.

Over the next 20 years many local acts were passed but public health provision was

Many towns and cities were provided with sewage and water supplies, for which the engineers deserve great credit.

piecemeal. In 1866 the Sanitation Act compelled local authorities to appoint sanitary inspectors, and in 1872 the Public Health Act divided the country into districts which were to set up health boards with a Medical Officer and staff. It did not impose clear duties on them, however.

The **Public Health Act** of 1875, the work of R.A. Cross, compelled local authorities to ensure that there was adequate water supply, drainage and sewage disposal. Regulations were laid down for removal of nuisances, burials, destruction of contaminated food and notification of infectious diseases.

> For the first time this Act ensured an effective system of public health throughout the country. It has been described as the single most important Act of Parliament of the century.
>
> **KEY POINT**

Housing

OCR ▶ M5 (synoptic)

This made the political reputation of Joseph Chamberlain, who was Mayor of Birmingham.

Progress in tackling the problem of poor housing was even slower. It was Cross who took the crucial first step. The **Artisans' Dwellings Act** of 1875 gave local authorities power to buy and clear insanitary property. Unfortunately, in deference to opponents who objected to this interference with the rights of landlords, Cross made the Act permissive rather than compulsory. Nevertheless, it did lead to slum clearance schemes in a number of towns, notably Birmingham. Two later Acts in 1890 and 1900 made the clearance of insanitary property a compulsory duty of local authorities.

In the 20th century two important developments occurred. The state, working through local authorities, undertook the responsibility for providing housing for the working class. It also took powers to regulate housing and other developments through planning laws. The most important Acts were:

- The **Housing and Town Planning Act** (1909) allowed local authorities to introduce town planning schemes. Since it was permissive, it had little effect.
- The **Addison Housing Act** (1919) provided government funds for local authorities to build council houses. This introduced the principle that provision of adequate housing was the responsibility of the state.
- The **Wheatley Housing Act** (1924) provided government grants to local authorities to build council houses and let them at affordable rents.
- The **Greenwood Housing Act** (1930) provided government grants to local authorities to clear slums and build new houses to replace them. By 1939 over 700 000 council houses had been provided.
- The **New Towns Act** (1946) introduced a new approach to the problem of providing a healthy environment. To reduce overcrowding in the big cities the government decided on sites for new towns. The first was at Stevenage. By 1951 there were 14 of them.
- The **Town and Country Planning Act** (1947) required local authorities to produce development plans for the next 20 years.

You should be able to explain the significance of each of these dates.

1842	Report on Sanitary Condition of the Labouring Population	
1848	Public Health Act allows local Boards of Health to be set up	**KEY DATES**
1875	Public Health Act compels local authorities to deal with major public health problems. Artisans' Dwellings Act	
1919	Addison's Housing Act	
1946	New Towns Act	

Factory legislation

OCR M5 (synoptic)
WJEC M6 (synoptic)

At the beginning of the 19th century working conditions in factories and mines were unregulated. Consequently many were dangerous and unhealthy. Hours of work were excessive, especially for children, who were commonly employed from the age of seven and sometimes younger.

Pressure for government action came from the humanitarians, many of whom, such as Ashley (later Lord Shaftesbury), were members of the Evangelical movement in the Church of England. In the prevailing climate of laissez faire, however, many of the upper and middle classes opposed government intervention on principle. Moreover, factory owners claimed that shorter hours would push up costs and make British exports uncompetitive.

Textile mills

In 1830 a Yorkshire Evangelical, Richard Oastler, founded the **Ten Hours Movement**. With the help of Lord Ashley the movement succeeded in getting Parliament to accept the **Factory Act of 1833**. There had been previous Factory Acts but this was the first one to be effective because it provided for four inspectors to be appointed to enforce it. The Act prohibited the employment of children under the age of nine. Children aged nine to 13 were limited to eight hours' work a day and young people aged 14–18 to 12 hours a day. But the Act was a disappointment to the Ten Hours Movement. By using a relay system for child labour, factory owners were still able to require adults to work 12 hours or more.

The Ten Hours campaign therefore continued and achieved most of its aims in three Acts passed between 1844 and 1850.

- The Factory Act of 1844 imposed a 12-hour limit on women's work. The age at which children could work in the mills was lowered to eight but hours of work for those aged eight to 13 were reduced to six-and-a-half. Mill owners were also required to fence dangerous machinery.

> The prime mover for this Act was John Fielden, a Lancashire millowner.

- The Factory Act of 1847 brought in a ten-hour day for women and young people aged 14–18. The Ten Hours Movement appeared to have achieved its goal. Some mill owners, however, got round the Act by using a relay system for women and children and requiring men to work for 12 hours or more.

> Note that all these Acts only applied to textile mills.

- The Factory Act of 1850 limited the opening hours of textile mills to 12 a day, of which one-and-a-half hours had to be for meals. Women and young people were only allowed to work for ten-and-a-half hours a day and were to have a Saturday half-holiday. The effect was that the working day for men was also limited to ten-and-a-half hours.

Coal mines

Ashley also spearheaded a campaign to improve conditions in mines. The report of a Royal Commission on the Employment of Women and Children in Mines in 1842 shocked public opinion and resulted in the Mines Act, which prohibited the employment of females in mines and also of boys under the age of ten. One inspector was appointed to enforce the Act.

The development of factory legislation after 1850

Attitudes towards government regulation of conditions in factories and other places of work gradually changed after 1850. The Factory and Mines Acts of the 1840s had shown that employers' fears that restrictions would destroy the profitability of their industries were unfounded. Regulations concerning hours of work and the age at which children could be employed were gradually extended to other industries. The Factory Act of 1874 reduced the working day to ten hours and raised the age at which children could be employed to ten. In 1891 the minimum age was raised to 11, in 1901 to 12 and in 1920 to 14.

> The Factory Acts established the principle of regulation of working conditions by law. They were the foundation of modern health and safety law.
>
> **KEY POINT**

2.4 Education

After studying this section you should be able to:

- *describe the provision for elementary education in England in the first half of the 19th century*
- *explain the development of state education from the Forster Act to the Butler Act*

LEARNING SUMMARY

The provision of schools before 1870

OCR ▸ M5 (synoptic)

In the early 19th century about 60 per cent of English children went to a school of some sort at some time but only 10 per cent were at schools of a reasonable educational standard. Few attended regularly. In the industrial areas the great majority of children gained what education they had from Sunday Schools. There was a good deal of prejudice against educational reform, and even more indifference.

The impetus for the development of education for the poor came first from the churches and especially the Evangelicals, who saw it as a duty to educate children in the principles of religion. Schools were provided mainly by two religious societies: the **National Society**, a Church of England Society founded in 1811, and the **British and Foreign School Society** (1814). Both placed more emphasis on religious instruction than general education and used the monitorial system.

> The older children (monitors) were used to help the schoolmaster teach the younger ones.

> Because education for the working classes was first provided by religious societies, the development of elementary education in the later 19th century was bedevilled by denominational rivalry and disputes about the place of church schools in the state system of education.
>
> **KEY POINT**

By 1830 it was clear that the religious societies did not have the funds to provide for more than a minority of children. Moreover, the Factory Act of 1833 required that factory children should have two hours of schooling a day. In order to make this possible the **first government grant for education** was made in 1833. Thus the principle of state responsibility for education had been established, though in a very small way – £20 000 a year at first. In 1839 this was increased to £30 000 and a committee of the Privy Council was set up to supervise the way it was spent. The secretary of the committee, Sir James Kay-Shuttleworth, sent inspectors into the schools. They found the monitorial system to be very inefficient. A new system was therefore set up by which able pupils were selected to work as pupil teachers for five years, after which they were sent to training colleges. By 1857 the grant was over £500 000.

The **Newcastle Commission** (1862) reported that most children received some education but the vast majority did not attend school for long enough and the quality of the education they received was poor. In response the government set up a system of 'payment by results': teachers' salaries and grants to schools were linked to the results of testing of children by inspectors. Unfortunately this led to much rote-learning and narrow concentration on the three Rs.

Forster's Education Act (1870)

OCR ▶ M5 (synoptic)

As Robert Lowe, a Liberal minister, remarked, 'We must educate our masters'.

By the 1860s the need for a national system of education was generally accepted. English education compared unfavourably with that of many continental countries, particularly Prussia. The 1867 Reform Act pointed to the need to provide education for the newly enfranchised urban working class. The religious societies were unable to keep pace with the population growth in industrial areas. A vigorous campaign for state provision of education was being waged by Joseph Chamberlain's National Education League, founded in Birmingham in 1869. The outcome was the **Education Act of 1870**.

This angered the Nonconformists.

- The denominational schools (known as Voluntary Schools after this) were left untouched, though with increased government grants.

And this offended Anglicans, who regarded the Board Schools as 'godless'.

- Elsewhere elected school boards were given power to levy rates, build schools for children aged five to 12 and employ teachers.
- Religious education in the Board Schools was to be non-denominational (the Cowper-Temple clause).

> **KEY POINT**
>
> The Forster Act laid the foundation for the system of state education.

Though the fees were low and poor children could be excused them.

The Forster Act did not make attendance compulsory nor was schooling free. Three further Acts dealt with these issues. **Sandon's Act (1876)** set up School Attendance Committees to encourage as many children as possible to attend school and **Mundella's Act (1881)** made attendance compulsory between the ages of five and ten. The Education Act of 1891 made elementary education free.

The Balfour Education Act (1902)

OCR ▶ M5 (synoptic)

By the end of the 19th century further reform was needed. There were three problems:

- Voluntary Schools were inferior to Board Schools because of lack of money
- secondary education was provided by three overlapping types of school – ancient grammar schools, 'higher grade' elementary schools run by the School Boards and technical schools run by county and county borough councils under the Technical Instruction Act (1889)
- England was lagging behind the USA and Germany in the provision of technical education.

Known as local education authorities.

The Balfour Act abolished the School Boards and transferred their functions to county and county borough councils, which were to run the Voluntary and the Board Schools and be responsible also for technical and secondary education. To improve the quality of the Voluntary Schools, they were to receive money from the rates, which angered nonconformists, especially in Wales, where the Anglican school was often the only one available. The local authorities were to provide fee-paying secondary schools and could also assist existing grammar schools from the rates. From 1906 more scholarships were made available so that poor but able children could go to secondary schools.

The 20th century

OCR ▶ MS (synoptic)

In 1918 **Fisher's Education Act** raised the school leaving age to 14. It also proposed that 'day continuation classes' should be set up for young people aged 14 to 18 but little came of this because of cuts in the education budget. For the same reason little was done to implement the **Hadow Report (1926)**, which recommended raising the leaving age to 15 and providing secondary education from the age of 11 for all children in either grammar schools or 'modern schools'.

The next major step forward was the **Butler Education Act (1944)**, which made secondary education available to all, free of charge. The school leaving age was to be raised to 15 in 1947. Local education authorities were required to provide sufficient secondary schools to enable all children to be educated in accordance with their 'ages, aptitudes and abilities'. In practice most local authorities carried this out by providing grammar schools, secondary modern schools and (in some cases) technical schools, i.e. the system recommended by the Hadow Report nearly 20 years earlier.

> By 1947 the state system provided free and compulsory primary and secondary education for all children from five to 15.
>
> **KEY POINT**

You should be able to explain the significance of each of these dates.

1833	First government grant for education	**KEY DATES**
1870	Forster's Education Act	
1902	Balfour Education Act	
1944	Butler Education Act	

Sample question and model answer

Study Sources A to C and answer questions (a), (b) and (c) which follow.

Source A

From an article by N. McCord in *The Long Debate on Poverty*, 1972.
The 1834 Poor Law Amendment Act, accepted by an overwhelming majority of the influential groups in society, aimed at removing any disincentive to independence and individual effort, while at the same time providing relief in cases of genuine need. Cutting down outdoor relief for the able-bodied was intended to coerce able-bodied workers into looking to their own resources; while from the beginning [there were] exemptions providing for relief in cases of sickness, accident and other urgent necessity. The harsher aspects of the 1834 system were mitigated in practice by the exercise of flexibility either locally or at the centre.

Source B

From the Majority Report of the Royal Commission on the Poor Law, 1909.
We feel strongly that pauperism and distress can never be successfully combated by administration and expenditure. The causes of distress are not only economic and industrial; in their origin and character they are largely moral. Government by itself cannot correct or remove such influences.

Source C

From *Ten Lean Years* by Wal Hannington, 1940. Hannington was a Communist who organised the National Unemployed Workers Movement.

[The Means Test] was the most savage and dangerous part of the economy measures of 1931. It constituted a serious step backwards in the field of social legislation because it violated the principle of state responsibility for making provision for able-bodied unemployed. The first Unemployment Insurance Act had been placed on the statute book in 1911 but by subsequent legislation Unemployment Insurance had been extended until practically the entire wage-earning population had been covered. Step by step the ruling class had been compelled to recognise the justice of the demand for state protection for all unemployed workers and now this principle was being smashed down again by the application of the Means Test.

(a) Study Sources A, B and C. What do these sources reveal about the attitudes of influential groups in society towards the poor in the period c.1830–1939? [4]

This question focuses on understanding of the sources.

(a) Source A recognises that some, e.g. the sick, had genuine needs but regards most poor people as needing to be forced to find work. I.e. the fault lies in their character. By 1909 source B accepts that poverty is sometimes caused by economic problems but still argues that poverty is largely caused by moral weakness. Source C argues that the Unemployment Insurance schemes (1911 on) marked the acceptance of the principle that the state should protect workers against unemployment, i.e. that it was caused by economic circumstances beyond their control.

(b) Use your own knowledge. In what ways may the publication of the surveys of Booth and Rowntree be seen as a turning point in public attitudes towards the poor?

[10]

(b) They provided hard evidence that
  • Thirty per cent of the population of London and York were living in poverty. This was most serious at certain stages in life, particularly when children were young and in old age.
  • It was impossible for many of the working class to save for old age.
  • Often men were unemployed simply because there was no work available.

The Poor Law Amendment Act was based on this assumption.

These findings challenged the assumption that poverty was something which could be avoided if only the poor made the effort.

Sample question and model answer *(continued)*

(c) Study Sources A, B and C and use your own knowledge. How far were changes in government policies towards the problems of the poor in the period 1830–1939 the result of changing perceptions of the causes of poverty?

[16]

This is an outline answer, to which you should add more detail.

(c) Outline main changes: 1834 Poor Law; Liberal reforms (especially old age pensions and National Insurance); between wars – extension of unemployment insurance, abolition of the Poor Law and replacement by public assistance, Means Test.

Perceptions of causes of poverty: 1834 Royal Commission report – Benthamite – argued that help for the poor was bad for their character because it undermined their self-reliance; poverty was the result of idleness – therefore recommended disincentives (the workhouse test). But it accepted that sometimes poverty was the result of circumstances, e.g. sickness, accident (source A). It ignored the cyclical unemployment characteristic of industries such as textiles.

Note that references to sources are woven into the argument.

Perceptions began to change in the late 19th century. Booth and Rowntree showed that poverty was often unavoidable because of low wages, unemployment (especially during the long depression of 1873–96) and old age. Their surveys provided support for the ideas of the 'New Liberals' and underlay the Liberal reforms. But the old view that poverty was often the result of character defects persisted (see source B). Neither the Majority nor the Minority Report was acted on, so the workhouse continued alongside the Liberals' 'social service state'.

The Minority Report disagreed.

In the inter-war years the view that poverty was primarily caused by economic factors outside the control of the individual (especially unemployment in this period) was the basis for most changes in provision for the poor: the Poor Law was finally abolished, unemployment insurance extended (see source C) and assistance was made available to those not covered by it. But attitudes were still ambivalent in the face of the cost of the 'dole' (source C).

You can refer to source A again here.

Other factors were also important. The cost of poor relief not only led to the Means Test in the 1930s but was a major factor in the substitution of the workhouse for the Speenhamland System in 1834. As early as the 1840s humanitarian concern led to some mitigation of the worst excesses of the workhouse system. The extension of the franchise made political parties from the late 19th century more responsive to the needs of the working class. Economic changes (industrialisation and urbanisation) put the 1834 system under increasing pressure, especially during the depression of 1873–96. By the 1930s there were some who argued that long-term unemployment was wasteful and government should therefore actively intervene in the economy and try to bring industry to depressed areas.

Practice examination questions

1 'Throughout the period 1830–1939 there was tension between awareness of the needs of the poor and the cost of meeting those needs.' How far does this explain changes in provision for the poor? [30]

2 'Significant social reforms only took place when the government was pressurised by outside factors.' How valid is this assessment of the response of government to demands for social reform in the period 1834–1948? [30]

3 Why did the state take an increasingly active role in tackling the problems of public health and housing in an industrialised society in the period c.1840–1948? [30]

Chapter 3

Britain and Ireland, 1798–1921

The following topics are covered in this chapter:

- *Irish nationalism*
- *Support for the Union*
- *British policies towards Ireland*
- *The Irish economy*

3.1 Irish nationalism

LEARNING SUMMARY

After studying this section you should be able to:

- *assess the importance of the United Irishmen, O'Connell, Young Ireland and the Fenians in arousing opposition to the Union*
- *explain the rise and decline of the Home Rule (Irish Nationalist) Party*
- *show how the Easter Rising and the rise of Sinn Fein brought about the establishment of the Irish Free State in 1922*

Ireland at the end of the 18th century

| OCR | M5 (synoptic) |
| NICCEA | M5 (synoptic) |

Politically Ireland was subordinate to the British government in London. It had its own parliament but until 1782 the laws it passed had to be approved by the British Parliament. Even after 1782 the British government still appointed the Viceroy and his officials.

In **religion** Ireland was divided between Protestants and Catholics. The majority of the Irish were Roman Catholics and as such were denied many of the rights of citizenship, including the right to be MPs. It was only in 1793 that they were given the right to vote. The established church, the Church of Ireland, to which the greater part of the aristocracy and gentry belonged, was to all intents and purposes a branch of the Church of England. The one part of Ireland where Protestantism predominated was Ulster.

> But most Ulster Protestants were Presbyterians of Scottish descent, not members of the Church of Ireland.

The United Irishmen, the Rebellion of 1798 and the Act of Union

| OCR | M5 (synoptic) |
| NICCEA | M5 (synoptic) |

The Society of United Irishmen was formed in 1791 to demand reform of the corrupt Irish parliament and full civic rights for Catholics, i.e. Catholic emancipation. An Ulster Protestant, **Wolfe Tone**, rapidly became its leading member. Rebellion broke out in 1798, but the British had little difficulty in suppressing it. The most dangerous rebel force was defeated at Vinegar Hill. Protestants portrayed the rebellion as a Catholic uprising, though the Society was originally supported by both Protestants and Catholics.

> The rising was particularly dangerous because it was supported by revolutionary France, with which Britain was at war.

Pitt's solution to the danger from Ireland was to propose the union of Ireland with Great Britain and at the same time to grant Catholic emancipation. By the Act of Union the Irish parliament was abolished. Ireland was to return 100 MPs to the United Kingdom parliament at Westminster. Unfortunately George III blocked the second part of the plan, Catholic emancipation.

> He claimed that it was against his coronation oath, when he swore to protect the Protestant religion.

> **KEY POINT**
> - Nationalists looked back to 1798 as a heroic rising against oppression and Wolfe Tone as a martyr to the Irish cause.
> - The failure to grant emancipation left Catholics feeling cheated.

O'Connell

OCR ▶ M5 (synoptic)
NICCEA ▶ M5 (synoptic)

In the 20 years after the Union Catholics made no progress with the demand for emancipation because of opposition from the Tories. In 1823 Daniel O'Connell founded the Catholic Association to press their claims. From 1824 money was raised by the 'Catholic rent' of a penny a month. This produced considerable sums and also gained mass support for the movement. The repeal of the Test and Corporation Acts in 1828, removing the disabilities imposed on Protestant nonconformists, made the case for Catholic emancipation more difficult to resist. The crucial moment was the election of O'Connell as MP for County Clare in a by-election in 1828. The law did not prevent him from standing for election but as a Catholic he would be unable to take his seat. Wellington and Peel realised there was a danger of civil war in Ireland unless concessions were made and in 1829 the **Catholic Relief Act** was passed.

> The Act allowed Catholics to hold all but a very few public offices.

O'Connell's long-term aim was repeal of the Union. After the success of the campaign for emancipation he led a group of Irish MPs who stood for repeal, but used his position to bring pressure on the Whigs to introduce Irish reforms. In 1840 he founded the Repeal Association but was soon challenged by 'Young Ireland'. In response O'Connell stepped up the pressure for repeal by holding a series of mass meetings. The climax of the campaign was to be a meeting at Clontarf in 1843 but when Peel banned it, O'Connell called it off. He died in 1847.

> In the Lichfield House Compact (1835) he agreed to support the Whigs in return for reforms in Ireland.

'Young Ireland' and the Fenians

OCR ▶ M5 (synoptic)
NICCEA ▶ M5 (synoptic)

The members of 'Young Ireland' wanted to see a revival of Irish culture and the development of a sense of Irish nationhood. They were impatient of O'Connell's methods and advocated more violent measures. The movement was, however, overtaken by the Great Famine. In the excitement of the revolutions of 1848 in Europe they attempted to start a rebellion in Ireland, led by Smith O'Brien, but it was quickly suppressed. The leaders were transported to Australia and the movement faded out.

> **KEY POINT**
> Although Young Ireland was a failure, it played an important part in the development of nationalist ideas.

> The name refers to the warriors of ancient Ireland.

Fenianism emerged in the late 1850s, developing from revolutionary groups formed among Irish immigrants in New York. In 1858 James Stephens founded a revolutionary society in Dublin with financial backing from the USA. This later became known as the Irish Republican Brotherhood. It quickly gained adherents in Ireland itself and among Irish immigrants in the USA and Great Britain. It was strongly nationalist and anti-English and its methods were conspiratorial and revolutionary.

In 1867 the Fenians were involved in a series of terrorist outrages. In Manchester a policeman was shot during an attempt to rescue Fenian prisoners from a police van. Another Fenian rescue attempt, this time at Clerkenwell prison, caused an explosion in which 12 people were killed. These actions achieved little in themselves but drew attention to the Irish question.

> **KEY POINT**
> The American connection marked an important step in the growth of Irish-American political and financial support for Irish nationalist movements.

The Home Rule Party

OCR → M5 (synoptic)
NICCEA → M5 (synoptic)

Home Rule meant a separate parliament and government for Irish domestic affairs.

There was a considerable rise in evictions which led to the Land War of 1879–82.

Key points from AS

• **Gladstone, Parnell and Ireland**
  Revise AS pages 33–35

In 1882 the Chief Secretary for Ireland, Lord Frederick Cavendish, and the Under-Secretary, T.H. Burke, were murdered in Phoenix Park, Dublin, by the Invincibles, an extremist organisation.

But was suspended – see below, p. 51.

The Home Rule Association was founded in 1870 by Isaac Butt. In the 1874 election the Home Rule Party won 59 seats. In the late 1870s it came under the influence of Parnell, who became its leader in parliament in 1880. The party gained publicity for its aims by pursuing obstructionist tactics in parliament.

The development of the party was profoundly affected by the agricultural depression of the late 1870s, which led in 1879 to the formation of the Land League. The moving force in this, Michael Davitt, persuaded Parnell to become its President, thus bringing together the agitation for land reform and for self-government. This **'new departure'** was also supported by some Fenians, particularly the Irish-American John Devoy. The Home Rule Party (Irish Nationalist Party) was thus closely linked with the militant tactics of the Land League in the 'land war' of 1879–82.

In the 1885 general election the Irish Nationalists won 86 seats, which gave them the balance of power in the House of Commons. Parnell gave his support to Gladstone when it became known that he had become converted to Home Rule. The First Home Rule Bill, however, split the Liberal Party and was defeated in the Commons. The subsequent general election produced a Conservative government, though the nationalists again won most of the Irish seats.

Parnell's policy was now to await a shift in electoral fortunes which would bring the Liberals to power. An attempt to discredit him by *The Times*, which published letters allegedly implicating him in the Phoenix Park murders, backfired when it was proved that the letters were forged. Parnell was at the peak of his power, but a year later his authority was undermined by the O'Shea divorce. His fight to retain control over the Irish Nationalist Party in the face of the disapproval of the Catholic bishops split it and left it weakened on his death in 1891.

With the failure of Gladstone's two Home Rule Bills and the splits in the Nationalist Party, the movement for Home Rule lost its momentum. The party was reunited in 1900 under Redmond, but it was not until 1910 that Home Rule again became a serious possibility. The crisis over the House of Lords made the votes of the Irish Nationalists vital to the Liberal government and Redmond demanded Home Rule as the price of Irish Nationalist support. As a result a Home Rule Bill was passed by the House of Commons in 1912 and became law, under the provisions of the Parliament Act, in 1914.

Sinn Fein and the Easter Rising

OCR → M5 (synoptic)
NICCEA → M6

Sinn Fein means 'Ourselves Alone'.

Like the dual monarchy in Austria–Hungary before the First World War.

The IRB developed from the Fenians.

The origins of Sinn Fein lie in the Irish cultural renaissance of the 1890s. The Gaelic League, founded in 1893, aimed to revive the Irish language as a means of building up a sense of nationhood. This emphasis on the special cultural identity of Ireland led several writers to advocate the separation of Ireland from Britain. Arthur Griffith, who founded Sinn Fein in 1907, argued for a dual monarchy of Britain and Ireland under the British crown. Sinn Fein remained a relatively small organisation on the nationalist fringe until after the Easter Rising.

The Easter Rising was the work of a small group of extremists, most of whom were members of the Irish Republican Brotherhood. On Easter Monday 1916, 1500 rebels occupied the General Post Office and other buildings in Dublin. Patrick Pearse declared a new Irish Republic. The rebels gained little support and within a week the rising had been crushed. One hundred and fifty rebels and over 100 soldiers and policemen were killed.

The harsh response of the British authorities turned the rebels into martyrs. Martial law was declared throughout Ireland, thousands were arrested and 15 of the

The only one not executed, because he had American nationality, was de Valera, the future President of Ireland.

leaders of the rising were executed. Irish opinion swung decisively away from Redmond's Irish Nationalist Party to Sinn Fein, which was taken over by the republicans. In the 1918 election Sinn Fein swept the board in southern Ireland, winning 73 seats. The Nationalist Party was almost wiped out.

> **KEY POINT**
> The Easter Rising was a turning point. Thereafter Home Rule was no longer enough to satisfy majority opinion in Ireland outside Ulster.

The Anglo-Irish War 1919–21

OCR M5 (synoptic)
NICCEA M6

The Irish Volunteers had been formed in 1914 in opposition to the Ulster Volunteers. See p.50.

The Irish Free State comprised 26 counties – all of Ireland except six counties in the north-east – Antrim, Armagh, Down, Fermanagh, [London]derry and Tyrone.

The Sinn Fein MPs elected in 1918 refused to take their seats at Westminster and instead constituted themselves as the Dail, or Parliament, of Ireland. The Irish Republican Army (successor to the Irish Volunteers) conducted a campaign of violence, particularly against the police. The overwhelming victory of Sinn Fein in Southern Ireland in the 1921 elections held under the Government of Ireland Act (1920) showed that for the majority of Irish people outside Ulster Home Rule was no longer enough. At the end of 1921 Lloyd George made an agreement (the Anglo-Irish Treaty) by which most of Ireland became the Irish Free State, with dominion status, in 1922. Northern Ireland remained in the United Kingdom.

> **KEY POINT**
> The Sinn Fein leaders had to accept partition as the price for independence for southern Ireland, but the result was civil war between supporters and opponents of the Treaty.

3.2 Support for the Union

> **LEARNING SUMMARY**
> After studying this section you should be able to:
> * explain the importance of the Protestant Ascendancy and its decline after 1870
> * assess the importance of Ulster Unionism in shaping Irish history from the 1880s to 1921

The Protestant Ascendancy

OCR M5 (synoptic)
NICCEA M5 (synoptic)

In the 18th century government and society in Ireland were dominated by a landowning class which was Protestant (Church of Ireland) and Anglo-Irish. This constituted the Protestant Ascendancy. For much of the 19th century, it continued to dominate Ireland. Tenants voted as the landowners decided and most Irish MPs at Westminster thus represented the Ascendancy.

Voting by secret ballot allowed Irish tenants to vote for Home Rule candidates without fear of eviction.

The power of the Ascendancy declined after 1870 as a result of the disestablishment of the Church of Ireland in 1869 and changes in the land law by which Irish tenants gained more security and eventually became owner-occupiers. Moreover the Ballot Act (1872) deprived the landowners of their electoral power and led to the rise of the Home Rule Party.

The Orange Order and Ulster Unionism

OCR M5 (synoptic)
NICCEA M5 (synoptic)

The Orange Order was founded in 1795 after a clash between Protestants and Catholics in County Armagh. Its members swore to defend the King 'as long as he

'Orange' in memory of William of Orange (William III), who preserved British supremacy in Ireland against the Catholic James II.

supports the Protestant Ascendancy'. The Order opposed the Union at first but became fiercely pro-Union in response to O'Connell's Repeal Movement. It had members throughout Ireland but was heavily concentrated in the north. With the growth of Belfast it gained strength among the working classes there. From the 1870s onwards, in opposition to the Home Rule movement, it was at the heart of Ulster Unionist opposition to Home Rule.

The rise of Ulster Unionism was a direct response to the Home Rule movement. Up to 1880 Ulster elections were fought mainly between Liberals and Conservatives. But when Gladstone declared for Home Rule in 1886, alarm bells rang. Ulster politics was reshaped along sectarian lines. Rallies and demonstrations were organised by the Orange Order. At a mass meeting in Belfast, Lord Randolph Churchill, a leading English Conservative, played 'the Orange card', threatening 'Ulster will fight and Ulster will be right'. In the 1886 election, 17 Unionists were elected in Ulster. In the rest of Ireland Nationalists swept the board.

Two main factors lay behind this development.

- Religion. Protestants were a majority in Ulster but a minority in Ireland as a whole. 'Home Rule', they believed, would be 'Rome rule'.
- The economic development of the north-east of Ireland, and especially the growth of Belfast, placed the industrial wealth of Ulster behind Unionism. Ulster's business leaders were overwhelmingly Protestant.

They also believed the Union was vital for Belfast's prosperity.

Ulster Unionists threatened armed resistance to Home Rule. When the House of Commons passed the Third Home Rule Bill in 1912, drilling of volunteers began and in 1913 the **Ulster Volunteer Force** was formed. In 1914 the UVF successfully landed a large cargo of arms and ammunition at Larne (the Larne gun-running). Meanwhile the Unionists' leaders, Carson and Craig, organised a 'Solemn League and Covenant' which attracted 250 000 signatures. The signatories pledged to use 'all necessary means' to defeat Home Rule. Sympathy for Ulster Unionism in the army led to the so-called **'Curragh mutiny'**, in which a number of cavalry officers said they would rather resign than fight in Ulster to enforce Home Rule. Unionist preparations for armed resistance naturally led to similar preparations by the Nationalists. The realisation that civil war would result from any future attempt to enforce Home Rule on Ulster explains why Ireland was partitioned in the settlement of 1921.

> By 1914 Ulster Unionists' opposition to Home Rule had brought Ireland to the verge of civil war.
>
> **KEY POINT**

You should be able to explain the significance of each of these dates.

		KEY DATES
1798	Rebellion of United Irishmen	
1800	Act of Union	
1829	Catholic emancipation	
1845–49	Great Famine	
1869–70	Irish Church disestablishment and First Land Act	
1879	'New departure'	
1886	First Home Rule Bill	
1912–14	Third Home Rule Bill brings Ireland to verge of civil war	
1916	Easter Rising	
1922	Partition	

3.3 British policies towards Ireland

After studying this section you should be able to:

- *outline the policies of British governments towards Ireland, 1800–1922*

LEARNING SUMMARY

Irish reforms 1829–1881

OCR   M5 (synoptic)

There was a 'tithe war' in 1830–33 – violent protests against paying tithes to the Church of Ireland.

Key points from AS

- **Gladstone, Parnell and Ireland**
  Revise AS pages 33–35

The most important Irish reform in the first half of the 19th century was **Catholic emancipation**, which was finally passed in 1829 under pressure from O'Connell's Catholic Association. Peel, who had previously affirmed his opposition, agreed with the Prime Minster, Wellington, that the alternative was civil war in Ireland.

In the 1830s the Whigs tried to win Catholic support for the Union by reforming tithes and introducing a national system of elementary education into Ireland. **Peel** (Prime Minister 1841–46) also tried to win Irish support for the Union by increasing the grant for Maynooth College (a training college for catholic priests) and establishing three new non-sectarian university colleges (the Queen's Colleges) at Belfast, Galway and Limerick. At the same time he acted firmly against O'Connell's Repeal Association, banning the Clontarf meeting in 1843. His measures to deal with the Great Famine are discussed below.

In his first two ministries (1868–74 and 1880–85) Gladstone tried to 'pacify Ireland' by disestablishing the Irish Church (1869) and tackling the land problem (First Land Act, 1870, and Second Land Act, 1881).

Home Rule and partition, 1886–1922

OCR   M5 (synoptic)

Ninety-three Liberals, led by Chamberlain and Hartington, voted against the Bill. In 1895 most of them followed Chamberlain into alliance with the Conservatives.

By 1885 Gladstone had come to the view that the only solution to the Irish problem was Home Rule, but his First Home Rule Bill (1886) split the Liberal Party and was defeated in the Commons. The Second Home Rule Bill was passed in the Commons but overwhelmingly defeated in the Lords.

> Gladstone's efforts to solve the Irish problem became almost obsessive, but it can be argued that he failed because he offered 'too little too late'.
>
> **KEY POINT**

This involved offering a 'fair rent' and refusing to pay if the landlord rejected it. It led to a renewal of unrest and agrarian crime in the west of Ireland.

Key points from AS

- **The Liberals and Ireland 1912–14**
  Revise AS pages 55–56

The Conservative ministries of 1886–92 and 1895–1905 followed a policy of 'constructive Unionism', or 'killing Home Rule with kindness'. The centrepiece of this was land purchase, which they encouraged in a series of Acts culminating in Wyndham's Land Purchase Act of 1903. This was not the whole story, however. Faced by the 'Plan of Campaign', Balfour as Chief Secretary for Ireland employed coercion and was nicknamed 'Bloody Balfour'.

The Liberals returned to office in 1905 but it was not until after the 1910 elections, which gave the Irish Nationalists the balance of power in the House of Commons, that they introduced a Third Home Rule Bill. Under the Parliament Act this would have come into force in 1914 but was suspended on the outbreak of war. At this point Ireland was on the verge of civil war. The Conservatives backed Ulster Unionist opposition to the implementation of Home Rule and their leader, Bonar Law, came dangerously close to encouraging armed rebellion.

At the end of the war Irish opinion had shifted because of the Easter Rising. Faced by armed rebellion in 1919, Lloyd George sent in troops and ex-soldiers (the Auxiliaries and the Black and Tans). Home Rule was clearly no longer practical and the eventual settlement achieved by Lloyd George involved acceptance of **partition** with Home Rule for the six counties of northern Ireland and a separate state, with dominion status, in southern Ireland.

3.4 The Irish economy

After studying this section you should be able to:

- explain the main features of the Irish economy in the 19th century
- assess the reasons for and consequences of the potato famine
- explain the Irish land problem and show how it was resolved in the late 19th and early 20th centuries

LEARNING SUMMARY

The land problem

OCR — M5 (synoptic)
NICCEA — M5 (synoptic)

> This was in spite of emigration, which was already significant before the Great Famine of 1845–9.

Early 19th-century Ireland was poor and economically backward. There were three key reasons for this.

- Rapid population growth. Between 1791 and 1841 the population almost doubled from 4.4 million to 8.2 million.
- Lack of industrial development, except in the north-east.
- The land tenure system.

Most land in Ireland was owned by members of the Protestant Ascendancy. Many landowners, especially the wealthiest, managed their estates through land agents.

Most Irish **tenant farmers** held their land on short leases. From the early 19th century it was increasingly common for them to hold annual tenancies, which meant that rents could be raised each year. Except in Ulster, they were not entitled to compensation for improvements at the end of the lease or tenancy. Consequently it was not worth their while to invest in improvements. As the population grew and pressure on the land increased, farms were sub-divided into smaller and smaller holdings. This in turn led many farmers to depend on potato growing.

> Because of the lack of industry, it was only possible to escape from rural poverty by emigration.

The system was extremely inefficient. Much of the Irish rural population was living at subsistence level. The right of the landlords to raise rents and evict tenants led to much unrest and at times serious disorder. This in turn made it difficult for landlords to consolidate holdings into bigger farms which would permit the introduction of improved agricultural techniques. Agriculture therefore remained backward. Landlords themselves were often in debt.

> **KEY POINT**
>
> The land tenure system meant that the ability of Irish agriculture to feed the growing population was increasingly precarious. If the potato crop failed, there would be widespread hunger.

The potato famine 1845–49

OCR — M5 (synoptic)
NICCEA — M5 (synoptic)

> Diseases, especially typhus and relapsing fever, spread rapidly in a population weakened by malnutrition.

In 1845, 1846 and 1848 potato blight virtually wiped out the crop. Because the potato was the staple diet of so much of the population, this was disastrous.

- Between 1845 and 1851 it is estimated that over 1 000 000 people died from starvation or disease. Large numbers emigrated to Britain, Canada or the USA. The population declined by one-fifth.
- The British government responded in various ways. Peel brought in maize from America and inaugurated a programme of public works. The Whig government, which came to power in 1846, expanded this and set up kitchens to supply meals throughout the country. But it refused to intervene to stop export of agricultural produce from Ireland.
- Landlords lost income from rents and faced high rates to pay for poor relief.

Many were already indebted and the Encumbered Estates Act (1849) enabled them to sell up. By 1857, 3000 estates had been sold. Nevertheless the bulk of the land remained in the possession of the old landed families.

- Evictions increased greatly. Many small farms disappeared as holdings and were consolidated into larger farms. There was, however, still a substantial number of small farms and most tenants, whatever the size of their farms, were still faced by the problems of short leases, high rents and evictions without compensation.
- There was a sharp fall in the number of agricultural labourers after the famine. High mortality among this class was followed by heavy emigration.
- Irish opinion, especially among the Irish who emigrated to America, blamed the British for the famine. This helps to explain the support of the Irish-American community for Irish nationalism, beginning with the foundation of the Fenian Society.

> Could the British government have done more? Some would argue that in the context of the laissez faire ideas of the time, it did as much as could be expected. Others claim that it would have acted differently if a famine of such proportions had occurred in England.
>
> **KEY POINT**

The Land and Land Purchase Acts

OCR ▷ M5 (synoptic)

NICCEA ▷ M5 (synoptic)

Gladstone identified the land problem as one of the main sources of Irish unrest in the 1860s. He attempted to solve it by the Land Act of 1870, which provided for tenants to be compensated for improvements and for disturbance if evicted other than for non-payment of rent. The weakness of the Act lay in the fact that there was no effective provision to prevent landlords raising rents and then evicting tenants. The agricultural depression which began in 1877 led to a big increase in evictions and the Land War of 1879–82.

Gladstone's Second Land Act (1881) granted Irish tenants the three Fs – fixity of tenure, free sale of the lease and fair rents. This went a long way to solving the problems of Irish land law. What Irish tenants really wanted, however, was to own their land. A series of Land Purchase Acts – Ashburne's Act (1885), Balfour's Act (1891) and Wyndham's Act (1903) – facilitated this.

Wyndham's Act provided cheap loans for tenants to buy their land and generous cash payments to landlords for releasing land for sale to tenants.

> By 1909 over half of Ireland's tenant farmers had become owner-occupiers, thus effectively solving the land problem.
>
> **KEY POINT**

Sample question and model answer

This question incorporates synoptic assessment.

This is an outline answer, to which you should add more detail.

Founded Repeal Association and organised a series of mass rallies.

Mention Isaac Butt and Michael Davitt.

Explain this in some detail.

Conclusion: aims changed in response to failure of British governments to satisfy Irish grievances.

In what ways, and why, did the aims of Catholic and nationalist movements in Ireland change between 1798 and 1921? [30]

In the early 19th century Catholic opinion was divided about the Union itself but united in demanding emancipation. O'Connell's Catholic Association and his victory in the County Clare election achieved this in 1829. In the 1830s O'Connell's approach was pragmatic: he aimed for repeal but used his position as leader of a group of Irish MPs to put pressure on the Whigs for reforms. In the 1840s O'Connell stepped up the pressure for repeal. This was partly because of the rise of Young Ireland. He was not prepared to resort to violent methods and acquiesced when Peel banned a meeting at Clontarf in 1843.

Young Ireland aimed to revive an Irish sense of nationhood and criticised O'Connell's reluctance to use force to oppose the Union. But it failed to gain mass support and its 1848 rising was a fiasco.

After the Famine and the collapse of Young Ireland, Catholic and nationalist demands were comparatively muted. But in the 1860s and 1870s three new strands emerged. The Fenians aimed to break away from Britain. They blamed England for Ireland's ills, especially the famine, and their methods were revolutionary. They did much to raise Irish consciousness of grievances. The Home Rule Association sought to modify the Union by giving Ireland self-government in domestic affairs while the Land League arose as a result of the agricultural depression.

In 1879 these three strands came together in the New Departure. As a result Parnell became the leader of nationalist opinion. The Land League campaign secured the 1881 Land Act, after which Parnell focused nationalist aims on Home Rule. By 1886 the strength of the support for Home Rule in Ireland convinced Gladstone that this was the right policy. Parnell allied with the Gladstonian Liberals. The achievement of Home Rule by Act of Parliament remained the aim of the Irish Nationalist Party through nearly 30 years of disappointment – the failure of Gladstone's Home Rule Bills, the divisions in the party after the fall of Parnell, the long period of Conservative government. When the Third Home Rule Bill finally became law in 1914, opposition in Ulster brought Ireland to the verge of civil war. The failure to achieve Home Rule helps to explain the swing of Irish opinion away from the Nationalist Party.

The Easter Rising of 1916 was a turning point. The rising was the work of a small group of extreme nationalists who rejected the policy of co-operating with the British government in the First World War. They had comparatively little support at first but after the execution of the leaders nationalist opinion swung dramatically to Sinn Fein, which aimed to make Ireland an independent republic. It also aimed for a united Ireland rather than partition, which came to be the aim of the Ulster Unionists.

Practice examination questions

1 'They conceded too little, too late.' How far is this a fair assessment of the response of British governments to Irish grievances in the period 1798–1921? [30]

2 What were the major obstacles in Ireland and at Westminster to the settlement of the Irish problem during the period 1798–1921? [30]

Chapter 4

German nationalism 1815–1919

The following topics are covered in this chapter:

- The origins and development of German nationalism to 1860
- Economic nationalism
- Bismarck
- German nationalism and the German Empire, 1871–1919

4.1 The origins and development of German nationalism to 1860

After studying this section you should be able to:

- explain the origins of liberal and nationalist movements in Germany
- assess the importance of Metternich in repressing nationalist ideas
- discuss the place of the 1848 revolutions in the history of German nationalism

LEARNING SUMMARY

Germany in 1815

OCR ▶ M5 (synoptic)

Make sure you understand the concepts of liberalism and nationalism and the connection between them.

The French Revolution and the Napoleonic Wars had a massive impact on Germany. The French armies which occupied much of Germany brought with them **liberal** ideas of freedom and equality. By the end of the Napoleonic period, however, the French were resented as an occupying power rather than as the liberators they professed to be. This stimulated the growth of **nationalism**, which was closely linked with liberalism since freedom came to be seen in terms of freedom from foreign domination as well as freedom from oppressive rulers. The defeat of Napoleon at Leipzig in 1813 gave a considerable boost to German national feeling.

The Napoleonic period also produced major changes in the way Germany was governed. The political map of Germany was completely re-drawn. The Holy Roman Empire was abolished, as were many of the smallest of the 300 German states. The creation of the Confederation of the Rhine from the remaining German states except Prussia and Austria was another stimulus to the idea of a unified Germany. At the same time some of the German states, following the example of Napoleonic France, modernised their legal and political systems. The most important was Prussia, where Stein and Hardenberg abolished serfdom and reformed the administration, the regulation of trade, the army and education.

Metternich and the German Confederation

OCR ▶ M5 (synoptic)

Some of the individual states had parliaments but there was no federal parliament.

In the Vienna settlement (1815) the political map of Germany was revised again. It was divided into 39 states, of which Prussia and Austria were far and away the biggest. Prussia not only regained the territory taken away by Napoleon but also gained the Rhineland and part of Saxony. A new **German Confederation** was set up, with a Federal Assembly (Bundestag) consisting of delegates from the states meeting under Austria's presidency. Essentially, therefore, Germany was a federation of princes.

The Confederation was dominated from 1815 to 1848 by the Austrian Chancellor, **Metternich**. Under his influence it became an instrument of repression. The universities were the main centres of liberal and nationalist ideas. In 1819 Metternich persuaded the Bundestag to issue the Carlsbad Decrees, which brought all German universities under close supervision and instituted rigorous censorship.

He also put pressure on those German states which had constitutions to limit the powers of their assemblies. The power of the Bundestag to act against liberals in the German states was further increased by the Six Acts of 1833.

They also strengthened press censorship.

After the reforms of Stein and Hardenberg nationalists saw Prussia as the potential focus of unification, but Frederick William III was content to follow Metternich's lead. The accession in 1840 of Frederick William IV, who appeared to have more liberal leanings, raised their hopes once again.

> Between 1815 and 1848 neither liberals nor nationalists made much progress towards achieving their aims.
>
> **KEY POINT**

The 1848 revolutions

OCR ▸ MS (synoptic)
NICCEA ▸ M4

In 1848 there were revolutions throughout Germany. In Prussia Frederick William IV appointed a liberal ministry and summoned a National Assembly to draw up a constitution. In Austria Metternich was overthrown after demonstrations in Vienna. A *Vorparlament* (pre-parliament), with members drawn from the assemblies of the various states, met in March and arranged for the election of a parliament for the whole of Germany, the **Frankfurt Parliament** of 1848–9. The purpose of the Frankfurt Parliament was to draw up a constitution for a united Germany. Its members – largely middle class liberals – engaged in endless debate, which revealed deep divisions about the definition of 'Germany'. There were two possibilities.

Study the map in *Revise AS*, p.108. Note the overlap between the Austrian Empire and the German Confederation.

- **Great Germany** (Grossdeutschland), which would include the Austrian lands except Hungary and would therefore include many Slav peoples. Since Austria was the biggest Catholic state, Catholics in the other south German states tended to support Great Germany.
- **Little Germany** (Kleindeutschland), which would exclude the Austrian lands altogether but would include the whole of Prussia. This view was more attractive to north German Protestants. Frederick William IV of Prussia was offered the crown in April 1849 but he would not accept 'the crown from the gutter'. He ordered the Prussian delegates to resign from the Parliament and soon afterwards it collapsed.

The events of 1848 left many Germans disillusioned with liberalism: the attempt to set up a united Germany by constitutional means had failed. Nevertheless, nationalist sentiment remained strong. If liberalism had failed to create a German nation state, other means must be found. The legacy of 1848 was that many Germans regarded parliamentary democracy as ineffective.

The failure of the Frankfurt Parliament allowed Austria to revive the Confederation. An attempt by Prussia to set up a new federation which excluded Austria (the Erfurt Union) failed and in 1850, in the **Submission of Olmütz**, Frederick William IV of Prussia rejoined the revived Confederation.

Thus Prussia accepted the renewal of Austrian pre-eminence – to the disgust of Bismarck.

Austria did not, however, recover the dominant position in Germany it had had under Metternich. Bismarck, as leader of the Prussian delegation to the Bundestag, constantly challenged Austria. The Crimean War isolated it from Russia. Its defeat by France and Piedmont in Italy in 1859 lowered its military prestige.

You should be able to explain the significance of each of these dates.

1813	Battle of Leipzig	**KEY DATES**
1815	Establishment of the German Confederation	
1819	Carlsbad Decrees	
1848	Revolutions in many German states. Overthrow of Metternich	
1848–9	Frankfurt parliament	
1850	Submission of Olmütz	

4.2 Economic nationalism

After studying this section you should be able to:

- *assess the importance of the Zollverein and the economic development of Prussia in the achievement of political unification*

The Zollverein

OCR	M5 (synoptic)
NICCEA	M4

Free trade was established within Prussia in 1818 and extended by negotiation to several other north German states in the 1820s. In 1834 negotiations with the Bavaria-Württemberg customs union led to the establishment of the Zollverein (customs union) of 17 states with a population of 25 000 000. Crucially, the Zollverein excluded Austria and thus gave Prussia economic leadership in Germany. Economic integration thus preceded political unification by several decades.

Until the middle of the century German economic development was comparatively slow. Agriculture still employed more than two-thirds of the population and the size of the middle class was small. The building of railways from the 1840s was the turning point: transport costs were reduced by 80 per cent and trade was stimulated. By 1860 Germany was producing more coal than France and the output of iron and steel was growing rapidly. Much of this expansion took place in Prussia, which not only had great natural resources but also the capital to exploit them and to finance the building of railways and investment in industry. Prussia's economic growth went hand in hand with the development of its military strength by Roon and William I, who came to the throne in 1861.

> The economic and military power of Prussia provided the foundation for the unification of Germany under its leadership.
>
> **KEY POINT**

4.3 Bismarck

After studying this section you should be able to:

- *explain how Bismarck brought about the unification of Germany*

The Danish and Austrian wars

OCR	M5 (synoptic)
NICCEA	M4

> There is a discussion of Bismarck's claim that he planned the unification of Germany from the beginning on p.139.

> **Key points from AS**
>
> - **Bismarck and the wars against Denmark and Austria, 1864–66**
> *Revise AS pages 110–111*

Bismarck was appointed Prime Minister of Prussia in 1862. William I was in dispute with the liberals in the Prussian parliament over new taxes to finance the expansion of the army. Bismarck had a reputation as a tough reactionary and he used a dubious constitutional technicality to enforce the taxes against liberal opposition.

His principal aim was to defeat Austrian claims to predominance in Germany. The steps by which he achieved this were as follows.

- He gave full backing to the expansion of the Prussian army. The result was the decisive victory at Sadowa in the Seven Weeks' War in 1866.
- He used the crisis in Schleswig-Holstein to further his aims. By going to war in alliance with Austria against Denmark he won the support of German nationalists and he manoeuvred Austria into a position where he could pick a quarrel over Holstein when it suited him.

He also secured the alliance of Italy.

- He isolated Austria from potential allies.
- When Austria called a conference of princes to propose reform of the Confederation, he pressurised William I into refusing to attend. He realised that Austria's plans were designed to consolidate its position in Germany,

> **KEY POINT**
>
> Austria was defeated in the Seven Weeks' War, the Confederation was abolished and the Prussian-dominated North German Confederation was set up in its place.

The Franco–Prussian War

OCR	MS (synoptic)
NICCEA	M4

Key points from AS

- **The Franco–Prussian War**
  Revise AS pages 111–112

Bismarck may have promoted the Hohenzollern candidature in order to provoke a war – see pp.140–141.

Prussia's gains in the Seven Weeks' War were greatly resented by the French. At the end of the war Napoleon III raised the question of compensation for France in Luxemburg or Belgium. Between 1866 and 1870 relations between France and Prussia deteriorated. For this reason Bismarck made military agreements with the south German states in 1866. Soon both Prussia and France were engaged in an arms race.

The issue which sparked off the Franco–Prussian War was the **Hohenzollern candidature** for the Spanish throne. The way this was handled enabled Bismarck to portray the French as aggressors and there was therefore widespread support for Prussia in the south German states. This made it possible for Bismarck to begin negotiations with them for a new German Federation. The outcome was the establishment of the German Empire with William I as Emperor. Once again the military strength of Prussia and Bismarck's careful diplomacy, which left the French isolated, were crucial to victory.

The Reichstag was elected by universal male suffrage but had little power. Real power lay with the Emperor and (until 1890) the Chancellor, Bismarck.

The new Reich excluded Austria and thus conformed to the **kleindeutsch** view of the German nation state. It had a federal constitution, which preserved a degree of independence for the states. Prussia, Bavaria, Saxony and Württemberg even preserved their own armies, which came together to form the German army in times of war. The principal elements in the government of the Reich were the Kaiser (Emperor), Chancellor, Reichstag (Parliament) and Bundesrat (Federal Council, representing the states). Since Prussia was by far the biggest state, with over half the area and population of the Reich, a great deal of power lay with the Prussian landowners.

You should be able to explain the significance of each of these dates.

		KEY DATES
1862	Bismarck appointed Prime Minister of Prussia	
1864	War against Denmark over Schleswig-Holstein	
1866	Seven Weeks' War v. Austria	
1867	North German Confederation set up	
1870–1	Franco–Prussian War	
1871	Establishment of German Empire (the Second Reich)	

4.4 German nationalism and the German Empire, 1871–1919

After studying this section you should be able to:

- explain Bismarck's foreign and domestic policies between 1871 and 1890
- assess the significance of the issue of protection in the Second Reich
- discuss the impact of German nationalism and Weltpolitik upon international relations in the reign of William II

Bismarck, 1871–90

OCR ▸ M5 (synoptic)

Key points from AS

- **The German Empire 1871–90**
  Revise AS pages 113–115

The establishment of the Empire was an enormous boost to German national pride. It also transformed the European balance of power. The new state's political and military strength, combined with the rapid growth of its economy made it the most powerful state in continental Europe by the end of the century. While Bismarck was in charge, German nationalism was directed to consolidating and defending this newly created Empire, but in the reign of William II it became increasingly aggressive.

Bismarck's aim in the 1870s was to strengthen the central institutions of the Reich while preserving Prussia's predominance. Since the Liberals shared his desire to centralise, they were his political allies until 1879. In that year he parted company with them over the issue of free trade versus protection and relied thereafter on the Conservative and Catholic Centre parties.

Bismarck saw both external threats and internal tensions against which it was necessary to defend the Reich. The main external threat came from France and his foreign policy was therefore directed primarily towards keeping France isolated. Militarily, because of Germany's geographical position, the greatest danger it faced was a war on two fronts. Bismarck's diplomatic energies were therefore directed towards maintaining good relations with Austria and Russia, so that neither would ally with France. The problem was that the interests of Austria and Russia were fundamentally in conflict in the Balkans, and it required all Bismarck's diplomatic skill to maintain good relations with both. William II abandoned this policy, which was probably unsustainable in the long run.

> The cornerstone of his foreign policy was the Dual Alliance with Austria (1879), but he also made agreements with Russia.

Internally, Bismarck at first saw the greatest threat as coming from the Roman Catholics. The North German Confederation was predominantly Protestant but southern Germany was Roman Catholic. When the German Empire was set up in 1871, it therefore had a substantial minority of Catholics. Bismarck feared that their loyalty to Rome would conflict with their loyalty to the Empire. He was also aware that south German Catholics tended to support the idea of a Greater Germany, including Austria, as opposed to the Prussian-dominated German Empire Bismarck had set up. Furthermore, the doctrine of Papal Infallibility, proclaimed in 1870, seemed to be a challenge to the nation state. The **Kulturkampf**, Bismarck's struggle with the Catholics in the 1870s, was therefore in his view a defence of the new Empire against forces which threatened to pull it apart. By 1879, however, he judged that the issue of protection, over which he needed the support of the Catholic Centre Party, was more important than the Kulturkampf, which he therefore abandoned.

> The doctrine that the Pope's official pronouncements on matters of faith and morals are true.

> He also needed their support against the Socialists.

> **KEY POINT**
> In 1878–9 Bismarck 're-founded the Reich'. He made three decisive changes: he abandoned the alliance with the Liberals, adopted protection and introduced the anti-Socialist laws.

Free trade v. protection

OCR ▶ M5 (synoptic)

Junkers: Prussian nobles and gentry.

Protection was a major issue in the Second Reich. Bismarck's alliance with the Liberals in the 1870s was partly based upon a policy of free trade. The onset of the Great Depression in 1873 led to loud demands from industrialists for protective tariffs. At the same time agricultural interests, spearheaded by the Junkers in Prussia, began to demand protection against cheap grain imports from the American prairies. In 1879 Bismarck decided to break with the Liberals and abandon free trade. This not only won him support from these powerful interest groups but it had the further advantage that these groups were as strongly opposed as he was to the socialists.

Protection remained a sensitive issue in the reign of William II. In 1892–4 Caprivi made a series of trade treaties which benefited German industry but involved the reduction of agricultural tariffs. As a result the Agrarian League was founded in 1893 to campaign for protection for agriculture. Eventually in 1902 Bülow introduced new agricultural tariffs along with new tariffs to protect key manufactures. This resulted in the 'Alliance of Rye and Steel'. Nevertheless, some agricultural interests still felt the new tariffs were too low.

William II and Weltpolitik

OCR ▶ M5 (synoptic)

Key points from AS

- **Foreign policy**
  Revise AS pages 118–119
- **The Balkans**
  Revise AS pages 120–121

It is important to understand the change of tone resulting from the impact of William's personality.

In the reign of William II German nationalism became more aggressive and had an increasingly unsettling effect upon relations between the Great Powers. In some historians' eyes it was the main cause of the First World War. This was partly due to William II himself. In 1890 he dismissed Bismarck and thereafter he exercised considerable personal control over the government, particularly in foreign affairs. He then embarked on the policy of **Weltpolitik**, a term first used in 1896. Nothing in Europe or elsewhere in the world, he claimed, should be settled without the intervention of Germany. In practice Weltpolitik meant colonial expansion, the extension of German influence in the Balkans and the construction of a powerful navy.

Weltpolitik was not simply William's personal hobbyhorse. It both responded to and encouraged important aspects of the German mentality.

- Militarism. The army had played a key role in unification with victories over Austria (1866) and France (1870–1) and had a unique status as a result. William took his role as head of the army very seriously and relied heavily on the generals for advice. By 1914 the General Staff probably had more influence than the Chancellor.
- Economic dynamism. The growth of industry gave Germans an increasing sense of their country's power. German industrialists pressed the need for expansion into world markets and drew attention to the fact that other powers, especially Britain and France, had much bigger overseas empires.
- An aggressively nationalist foreign policy was seen as a means of uniting the nation and diverting attention from internal political divisions. In particular it could win over the working classes from the Socialists. This was the explicit aim of the 'social imperialism' pursued by Bülow (Chancellor, 1900–09).

Industrialists financed these pressure groups because they supported Weltpolitik.

The fact that the aggressive nationalism of Weltpolitik was in tune with much German opinion is demonstrated by popular support for the **Pan-German League** (founded 1891) and the **Navy League** (founded 1898). The aims of the Pan-German League were strikingly similar to those of Hitler: the union of all Germans in one great German state, including not only Austria but also the Low Countries, Hungary, Poland and parts of the Balkans. The League also asserted the claims of this state to world domination and was strongly tinged with anti-semitism and anti-Slavism.

Kaiser William II

> The way in which nationalistic feeling was whipped up at this time may be regarded as sowing the seeds for National Socialism.
>
> **KEY POINT**

Many historians argue that the main purpose of Weltpolitik was to win the loyalty of the masses and divert them from socialism. In other words domestic political considerations were paramount. But it was bound to appear threatening to other powers and was therefore a destabilising factor in international relations.

- It caused tensions with Britain over German support for the Boers in the Kruger Telegram (and the Boer War).
- It drew Germany into colonial rivalries in China.
- It led to financial and commercial penetration of the Middle East, symbolised by the Berlin–Baghdad railway project. This caused tension with Russia and Britain.
- It was one of the causes of the two Morocco crises (1905–6 and 1911).
- It led to the naval race with Britain. The German naval laws of 1898 and 1900 and the race to build Dreadnoughts after 1906 were perhaps the main cause of anti-German feeling in Britain.
- Above all, by destroying the Bismarckian balance of power in Europe, it created the fear of a German-dominated Europe and thus was a major cause of the First World War.

You should be able to explain the significance of each of these dates.

1871	Proclamation of the Second Empire	**KEY DATES**
1879	Bismarck breaks with the Liberals and adopts protection	
1890	Dismissal of Bismarck	
1898	Tirpitz's First Naval Law. Foundation of Navy League	
1914	Outbreak of First World War	
1918	November Revolution. Armistice	

Sample question and model answer

This question incorporates synoptic assessment.

'Nationalism had more appeal to the German people than liberalism.' How far do you agree with this view of German political attitudes in the period 1815–1919?

[30]

This is an outline answer, to which you should add more detail.

1815–48: nationalism had a limited appeal, mainly in intellectual circles which were also engaged by the ideas of liberalism. For many Liberals the more immediate goal was constitutional government of the states into which Germany was divided and which were the focus of loyalty for many. The German Confederation represented princes, not people. Under Metternich's influence it served mainly to maintain legitimism against liberalism, and to uphold Austria's predominance among the German states.

Legitimism = upholding the rights of hereditary princes.

1848: Liberals failed to achieve unification. Frankfurt Parliament aimed to set up a unified constitutional state in Germany but was unable to agree about definition of Germany. 'Grossdeutschland' raised problems of Austria's non-German territories. 'Kleindeutschland' would leave out substantial numbers of German-speaking peoples. Religion was a further complication – Grossdeutschland would be dominated by Catholic Austria, Kleindeutschland by Protestant Prussia. Result: collapse of Frankfurt Parliament and return to status quo. But attempt at unification gave a boost to nationalism.

Explain these concepts.

1862–71: Bismarck. Appointed Prime Minister of Prussia because of conflict between King and Liberals in parliament. By skilful diplomacy and use of Prussian military power won successive wars against Denmark, Austria and France. As a result, united first north German states, then all Germany except Austria. Bismarck had succeeded where Liberals had failed. The German Empire was 'kleindeutsch' and Prussian-dominated. The constitution established a Reichstag elected by universal suffrage, which satisfied the Liberals; but in reality power lay with the emperor. The constitution entrenched the power of the Prussian Junkers (Bismarck was a Junker).

You can add some detail here.

They controlled the Prussian parliament, which controlled the biggest group of votes in the Bundesrat.

1871–1914: Bismarck worked with the Liberals in the 1870s, partly because he needed their support in his battle with the Catholics (the Kulturkampf), but broke with them in 1879. Thereafter they were increasingly marginalised. Meanwhile united Germany developed into the most powerful industrial country in continental Europe. Bismarck's cautious diplomacy (based on the need to avoid war on two fronts) was replaced after 1890 by William II's Weltpolitik, a more aggressive form of nationalism which matched Germany's political, economic and military power and asserted its right to be involved in all major international questions. Support for this aggressive nationalism was demonstrated by the appeal of pressure groups such as the Navy League and the Army League.

Before Bismarck liberalism and nationalism went hand in hand, though the appeal of both was primarily to intellectuals. Bismarck 'amputated nationalism from liberalism' and produced 'a new synthesis in German political attitudes between German nationalism, Prussian militarism and Hohenzollern authoritarianism' (O. Pflanze). In the Kaiserreich nationalism undoubtedly had the greater appeal.

Practice examination questions

1 'The emergence of a unified and powerful German state was rooted in its economic development.' How far do you agree with this view of German history in the period 1815–1914? [30]

2 Why did German liberalism achieve so little in the period 1815–1919? [30]

3 How successful were German rulers and statesmen in resisting the demands of liberals and socialists in the period 1815–1919? [30]

Chapter 5

Economic modernisation in Germany, c.1880 – c.1980

The following topics are covered in this chapter:

- The German economy 1880–1914
- The First World War and its aftermath
- The German economy under the Nazis
- Post-war Germany

3.1 The German economy 1880–1914

LEARNING SUMMARY

After studying this section you should be able to:

- explain how and why Germany's industrial power grew so rapidly in this period

The growth of German industry

AQA ▸ M4 (synoptic)
OCR ▸ M5 (synoptic)

Zollverein: a customs union between most German states, except Austria. Dominated by Prussia.

Industrialisation made rapid progress in Germany after 1850. The combination of the Zollverein, which established internal free trade in 1834, and the development of the railways from the 1840s opened up a home market of 25 million Germans. Railway-building was a major stimulus to the iron and steel and engineering industries. Unification in 1871, bringing with it a single currency and a uniform body of commercial law, provided a further stimulus.

Nevertheless, in 1880 German industrial output was still well below that of Britain, as is shown by a comparison of key indicators.

Germany and Britain, 1870

	Germany	**Britain**	
Coal (million tons)	34	112	
Pig iron (million tons)	1.3	6.0	
Steel production (million tons)	0.3	0.7	
Length of railroad (thousand km)	19.5	24.5	

By 1914, Germany's industrial strength rivalled Britain's. Coal production rose to 277 million tons in 1914. Production of pig iron rose by a factor of ten. In the newer industries of electrical engineering and chemicals Germany was well ahead of all other European countries. Between 1880 and 1914 Germany's share of world manufacturing rose from 8.5 per cent to 14.8 per cent. The value of Germany's exports more than trebled. The most dramatic growth of German trade was in European markets, but overseas trade also grew rapidly. By 1914 Germany's merchant navy was the second largest in the world after Britain's.

The growth of the German economy

	Population (millions)	**Coal production (million tons)**	**Steel production (million tons)**	**Pig-iron production (million tons)**
1870	41	34	0.3	1.3
1890	49	89	2.3	4.1
1910	65	222	13.8	9.5

Many factors explain this growth.

- Germany was richly endowed with resources of coal and iron, including Europe's richest iron-ore deposits after the annexation of Alsace-Lorraine in 1871.

- The introduction of protection in 1879 enabled industry to exploit the potential of the largest domestic market in continental Europe to the full.
- The infrastructure was well developed. The railway system was approximately doubled in length between 1880 and 1914.
- A highly developed banking system, which by 1880 had total deposits of 2500 million marks, provided the capital for expansion.
- The formation of cartels – a particularly marked feature of German industrial organisation – enabled manufacturers to control and develop markets to their advantage. Some of the cartels, e.g. the Ruhr Coal Syndicate and the Rhenish Steel Syndicate, were extremely powerful.

> Combinations of industrial companies to organise production and markets in their own interests.

By 1914 Germany's industrial strength matched that of Britain.

KEY POINT

5.2 The First World War and its aftermath

After studying this section you should be able to:

- *discuss the impact of the war and post-war problems on Germany's economy*
- *assess how far the German economy recovered during the 1920s*

LEARNING SUMMARY

The wartime economy

AQA   M4 (synoptic)

> Walter Rathenau directed the 'war economy'.

Germany's industrial development and its reserves of coal and steel were sufficient to sustain a massive war effort. Central control of the economy, e.g. in direction of labour, helped, though there was a good deal of bureaucratic inefficiency. Germany's geographical position, however, made it vulnerable to the effects of the Allied blockade and imported raw materials such as cotton, rubber and lubricating oil became scarce. Total industrial production declined by 30 per cent between 1914 and 1918. German merchant shipping virtually came to a halt. At the same time the demands of the army for men and horses led to a drop of about 50 per cent in agricultural production. Not surprisingly, Germany was the first power to introduce rationing. There were severe food shortages in the 'turnip winter' of 1916–17. By the end of 1918 malnutrition was widespread. There were food riots in German cities in November 1918.

Post-war problems

AQA   M4 (synoptic)

At the end of the war Germany faced severe economic problems: food shortages, inflation, high unemployment and a large national debt. The Weimar government had to accept a peace treaty which deprived Germany of the rich mineral resources of Alsace-Lorraine and the Saar and required it to pay **reparations**. These were fixed in 1921 at £6600 million – a figure which many Germans claimed it was beyond their power to pay.

> The reasons were as much political as economic.

The government decided it was impossible to raise the sums required from taxation, so it resorted to printing paper money, which led to further inflation. In 1923 Germany defaulted on its reparations payments, resulting in the occupation of the Ruhr by France. The economic consequences were catastrophic. Passive resistance in the Ruhr brought Germany's greatest industrial area to a standstill. The government met the situation by printing yet more paper money and by November 1923 hyper-inflation left the mark worthless.

> The currency crisis wiped out the savings of the middle classes. The working classes were also badly affected but landowners and industrialists profited because their debts were effectively cancelled.
>
> **KEY POINT**

Economic recovery in the 1920s

AQA ▶ M4 (synoptic)

> Stresemann made this change and thus defused the crisis.

The foundation for recovery was laid by the ending of the campaign of passive resistance in September 1923 and the introduction of a new currency, the Rentenmark, in November. In 1924 the **Dawes Plan** was negotiated: the annual reparations payments were scaled down and a loan was arranged to rebuild the German economy.

> Note that cartels continued to be an important feature of German industry. IG Farben was a chemicals cartel.

As a result, between 1924 and 1929 Germany enjoyed a period of relative stability and prosperity. With a stable currency, industry entered on a period of expansion and output more than doubled by 1929. New industrial cartels were formed, notably IG Farben and United Steelworks. Unemployment, which reached 2 million in the winter of 1925–6, fell to 1.3 million in 1928. Living standards rose. The Young Plan (1929) reduced the annual burden of reparations by spreading payments over 59 years.

There were worrying features, however. Economic growth depended heavily on foreign investment, much of it from America. The balance of trade remained unfavourable and unemployment was still too high. Agriculture did not share in the general prosperity, as farm prices and farmworkers' living standards fell. The drop in farm prices foreshadowed an economic blizzard, which came from Wall Street in 1929.

> The prosperity of the late 1920s rested on shallow foundations.
>
> **KEY POINT**

5.3 The German economy under the Nazis

After studying this section you should be able to:

LEARNING SUMMARY

- *explain how Germany's economy revived under the Nazis*
- *assess the success of Nazi economic policies*

The Great Depression

AQA ▶ M4 (synoptic)

The Wall Street crash affected Germany particularly badly. As share prices collapsed in the USA, American investors withdrew their loans from Germany, ruining many businesses. This had a knock-on effect on other businesses which did not depend directly on American investment. Unemployment, which was already rising in 1929, shot up to four million in 1931 and six million in 1932. For those in work wages fell. For the unemployed benefits were cut. This was the situation which led to the collapse of the Weimar Republic and the rise of the Nazis.

The Nazi 'economic miracle'

AQA   M4 (synoptic)

Key points from AS

- **The economy under the Nazis**
  Revise AS pages 145–146

The main economic indicators show the extent of the German economic recovery under the Nazis.

- Unemployment fell from six million in 1932 to 1.75 million in 1935 and under 200 000 by 1939.
- Production of industrial goods, which had fallen by nearly a half during the depression, was back to the level of 1928 by 1936 and over 40 per cent above it in 1938.
- Coal production increased by 50 per cent between 1932 and 1938 and production of iron and steel more than doubled.

How was this achieved?

- The Nazis embarked on a massive programme of public works, the best known example being the building of 7000 km of Autobahns.
- Wages, food prices, rents, investment and foreign exchange were controlled.
- Spending on armaments increased massively. By 1938, 50 per cent of public expenditure went on the arms budget. Rearmament provided contracts for industry and reduced unemployment because conscription took half a million men out of the labour market.

> Spending more than was raised by taxation – the policy recommended by Keynes in a recession.

- Deficit financing was employed to make these schemes possible.
- Small farmers were helped by import controls, higher farm prices and laws to give them security of tenure.

> Eastern European countries which depended on Germany as the market for their food exports were forced to accept German manufactures in return.

- **Dr Schacht**, President of the Reichsbank, devised an elaborate system of exchange controls and negotiated a series of two-way (bilateral) trade agreements with Eastern European and South American countries to boost German exports and secure essential raw materials. As a result by 1935 exports exceeded imports.

> The showpiece of the Plan was the Hermann Goering Steelworks. Goering was in charge of the Plan.

- In 1936 a **Four Year Plan** was introduced with the explicit aim, stated in a memorandum from Hitler, of making Germany ready for war within four years. The state took control of all aspects of economic life – foreign exchange, distribution of raw materials, prices, wages and profits. The basic purpose was to achieve self-sufficiency (Autarky) by boosting domestic production and developing synthetic substitutes for oil, rubber and other imports.

How successful were Nazi economic policies?

Historians are divided about the success of Nazi economic policies. Undoubtedly they achieved their immediate objectives of reducing unemployment and reviving Germany's economic and military power. Many historians, however, doubt whether this success would have lasted. The massive cost of rearmament created a serious risk of runaway inflation. Despite massive investment, synthetic substitutes for oil and rubber only produced a small proportion of Germany's needs. Agriculture failed to meet its targets and Germany continued to depend on food imports. Imports of raw materials and food therefore continued to be a problem – one which could only be solved by a war for **Lebensraum**. This was the logic of the Four Year Plan which could only be completed by a war for which it aimed to prepare Germany.

> This was because Nazi agricultural policy provided support for a large number of small, inefficient farms.

Moreover the virtual elimination of unemployment had been achieved partly by luck (world trade was beginning to pick up when the Nazis came to power) and partly by measures which caused a massive increase in public spending and thus caused a long-term threat of inflation. The expansion of the civil service and the party organisation created jobs but both were over-staffed. Public works, conscription into the armed forces and compulsory labour service for young men aged between 18 and 25 all had to be paid for.

> Dr Schacht warned of the danger of runaway inflation in 1939.

> **KEY POINT**
> The outbreak of war in 1939 makes it impossible to judge the long-term success of Nazi economic policies, but it is likely that inflation and the balance of payments would have presented severe problems if there had been no war.

The Second World War

AQA ▶ M4 (synoptic)

The Nazis had been preparing for war since the Four Year Plan in 1936 but the economy faced serious problems from the start. There were shortages of food and raw materials, especially oil, and manpower problems. The overlapping functions of various Nazi agencies caused administrative inefficiency.

Much effort was put into overcoming these problems and in the early years of the war Germany achieved high levels of production. Food rationing was introduced in 1939 and food supplies were obtained from areas of Eastern Europe conquered by the Nazis. The occupied territories also provided labour to tackle manpower shortages: some eight million foreign workers were employed altogether, though most were either reluctant conscripts or slave labour. By 1944, too, half the female population was employed, despite Hitler's reluctance to employ women.

> *Also many were unskilled.*

The Armaments Minister, Todt, and his successor, Speer, tackled administrative problems with measures to co-ordinate production, notably the Central Planning Board set up in 1942. Unfortunately the activities of the SS under Himmler and of the Gauleiters often cut across Speer's planning.

> *Gauleiters: senior Nazi party officials, each responsible for the administration of a province*

From 1943 onwards, however, the economy was under increasing stress. Allied bombing raids on German cities caused terrible damage to industrial plant and to housing. The final invasion of Germany in 1944–45 and Hitler's refusal to contemplate surrender led to enormous physical destruction.

> *Most notoriously Dresden.*

> **KEY POINT**
> By the end of the war the Germany economy was in ruins.

5.4 Post-war Germany

After studying this section you should be able to:

LEARNING SUMMARY

- explain the post-war 'economic miracle' in Western Germany
- compare the economic development of West and East Germany

West Germany

AQA ▶ M4 (synoptic)

In 1945 Germany faced terrible problems. The cities were in ruins. The infrastructure had been wrecked. Industry was at a standstill. There were widespread food shortages. There were some 15 million refugees from Eastern Europe, over half of them ethnic Germans expelled from Poland, Czechoslovakia, Hungary, Rumania and Yugoslavia.

With the collapse of the Nazi regime, Germany came under the control of the four Allied occupying powers. As early as 1947 Britain and the USA set about restoring the German economy by linking their zones together. The American Marshall Plan, designed to bring about the economic regeneration of Western Europe, played a major part in the revival of the economy of western Germany. A further important step was the introduction of a new currency, the **Deutschmark**, in 1948. The Russians, however, opposed these developments and embarked on the Berlin blockade to keep out the new currency and, they hoped, to expel the west from Berlin. Thus western policies towards Germany were a major cause of the hardening of divisions between east and west in the Cold War.

> The blockade was overcome by the airlift.

With the establishment of the Federal Republic in 1949 economic recovery gathered pace. In the 1950s the growth rate of the West German economy was 8 per cent per annum. By 1952 it had a positive balance of trade and by 1960 its economy was the strongest in Europe. Apart from the kick-start given by the Marshall Plan, there were other factors assisting this 'economic miracle'.

> The 'economic miracle'.

- West German factories were re-equipped with modern machinery after the destruction at the end of the war. This enabled West Germany to develop strong exports of industrial goods.
- The Federal Republic spent nothing on armaments for several years because it had been demilitarised.
- The Korean War provided a stimulus for the steelworks of the Ruhr.
- Labour relations were good and there was comparatively little disruption from strike action.
- The division of Germany freed West Germany from the demands of Prussian agricultural interests, which had been a continual problem from the time of Bismarck onwards. Post-war West German economic policies therefore promoted industry, and the agricultural sector declined in size.
- The Economics Minister, **Erhard**, followed free market economic policies and kept interest rates low to encourage investment. He avoided state intervention in the economy except for investment in education and the infrastructure.
- The Bundesbank, established in 1957, was independent of the government and pursued policies which made the Deutschmark one of the world's leading currencies.
- The European Coal and Steel Community (founded 1951) created a much bigger 'domestic' market for these basic industrial products. This process was expanded by the creation of the **European Economic Community** in 1957. This development also ensured that the revival of Germany's economic strength would not be seen as a threat by its neighbours, since Germany's economy was integrated into the wider European economy. Indeed, Germany was a motor for growth and prosperity in the EEC as a whole.

Economic growth slowed in the 1960s and unemployment rose. Nevertheless, West Germany remained the economic powerhouse of Europe.

> The 'economic miracle' produced a marked contrast in standards of living between West and East Germany.
>
> **KEY POINT**

East Germany

AQA   M4 (synoptic)

> This is known as a command economy in contrast to West Germany's free market economy.

The Russian zone of Germany developed quite differently. As Germany became the focus of east–west tension after the end of the war, the Russians turned their zone into a satellite state, the German Democratic Republic. This was a single-party communist state and its economy was run on Stalinist lines.

- After the end of the war the Russians stripped their zone of machinery and industrial assets worth £7 billion as reparations.
- They seized the landed estates of the gentry and distributed the land to peasants and refugees. This was popular with the recipients but created a lot of small, inefficient farms. In 1949 a programme of collectivisation began and by 1961 90 per cent of agricultural production came from collective farms.

The Council for Mutual Economic Assistance – set up by the USSR to co-ordinate the economies of the Soviet bloc.

- Banks and large companies were nationalised. By 1948 only 39 per cent of industry remained in private hands.
- Following the example of the USSR, a Two Year Plan was introduced in 1948, followed by a Five Year Plan in 1950. As in Stalin's Russia, the emphasis was on heavy industry and consumer goods were comparatively neglected. The targets were hopelessly over-ambitious.
- Its economy was integrated into the Soviet economic system through Comecon.

The unpopularity of the regime and its failure to match the economic progress of West Germany led many East Germans to leave for the west via West Berlin. By 1960 this had become a major problem, particularly since many of those who went were young and skilled. By 1961, 2.7 million East Germans had gone. This was the main reason for the erection of the Berlin Wall in 1961.

In the 1960s, however, East Germany achieved comparatively strong economic growth, partly because the rigidity of the Five Year Plans was replaced by the more flexible New Economic System in 1963. Living standards and industrial output were the highest in the Soviet bloc but even so they were well below those of West Germany. Prices of basic necessities such as food and housing were kept down but consumer goods such as cars were extremely dear.

Much of East Germany's industry was inefficient by western standards.	KEY POINT

Sample question and model answer

Study Sources A to D and answer questions (a) and (b) which follow.

Source A

From an essay by V. Berghahn in *German History since 1800*, edited by M. Fulbrook, 1997.
Late 19th-century Germany greatly benefited from the rapid expansion of electrical engineering and chemicals. These were new industries based on scientific breakthroughs and technical innovation that complemented the older industries of the first industrial revolution like coal, iron and textiles. In fact, it has been argued that the first and second industrial revolutions occurred in Germany virtually at the same time, as the new industries experienced their most spectacular growth. In chemicals and pharmaceuticals, in particular, Germany had by 1900 achieved a leading position in the world. By 1914 it had also outpaced Britain, the first industrial nation, in steel production.

Source B

From *A History of Germany 1815–1990*, by W. Carr, 1991.
It is sometimes said that Weimar Germany experienced boom conditions between 1924 and 1929 comparable to those in the Federal Republic in the 1950s. Certainly iron and steel, coal, chemicals and electrical products recovered quickly after the war – though even in 1929 they only attained the output and export levels of 1913. … On the other hand, the extent of the 'boom' has been greatly exaggerated. Germany experienced high growth rates and low unemployment between 1919 and 1924. In the late 1920s growth rates were unsteady, rising in 1924–5 and 1927 but falling in between to a minus rate by 1928–9. … Capital investment was already falling by 1929; unemployment consequent upon rationalisation was never less than 1.3 million and reached 3 million by February 1929. … The true position was disguised by two factors. First, the massive inflow of foreign capital. Second, the extensive welfare system.

Source C

From *Hitler and Nazi Germany*, by F. McDonough, 1999.
Economic growth in Nazi Germany from 1933 to 1938 was primarily due to the rapid growth in arms spending, not improved economic efficiency, increased exports or a major expansion in the German consumer goods industry. Even the low inflation rate Germany enjoyed in the Nazi period was created by the artificial government device of a wage and price freeze. This kept inflation much lower than it would otherwise have been in a free-market system. The claims of a Nazi 'economic miracle' can now be seen as largely a propaganda myth.

Source D

From *The Cambridge Illustrated History of Germany*, by M. Kitchen, 1996.
Aided by the economic upswing caused by the Korean War, the economy was soon growing at an annual rate of almost eight per cent, and maintained the growth throughout the 1950s. The basis of Erhard's policy was that the state should only interfere indirectly in the economy by encouraging those factors which would stimulate economic growth, especially investment. The state provided investment capital where this could not be provided by ploughing back profits. Investments were 22.8 per cent of GNP in 1950 and rose to 28.8 per cent by 1965. Exports formed the basis of the 'economic miracle' which the government encouraged by fiscal measures and an undervalued currency.

(a) Compare Sources B and C and use your own knowledge. Explain how fully these sources explain Germany's economic problems in the 1920s and 1930s.

[12]

(a) Both sources draw attention to problems of the growth rate, inflation and unemployment. Both claim the true position was worse than it seemed either in the late 1920s or under the Nazi 'economic miracle'. Source B

Sample question and model answer *(continued)*

admits there was high growth and low unemployment between 1919 and 1924 – but this was a period of high inflation, culminating in the crisis of 1923. The 'boom' of the late 1920s was uneven and based on foreign investment. It ended with the Great Depression. The recovery under the Nazis was to a large degree artificial. Source C points out that growth was largely due to rearmament and low inflation was achieved by a wage and price freeze. It could have added that the virtual elimination of unemployment was also achieved partly by artificial means and that by 1939 it was almost certain that rearmament would soon cause severe inflation.

Note that own knowledge is used as well as the sources.

Explain this carefully.

(b) With reference to these sources and your own knowledge of the period c. 1880 to c. 1980, explain how far, and why, the German economy was able to recover from the effects of wars and depression. [18]

This question incorporates synoptic assessment.

(b) The First World War led to economic exhaustion by 1918. In the following 27 years Germany suffered from the great inflation of 1923, the Great Depression of 1929–33 and destruction of industry and the infrastructure at the end of the Second World War.

This is an outline answer, to which you should add more detail.

Germany's ability to overcome these problems was rooted in its economic advantages and the strong industrial growth between unification in 1871 and the outbreak of war in 1914. It had considerable reserves of the natural resources required for industrial growth in the 19th century, especially coal (in the Ruhr and Silesia) and iron ore in Alsace–Lorraine. Its central geographical location in the continent was complemented by a well-developed rail and river transport system. The banking system was well-developed. Rapid population growth provided the workforce. Education, particularly technical education, was good. The result was rapid growth in industries characteristic of both the first and second industrial revolutions (source A). By 1914 Germany's industrial strength rivalled and in some respects exceeded Britain's.

Cartels could also be mentioned.

Note that references to sources are woven into the argument.

Nevertheless, the First World War exhausted the economy. Germany's geographical position made it vulnerable to the effects of the Allied blockade. Food and imported raw materials became scarce and industrial production declined by 30 per cent. Recovery during the 1920s was partial and uneven. In the early 1920s economic growth was high and unemployment low (Source B). But at the same time there was high inflation. A combination of inability and unwillingness to meet the demands for reparations exacerbated the problem and led to hyper-inflation in 1923. The Dawes Plan and a currency reform made for a comparatively quick recovery from this further economic disaster, but left Germany dependent on foreign investment. In the late 1920s growth rates were sharply down and unemployment rising (source B).

Explain main details of Dawes Plan.

Because its prosperity was so closely bound up with American loans, Germany was hit extremely hard by the Great Depression. This time recovery took the form of the Nazi 'economic miracle' (source C). Unemployment was virtually eliminated and inflation kept under control. This was achieved by various means – public works, control of wages and prices, an intricate web of foreign trade agreements negotiated by Schacht, above all rearmament. Economists doubt whether Nazi economic policies were sustainable: Schacht himself warned of the danger of runaway inflation in 1939. Nevertheless, Germany was the most powerful industrial

Sample question and model answer *(continued)*

state in continental Europe, as it had been throughout the inter-war years despite the problems it faced.

The end of the Second World War left Germany divided and with its economy in ruins. Unlike in 1919, it had suffered massive physical destruction. Nevertheless, by the end of the 1950s West Germany had witnessed another 'economic miracle' (Source D). There were many reasons for this: Marshall Aid, Erhard's free market economic policies, the establishment of the Bundesbank, the re-equipment of German factories with modern machinery, good labour relations, the economic stimulus of the Korean War, the development of the European Economic Community. All these factors enabled West Germany's underlying economic strengths to be developed to full advantage. East Germany, with a Soviet-style command economy, did not recover to the same extent, though it was the most industrially successful of the Soviet satellite states in Eastern Europe.

These points need to be amplified.

Practice examination questions

Study sources A to D and answer the questions which follow.

Source A

From *A History of Germany 1815–1990*, by W. Carr, 1991.
Under Stresemann's guidance the republic had survived its darkest hour; threats to the unity of the Reich were overcome, confidence in the economy restored and reparations put on a realistic footing. These were considerable achievements, for which much, though by no means all, of the credit must go to Stresemann. Yet his policies were not universally popular at home; mostly he had to fight for them in the teeth of bitter opposition and savage personal attacks from the extreme right and extreme left as well as from the right wing of his own party.

Source B

From *Did Hitler Want Total War?* By R.J. Overy, in *History Sixth*, 1989.
The effect of [the Four-Year Plan] was to bring the state into virtual control of the whole German economy. The Four-Year Plan had profound effects on the nature of the German economy. Almost all the extra growth in the economy was diverted to the needs of war. Living standards barely returned to the level of 1928, but the economy as a whole had grown 38 per cent by 1938 above the level of 1928 (in real terms). There were wide areas of poverty in the Germany of the 1930s and by the end of the decade living standards were beginning to decline.

Source C

From an article by Norman Taylor, an American expert on Germany, in the magazine *Foreign Affairs*, 1936.

Under the Nazis there has been much 'invisible unemployment'. The number of unemployed Jews is great but these are not counted as unemployed. Another source of 'invisible unemployment' has been the wholesale discharge from paid work of women whose husbands are employed, and of unmarried men under 25. None of these are included among the unemployed in the official statistics. Part-time workers are counted as fully employed. 'Artificially created' work accounts for some of the employment. The reintroduction of conscription has taken hundreds of thousands of men off the labour market.

Source D

From *Germany since 1945*, by L Kettenacker, 1997.
East Germany was at the top of the Comecon league. However, while the regime compared its performance with Poland and the Soviet Union, its citizens always looked to the West... Nowhere has the failure of the socialist command economy been more glaringly exposed than in East Germany: the ludicrous process of making Five- and Seven-Year Plans which were either totally without consequence or became excuses for wasting manpower in all kinds of unproductive jobs (such as academic sinecures for Party stalwarts). An already inflated public service was controlled by a huge Party bureaucracy. Almost incalculable are the costs incurred by the obsession with external and internal security.

(a) Compare Sources B and C and use your own knowledge. Comment on these sources as assessments of the success of Nazi economic policies. [12]

(b) With reference to these sources and your own knowledge of the period c.1880 to c.1980, assess the impact of government policies on the development of the German economy. [18]

Chapter 6
Dictatorship in Russia 1855–1956

The following topics are covered in this chapter:

- The tsarist autocracy 1855–1917
- The revolutions of 1917
- The Communist dictatorship
- The growth of opposition
- The Russian economy

6.1 The tsarist autocracy 1855–1917

After studying this section you should be able to:

- understand the pressures for and against westernisation in tsarist Russia
- explain and assess the effectiveness of reform and repression in Russia between 1855 and 1917
- account for the failure of the revolution of 1905

LEARNING SUMMARY

Russia in 1855

OCR ▷ M5 (synoptic)
WJEC ▷ M6 (synoptic)

The key features of Russian government and society in 1855 were:

- **Autocracy.** All political power was concentrated in the hands of the Tsar. Laws could only be made by his edicts. The Third Section operated a secret police and a strict censorship.
- **The Orthodox Church** had a key role in supporting the regime. It taught that the Tsar's authority was derived from God and required unquestioning obedience.
- **Serfdom.** Over half the Russian people were serfs, either the personal property of landowners or tied to estates owned by the Crown.
- The **nobility** were a powerful vested interest hostile to change (because their finances depended on the ownership of serfs). Their role in maintaining order in the provinces was vital to the tsarist system of government.

Landowners had almost absolute power over the serfs.

Russia's defeat in the Crimean War highlighted its backwardness and the need for reform. Reformers (**westernisers**) wished to modernise Russia on western lines. They sought to reform Russian government in accordance with liberal ideas from western Europe and they advocated the abolition of serfdom, which they thought was holding back Russia's economic development.

Liberal ideas circulated among university students from whom the administrators of the tsarist government were drawn.

But there were also powerful forces which resisted change. The nobility and the Church had a vested interest in the status quo and there were also many people who believed that Russia, the embodiment of Slav culture and Orthodox Christianity, must be preserved from western influences, which would destroy the soul of Russia. These **Slavophiles** also wanted to extend Russian influence over the Slav peoples within the Turkish empire.

This idea was known as Pan-Slavism.

> The tension between westernising and conservative ideas is a major theme running through Russian history.
>
> KEY POINT

Alexander II, the 'Tsar liberator'

OCR ▷ M5 (synoptic)
WJEC ▷ M6 (synoptic)

Alexander II was responsible for a series of reforms in the 1860s.

- The **emancipation of the serfs** was perhaps the most far-reaching reform by any European state in the 19th century.

Key point from AS

• **Alexander II, 1855–81**
  Revise AS pages 91–92

- The 'zemstva' (elected district councils) were potentially a step towards democracy, although the electoral system favoured the nobility and gentry.
- **Legal reforms**: trials in public, trial by jury and salaries for judges.
- **Army reforms**: the general staff was reorganised and all classes became liable for conscription.
- **Education**: universities were allowed to expand and given more freedom.

How effective were Alexander II's reforms?

The way the emancipation of the serfs was carried out had serious weaknesses. Generally the peasants got the poorer land and their farms were small. The land was not transferred to individuals but to the 'mir' or village commune. Since the land was communally owned, there was no incentive to improve it. Russian agriculture therefore remained inefficient. Because the 'mir' was collectively responsible for the redemption payments, it was very difficult for peasants to leave the village and there was little migration either to the under-populated territories of Siberia or to the towns. Industrial progress was therefore slow.

The government compensated the landlords for the loss of their serfs and reclaimed the money from the peasants over a period of 49 years.

He remarked, 'It is better to abolish serfdom from above than to wait until it begins to abolish itself from below'.

Moreover, the regime remained autocratic. Alexander intended the reforms to strengthen autocracy, not undermine it. He rejected a suggestion that delegates from the zemstva should come together in a central national body, which might have been the germ of a parliament.

After the Polish Revolt (1863) Alexander's rule became more repressive. Press censorship was strict and the secret police were active. Nevertheless, in the last years of his reign it was still uncertain whether the tsardom would remain repressive or move gradually towards a constitutional system of government. A wave of revolutionary violence in 1879–81 resulted in many executions, but at the same time, under the influence of Loris-Melikov, Alexander was on the point of calling a partly elected national assembly. His assassination in March 1881 killed the proposal.

By anarchists – see pp.81–82.

> Alexander II set Russia on the path to modernisation but left both westernisers and conservatives dissatisfied.
>
> **KEY POINT**

1881–1905: repression

| OCR | M5 (synoptic) |
| WJEC | M6 (synoptic) |

Key point from AS

• **Alexander III and Nicholas II**
  Revise AS pages 93–94

Alexander III and his chief minister, Pobedonostsev, believed firmly in autocracy and repression. Land Captains – nobles appointed by the Tsar – were put in charge of local government, overriding the powers of the zemstva. Revision of the franchise cut down the electorate for the zemstva. The Okhrana (secret police) were active and there was strict press censorship. The policy of Russification, which had been followed in Poland after the Polish Revolt of 1863, was extended to Georgia, Finland, Armenia and the Baltic Provinces. The government encouraged anti-semitism with pogroms and new restrictions on the movements and education of Jews.

Armed attacks on Jews.

Nicholas II continued his father's repressive policies. He began his reign by promising to 'uphold the principle of autocracy'. He was able to maintain this position until 1905, when he was faced with revolution.

See p.84. Witte played a great part in this.

Although there was no political reform in the period 1881–1905, Russia was undergoing considerable social and economic change. Some form of political adjustment would eventually be necessary.

The revolution of 1905

| OCR | M5 (synoptic) |
| WJEC | M4, M6 (synoptic) |

Key points from AS

- **The 1905 Revolution**
  Revise AS page 94

There was also a famous mutiny on the 'Potemkin'.

Soviet: committee of workers' representatives.

At the beginning of the 20th century there was widespread unrest in Russia. There were peasant disturbances in many parts of the empire and frequent strikes in the cities. Political repression was as fierce as ever. Discontent boiled over into revolution as a result of defeat in the **Russo-Japanese War (1904–5)**.

On January 22, 1905, (**Bloody Sunday**), several hundred people were killed in St Petersburg when troops opened fire on a procession of demonstrators carrying a petition to the Tsar. This atrocity provoked a wave of strikes and peasant uprisings. In September there was a general strike. In St Petersburg a **Soviet** was set up with Trotsky as co-chairman.

Nevertheless the revolution failed. Why?

- There was no central leadership: the strikes and peasant uprisings were spontaneous and not organised. Lenin and other revolutionary leaders were in exile abroad and arrived too late to influence events.
- At the critical moment the Tsar made concessions. In the **October Manifesto** he promised to set up a Duma (parliament) and granted freedom of speech, religion and assembly. This satisfied the Liberals and divided them from the workers in the Soviet. In November he cancelled the redemption payments still owed by peasants for land acquired after emancipation. This removed the alarming threat of a general revolt of the peasants.

The loyalty of the army and navy was a crucial difference between this revolution and 1917.

- The army and navy mostly remained loyal. This enabled the Tsar to suppress the revolution. The Soviet leaders were arrested and a rising in Moscow was brutally suppressed. By April 1906 the tsarist government was back in control.

Key points from AS

- **The Dumas and Stolypin**
  Revise AS page 95
- **Russia in 1914**
  Revise AS page 95

Consequences of the 1905 revolution

The tsarist system of government never fully regained the loyalty it lost on Bloody Sunday. Nevertheless, there were some hopeful results of the revolution:

- a step was taken towards a constitutional monarchy by the institution of the Dumas
- the creation of the Dumas led to the formation of legitimate political parties

Bloody Sunday 1905

See page 84.

- **Stolypin** introduced important agrarian reforms which were intended to win the support of the peasants.

Progress towards the modernisation of Russia was, however, limited.

- The regime remained fundamentally autocratic. The power of the Dumas was limited: they had no control over ministers and they were only allowed to make reforms which the Tsar approved.

He dismissed Witte in 1906 and Stolypin was assassinated in 1911.

- Nicholas II's outlook was reactionary. He only gave the Dumas grudging approval. He never gave his full confidence to his most able ministers, Witte and Stolypin.
- Modernisation was slow. Stolypin's agrarian reforms needed many years to have their full effect. Russia's industrial base was still comparatively small, while conditions for the industrial working class caused much discontent.

> Opinions are divided as to whether the tsarist regime would have evolved into a constitutional monarchy if it had not been overtaken by the First World War.

KEY POINT

You should be able to explain the significance of each of these dates.

1855	Accession of Alexander II
1861	Emancipation of the serfs
1881	Assassination of Alexander II and accession of Alexander III
1894	Accession of Nicholas II
1904–5	Russo-Japanese War, followed by revolution of 1905

KEY DATES

6.2 The revolutions of 1917

After studying this section you should be able to:

- *account for the overthrow of the tsarist government in February 1917*
- *explain the failure of the Provisional Government to establish a liberal democracy in Russia*

LEARNING SUMMARY

Causes of the February revolution

OCR	M5 (synoptic)
WJEC	M4, M6 (synoptic)

- The war exposed the inefficiency of tsarist Russia. Millions of men were drafted into the armed forces but were not provided with adequate clothing, training or equipment.
- The civilian population suffered great hardship. Germany and Turkey closed Russia's Baltic and Black Sea ports and thus virtually cut Russia off from its allies. The internal transport system was in chaos. Food and fuel became increasingly difficult to obtain in the towns and prices rose dramatically.
- Since the Tsar unwisely decided to take personal command of the army in September 1915, military defeats were blamed on him.

The influence of Rasputin undoubtedly discredited the regime but his importance is often exaggerated.

- The government became increasingly unstable. There were four prime ministers in two years. In the absence of the Tsar at army headquarters continuity was provided only by the Tsarina Alexandra and her favourite Rasputin.
- Liberal opposition grew in response to the failures of the government. In November 1916 a member of the Duma, Miliukov, accused it of incompetence.
- On February 23, 1917 (Russian calendar) a great wave of strikes and food riots broke out, particularly in Petrograd (formerly St Petersburg). Troops sent to quell the rioters joined them. Six days later the Duma established a Provisional Government. Most of its members were Liberals, but there was one socialist, Kerensky. The next day the Tsar abdicated.

He was a Trudovik (see p. 82).

The Provisional Government and the October Revolution

| OCR | M5 (synoptic) |
| WJEC | M4, M6 (synoptic) |

Key points from AS

• **Why were there two revolutions in Russia in 1917?**
Revise AS pages 96–97

An attempted right-wing coup headed by General Kornilov.

See Chapter 10.1.

The Provisional Government, led first by Prince Lvov and then from July by Kerensky, attempted to turn Russia into a liberal democracy. But it failed to solve the pressing problems Russia faced and only lasted for eight months.

• It failed to tackle **the land question**, with the result that in many areas peasants began to seize land. When rumours spread that this was happening, peasants in the army deserted and the Russian armies began to disintegrate.
• It decided not to make peace, so further **military disasters** followed. The offensive in Galicia in July collapsed. By the autumn the Provisional Government was discredited.
• Its authority was challenged by the **Soviets**, which claimed that they represented the people more faithfully than the Provisional Government.
• Its handling of the **Kornilov** affair seemed indecisive.

The Bolsheviks took advantage of the failings of the Provisional Government. They gained increasing support in the summer and autumn, partly because Lenin offered 'Peace, Land and Bread' and partly because they benefited from the reaction against the Kornilov affair. In September they gained a majority in the Petrograd and Moscow Soviets. At this point Lenin decided that the moment was opportune to seize power and persuaded the Bolshevik Central Committee to seize power in a coup.

> The Provisional Government was overthrown in a coup by a group of determined and ruthless revolutionaries.

KEY POINT

6.3 The Communist dictatorship

After studying this section you should be able to:

• *explain the system of power established by Lenin*
• *outline the main features of the Stalinist state*

LEARNING SUMMARY

Lenin

| OCR | M5 (synoptic) |
| WJEC | M6 (synoptic) |

Key points from AS

• **The consolidation of Bolshevik power**
Revise AS pages 150–151

The political bureau (central committee) of the Communist Party.

Lenin's aim was to create in Russia a new form of political, social and economic organisation. The liberal democracy of the Provisional Government was to be replaced by '**dictatorship of the proletariat**'.

By the new Soviet constitution, introduced in July 1918, Russia became the Russian Soviet Federated Socialist Republic. Russia was declared to be a classless society with no private ownership of property. Supreme power was nominally given to the All-Russian Congress of Soviets – representatives of city and village soviets elected by universal suffrage. The Congress elected an Executive Committee, which in turn elected the ten members of the Council of People's Commissars (ministers). Lenin was the Chairman of this Council and thus the head of the government.

There was only one political party, the Communist Party. All other parties were held to be counter-revolutionary. Real political power, therefore, lay with the Communist Party and especially its **Politburo**. Since there was only one party, membership was essential for political advancement.

To destroy counter-revolutionary forces, Lenin set up the **Cheka** (secret police) in December 1917. Between 1918 and 1922 over 140 000 people were executed in

See Chapter 10.1 for further discussion of the Red Terror, War Communism and the New Economic Policy.

Key points from AS

- **The New Economic Policy**
  Revise AS page 152

the 'Red Terror' carried out by the Cheka. He also formed the **Red Army**, which by 1920 numbered over five million men. It was the Red Army, under the dynamic leadership of Trotsky, which saved the new regime during the Civil War (1918–1920).

Finally, Lenin brought the economy under state control by instituting '**War Communism**' in June 1918. By 1921, however, War Communism, combined with the effects of the First World War and the Civil War, had brought the economy to the verge of collapse. Lenin realised that a change was needed and introduced the **New Economic Policy**.

> Lenin established a totalitarian police state which made Stalinism possible. But it is possible that he would have modified it if he had lived.
>
> **KEY POINT**

Stalin

OCR — M5 (synoptic)
WJEC — M6 (synoptic)

Key points from AS

- **Rise to power**
  Revise AS pages 153–154
- **Stalin's Russia**
  Revise AS pages 156–157

'Stalinism'.

The death of Lenin in 1924 left no obvious successor. Many people expected a form of collective leadership to emerge. By 1929, however, Stalin had overcome his rivals – Trotsky, Kamenev, Zinoviev and Bukharin – to become undisputed dictator. He had achieved this partly by advancing his cause through the party machinery established by Lenin. As General Secretary of the Communist Party from 1922, Stalin controlled party membership and he was able to use his position to secure the promotion of his allies.

Stalin established a totalitarian state. The main elements of Lenin's political system – the Soviet constitution, the Communist Party, the secret police and the Red Army – were developed into the '**Stalinist' dictatorship**. Lenin's 1918 constitution was replaced in 1924 by the Union of Soviet Socialist Republics. This brought the republics which had replaced the old national units of the Russian empire into a federation dominated by the Russian Soviet Federated Socialist Republic. The constitutional structure, however, was much the same, with an All-Union Congress of Soviets replacing the All-Russian Congress. As before, the real power lay with the Communist Party, and within the party with the Politburo. A new constitution in 1936 guaranteed freedom of speech and the press and the right to education and work – but only if exercised 'in order to strengthen the socialist system'.

The secret police were even more powerful than in tsarist Russia.

In practice Stalinist Russia was a police state. The Cheka was replaced in 1922 by the OGPU, which Stalin used to enforce collectivisation. In 1934 the OGPU was merged with the NKVD (People's Commissariat for Internal Affairs), which became

A cartoon published by Russian exiles in 1936 shows Stalin holding every position in the government

notorious as the instrument by which Stalin carried out the purges. Meanwhile the Red Army came more firmly under political control. Under a system of dual command, political commissars worked alongside military commanders.

See Chapter 10.2. Kulaks were the richer peasants.

The influence of the state was felt in all areas of life – nowhere more so than in economic policy. Stalin was ruthless in suppressing the opposition of the kulaks to the collectivisation of agriculture. Similarly, the success of the Five-Year Plans depended on the power of the state to drive them forward.

> The Stalinist system left Stalin in unchallenged control of Russia – more powerful than the Tsars.

KEY POINT

Stalin's Russia during and after the Second World War

Key points from AS

- Stalin's last years 1945–53
  Revise AS page 159

The Stalinist state and the industrial power that it had created helped Russia to eventual victory in the Great Patriotic War and provided the means by which Stalin pushed forward the reconstruction of the Russian economy after the war. Stalin's last years saw renewed repression by the secret police under Beria. Stalin's dictatorial powers were further increased: the Party Congress, the Central Committee and the Politburo rarely met. When he died in 1953 he was planning new purges.

> When Stalin died, Russia was one of the two superpowers, but it was ruled by a savagely repressive dictatorship.

KEY POINT

You should be able to explain the significance of each of these dates.

1917	October revolution; establishment of Bolshevik regime
1918–20	Civil War
1921	New Economic Policy
1924	Death of Lenin
1925	Fall of Trotsky
1929	Stalin in undisputed control as dictator
1953	Death of Stalin

KEY DATES

6.4 The growth of opposition

After studying this section you should be able to:

- *outline the development of revolutionary movements and political parties in tsarist Russia*
- *explain the methods by which Lenin and Stalin dealt with opposition*

LEARNING SUMMARY

Opposition groups under the Tsars

OCR	M5 (synoptic)
WJEC	M6 (synoptic)

Key points from AS

- **The consolidation of Bolshevik power**
  Revise AS pages 150–151

Alexander II's reforms raised the hopes of Russia's liberals, but by the 1860s many young intellectuals felt that they had not gone far enough. Their disappointment led to the formation of reformist movements. The two most important were the **populists** ('narodniki') and the **anarchists**. The former aimed to educate the peasants to demand reforms, but the results of a campaign in the countryside in 1874–5 were disappointing. The anarchists, who derived much of their inspiration from Bakunin, advocated terrorism. They made several unsuccessful attempts on the life of Alexander II in 1879–80 and succeeded in 1881.

> **KEY POINT**
>
> The growth of revolutionary movements strengthened reactionary influences around the Tsar.

Under Alexander III and Nicholas II revolutionaries were hunted down by the Okhrana (secret police) and many were executed or sent to Siberia. But despite repression, new opposition movements emerged.

- Probably the most important before 1917 were the Liberals, who were well represented in the zemstvos. In 1904 some zemstvo leaders formed the Union of Liberation which aimed for the establishment of a representative assembly. From this the Cadet Party developed in 1905 – a party of radicals which formed the biggest group in the First Duma. At the same time a more moderate liberal party emerged, the Octobrists. They favoured limited political reform within the framework of the October Manifesto and dominated the Third and Fourth Dumas.

- The next biggest group was the Social Revolutionaries. They aimed to unite intellectuals, peasants and urban workers. They demanded not only political reform but also redistribution of the land, which gave them their appeal to the peasants. Their terrorist wing was responsible for a number of high-profile assassinations between 1901 and 1905. Another non-Marxist socialist group, similar to the SRs in demanding land reform, was the Trudovik Party, the most important member of which was Kerensky.

- The other main socialist group was the Social Democratic Party, founded in 1898 by Plekhanov. Its ideas were Marxist and it sought support from Russia's newly emerging industrial working class. At its 1903 Congress, held in exile in Brussels and London, it divided into two wings. The Bolsheviks, led by Lenin, wanted membership restricted to a small number of dedicated activists who would bring about a socialist revolution and the dictatorship of the proletariat. The Mensheviks wanted a mass party of the working class which would aim to overthrow the Tsar, set up a democratic republic and then introduce an eight-hour working day and other social reforms. The Mensheviks – and especially Trotsky – dominated the St Petersburg Soviet in 1905.

- Opposition also developed in the form of nationalist movements in Finland, Poland, the Baltic provinces, the Ukraine, Georgia and Armenia.

Note the continuity between the populists and the SRs.

Including the Minister of the Interior, Plehve.

Bolsheviks = majority men, Mensheviks = minority men. In fact the Bolsheviks were in a minority for much of the proceedings.

The reaction of the national minorities to tsarist policies of Russification.

> **KEY POINT**
>
> Opposition to the tsarist regime was fragmented. This allowed Nicholas II to play off Liberals against Socialists in 1905. It also made it possible in 1917 for the most ruthless group to seize power.

Opposition after 1917

OCR ▸ M5 (synoptic)

The Whites

Key points from AS

- **The Civil War**
  Revise AS pages 151–152

The seizure of power by the Bolsheviks inevitably produced opposition, as did Lenin's subsequent moves: the dissolution of the Constituent Assembly (because the Bolsheviks did not have a majority in it), the signing of the humiliating peace of Brest-Litovsk and the institution of War Communism. By the middle of 1918 Russia had descended into Civil War.

The White forces in the Civil War consisted of a number of strands of opposition to the Bolsheviks.

The Whites failed to gain the support of Russian peasants, who feared they would return the land to the landlords.

- Members of other political parties or revolutionary groups, including Liberals and Social Revolutionaries. They aimed to restore the Provisional Government.
- Officers of the tsarist army, who were particularly incensed by the Treaty of Brest-Litovsk. Some wished to restore the Provisional Government, others aimed to bring back the Tsar.
- Various nationalist groups which aimed to break away from the Russian Empire. In Finland, the Baltic states and Poland they succeeded in gaining their independence. The Ukraine and the Caucasus, however, were eventually brought back into the USSR.

The Whites were also supported by foreign powers – Britain, France, Italy, the USA and Japan – but this played a minor part in the war. The Red Army, assisted by the activities of the Cheka, overcame all organised opposition.

> The fact that these groups had different aims was a source of weakness which contributed to their defeat.
>
> **KEY POINT**

Opposition from within the Communist Party

OCR ▸ M5 (synoptic)

Key points from AS

- **The purges**
  Revise AS pages 155–156

All the living members of the Lenin's politburo were liquidated except Stalin himself and Trotsky who was in exile in Mexico, where he was murdered in 1940.

The battle for the succession to Lenin revealed not only deep personal rivalries but fundamental political differences. The principal dispute was over whether the USSR should pursue 'socialism in one country' (Stalin) or 'permanent revolution' (Trotsky). There was also much argument about Lenin's New Economic Policy, which Trotsky and others attacked as too much of a compromise with capitalism.

Stalin's victory in the struggle for power appeared to settle these arguments but his economic policies, especially collectivisation, aroused opposition from within the Party. This was almost certainly part of the reason for the purges. Stalin could not feel safe until he had eliminated all critics, especially the Old Bolsheviks associated with the revolutionary era, and replaced them with his own creatures. Many of the victims were simply potential enemies who had shown no sign of disloyalty.

> Stalin displayed an almost paranoid suspicion of potential (and even imaginary) opponents and this continued right up to his death in 1953.
>
> **KEY POINT**

Key points from AS

- **The New Economic Policy**
  Revise AS page 152
- **The collectivisation of agriculture**
  Revise AS page 155

The peasants

Both Lenin and Stalin faced opposition from the peasants. The resistance of the peasants to the demands made upon them forced Lenin to abandon War Communism. As grain production dropped, famine set in and this led to widespread disturbances, culminating in the Kronstadt naval mutiny in 1921. Lenin, realising that a change was needed, introduced the New Economic Policy, by which peasants were allowed to sell their surplus on payment of a tax of a percentage of their crops.

In the 'procurement crisis' of 1927 the peasants refused to produce enough grain at the prices offered by the state.

This episode demonstrated how crucial the agricultural sector was to the Russian economy. Even under the New Economic Policy there were food shortages. It was to solve this problem that Stalin embarked on collectivisation in 1928. The policy met widespread resistance: the kulaks burnt their crops and slaughtered their cattle. The result was a famine in 1932–3. In the end Stalin triumphed and peace was restored but in the process, it is estimated, ten million kulaks were killed, died in the famine or were sent to Siberia.

> Collectivisation destroyed the resistance of the peasantry but was a disaster for Russian agriculture.
>
> **KEY POINT**

6.5 The Russian economy

LEARNING SUMMARY

After studying this section you should be able to:

● *outline the development of the Russian economy from c.1880 to c.1980*

The Russian economy under the last Tsars

AQA   M4 (synoptic)
OCR   M5 (synoptic)
WJEC   M6 (synoptic)

The rapid rise in the rural population made matters worse as farms were sub-divided into smaller holdings.

Russia was economically the most backward of the European great powers. Its economy was overwhelmingly agrarian but agriculture was grossly inefficient. The emancipation of the serfs in 1861 did little immediately to improve the economy. Most ex-serfs were still tied to the mir (commune) by the collective obligation to make redemption payments to the state.

Industry was under-developed but the pace of industrial growth began to increase in the reign of Alexander III. **Witte**, Minister of Finance from 1892 to 1903, achieved rapid industrial growth by increasing tariffs, encouraging foreign investment, especially from France, and stabilising the currency. The rate of growth of industrial production was the highest in the world. Even so, by 1910 only 30 per cent of Russia's gross national product came from industry. Moreover the rapid growth of the urban population produced appalling housing and working conditions, especially in Moscow and St Petersburg.

The main criticism of Witte is that he did little for agriculture. **Stolypin** turned his attention to this. There were three main elements in his reforms:

● peasants were allowed to turn their holdings into their own individual properties
● state land was made available through the Peasants' Bank
● government assistance enabled over three million people to migrate to Siberia.

There was a substantial increase in the number of peasants who owned their farms but productivity was still low.

Stolypin hoped that these measures would make agriculture more efficient and would create a class of prosperous peasant farmers. His reforms offered a solution to Russia's agrarian problems but they needed many years to succeed.

> **KEY POINT**
>
> By 1914 Russia still had a long way to go to catch up with western Europe and the USA.

Economic failure led to defeat and revolution.

The First World War revealed all too clearly the comparative weakness of the Russian economy. Russia was able to mobilise huge armies but its industry was unable to equip them adequately. Because of growing chaos in the transport system food shortages developed in the cities. Food prices rose dramatically. When the Bolsheviks seized power in the October Revolution, the economic situation was dire.

Lenin and Stalin, 1917–41

AQA   M4 (synoptic)
OCR   M5 (synoptic)

Grain crops were about half the 1913 total: peasants stopped producing more than they needed for themselves.

In 1918, faced by civil war, **Lenin** introduced **War Communism**, which he claimed was 'dictated not by economic but by military needs'. By 1921 the country was on the verge of economic collapse, partly because of seven years of foreign and civil war, but also because of War Communism. The result was famine, aggravated by droughts in 1920–21. People fled from the cities to the countryside. There were widespread disturbances, the most serious of which was the Kronstadt naval mutiny in March 1921. Lenin therefore abandoned War Communism and introduced the **New Economic Policy**. By 1926 production in both agriculture and industry approached pre-war levels.

Key points from AS

• **Economic policy: the Five-Year Plans and collectivisation**
Revise AS pages 154–155

The victory of **Stalin** in the struggle for the succession to Lenin was a victory for the aim of 'socialism in one country'. In practice this meant industrialisation. Stalin therefore embarked on a series of **Five-Year Plans**. Targets were set for all major industries, to be achieved by a mixture of rewards and punishments. The result of the Five-Year Plans was that the gross national product of the USSR increased much more rapidly than that of the western powers. Between 1928 and 1941 coal and steel production quadrupled.

> The Five-Year Plans transformed Russia into a major industrial power.   **KEY POINT**

Collectivisation was a disaster: it was enforced at huge cost in human suffering and caused long-term damage to Russian agriculture.

The transformation of Russian industry depended upon a parallel transformation of agriculture. Agriculture presented two problems. Firstly productivity was low because there were 24 million separate peasant farms, many of them too small to use modern agricultural machinery. Secondly the richer peasants (kulaks), who had profited from the New Economic Policy, wanted high prices for their produce. Stalin's solution was **collectivisation**.

The Second World War and after, 1941–80

AQA   M4 (synoptic)

The war caused enormous damage to the Soviet economy. Yet it was Russia's industrial strength, together with massive aid from the USA and Britain, which underlay victory. Stalin's industrialisation in the 1930s paid off. In the latter years of the war the USSR was producing more military equipment than Germany and of better quality.

The major task facing Russia in 1945 was reconstruction. The Fourth and Fifth Five-Year Plans rebuilt Russian industry. The output of heavy industry more than doubled between 1947 and 1950. Particular attention was given to the development of a nuclear industry. By 1949 the USSR had an atomic bomb. Agricultural productivity remained poor and food prices were high. This was partly a result of destruction in the war but mainly because of low investment and the inefficiency of the collective farms. The standard of living remained low, partly because of the emphasis on capital goods in the Five-Year Plans but also because of the high level of military expenditure.

> By 1950 the USSR was the world's second biggest industrial power, and also a nuclear power.   **KEY POINT**

Stalin's successors.

Khrushchev tried to solve the agricultural problem by the Virgin Lands policy. Volunteers were sent to Siberia and provided with tractors to bring new land into cultivation. This led to increased food production, but poor management and problems of soil erosion hampered the scheme. In 1963 Russia had to import American grain. **Brezhnev** tackled the problem by giving collective farms more freedom and raising farm workers' wages. Between 1966 and 1971 there were good harvests. However, a bad harvest in 1972 forced Russia once more to buy American grain.

Khrushchev also changed the emphasis of industrial policy. More attention was paid to production of consumer goods with the aim of improving standards of living. Brezhnev introduced bonuses for efficient workers in order to increase both productivity and consumer demand (since workers would have more to spend).

> Despite Russia's ability to produce sophisticated defence equipment and to take part in space exploration, much of its industry was still inefficient and standards of living still lagged behind those of the west.   **KEY POINT**

Sample question and model answer

This question incorporates synoptic assessment.

This is an outline answer, to which you should add more detail.

How far do you agree that Stalin was not only the most autocratic and repressive ruler of Russia during the period 1855–1953 but also the one who was most successful in modernising Russia? [30]

The USSR under Stalin was nominally a democracy but this was a façade. The guarantees of personal liberty meant little. The Supreme Soviet met only briefly each year. Real power lay in the Communist Party, of which Stalin was Secretary. Opposition, real and imaginary, was ruthlessly crushed. In his last years Stalin was believed to be planning yet more purges. The regime displayed all the characteristics of totalitarian dictatorship – the secret police, the gulags, censorship, manipulation of the arts for propaganda purposes. Stalin himself was the focus of an extraordinary personality cult which exceeded the veneration of the 19th-century Russian peasant for the Tsar.

Between 1855 and 1905 the tsarist regime was completely autocratic, in the sense that all government activity was based solely on the Tsar's authority. There was no parliament. Local elected assemblies (zemstva) were set up by Alexander II, but their powers were soon clipped by the Land Captains established by Alexander III. Execution or exile to Siberia awaited opponents of the regime identified by the secret police. Censorship was rigidly enforced. In all these ways the tsarist regime resembled Stalin's, though the fact that it was in the end less successful in crushing opposition is testified by a number of political assassinations carried out by revolutionaries and above all by the outbreak of revolution in 1905. Though there were no political parties, opposition groups did exist, though often underground or in exile.

Give examples of political assassinations and opposition groups.

The tsarist regime was shaken by the 1905 Revolution but recovered. The Tsar's authority was restored in Moscow in 1906 with great brutality. In the remaining years of tsarism, repression of opposition by executions, torture, imprisonment and exile to Siberia continued unabated, as did press censorship and suppression of trade unions. But the autocracy was mitigated by the Dumas, with legitimate political parties. Some historians claim that, but for the war, the regime might have developed in a constitutional manner.

The Dumas actually had very little power.

It is more difficult to reach a conclusion about Lenin's regime. It was undoubtedly repressive. One of his first acts after the October revolution was to establish the Cheka, which conducted the Red Terror. But debate within the Bolshevik Party was not suppressed, at least until the ban on factions in 1921, and Lenin's apologists claim that if he had lived he would have modified the terror.

The Lenin period was dominated by the Civil War, which helps to explain the terror.

On balance, therefore, the claim that Stalin's regime was the most ruthless in the period seems valid. What about modernisation? Under Stalin, nothing was allowed to stand in the way of economic modernisation. The human cost of collectivisation and dekulakisation was enormous. There can be little doubt, however, that the result was a transformation of the economy and Russian society. Agriculture was forcibly collectivised and a massive programme of industrialisation achieved by the Five-Year Plans. Although huge numbers of people were displaced by collectivisation, the counterpart to this was that Russian society became more urbanised and better educated. But revisionist historians have shown that in reality centralised control was much less effective than it appeared to be. The over-ambitious targets of the Five-Year Plans were not fulfilled. Agriculture remained inefficient.

Sample question and model answer (continued)

Lenin had less chance to modernise Russia, though he did embark on social and educational reforms. Pressure of events forced him to abandon War Communism for the New Economic Policy. For all the backwardness of Russia in 1917, the contribution of the last Tsars to the modernisation of Russia should not be under-estimated. Alexander II was responsible for the basic act of modernisation on which all else depended, emancipation (even though the way it was carried out did nothing to make agriculture more efficient). Substantial progress was made in industrialisation from the 1880s, particularly by Witte's policies. Some would claim that this was the real foundation for Stalin's industrialisation. Nevertheless it seems fair to conclude that the most rapid progress was made under Stalin, though at enormous cost. For all the weaknesses of the Soviet economy in 1953, it was by then the world's second biggest industrial power.

A brief discussion of the effects of emancipation would be useful here.

Practice examination questions

1 Study Sources A to D and answer questions (a) and (b) which follow.

Source A

From *Europe since Napoleon,* by D. Thomson, 1957.
Emancipation did not lead to any marked improvements in the methods or output of Russian agriculture. For the next 40 years the land was still mostly cultivated in strips and the time-honoured methods were used to grow the traditional crops. No fresh wind of scientific agriculture or progressive methods blew through the farmlands of Russia. Because productivity did not keep pace with population, famines and periods of great distress became more and more frequent. In all these ways the liberal and far-reaching measure of emancipation did little to improve either the economic lot of the mass of the peasants or the economic prosperity of the country as a whole.

Source B

From a speech by Stalin to a conference of students of agrarian problems in 1929.
Can the Soviet government and the work of socialist construction be, for any length of time, based on two different foundations – on the foundation of the most large-scale and concentrated socialist industry, and on the foundation of the most fragmentary and backward, small-commodity, peasant farming? They cannot. Sooner or later the end must be a complete collapse of the whole national economy. What, then, is the solution? The socialist way is to set up collective and state farms. This way leads to the amalgamation of the small peasant farms into large collective farms, technically and scientifically equipped.

Source C

From *The Making of Modern Russia,* by L. Kochan, 1962.
It was many years before Russian agriculture made its recovery from the turmoil and destruction of 1929–32. Not until 1934 did Stalin reveal the cost of the 'advance' to large-scale farming. There were 33 million horses in 1928 – and 15 million in 1933. The respective figures for horned cattle were 70 million and 34 million; for pigs, 26 million and 9 million; for sheep and goats, 146 million and 42 million. This is to say nothing of the millions of kulaks and their families deported to forced-labour camps and new industrial locations beyond the Urals.

Source D

From *A History of Russia,* by P. Dukes, 1998.
For agriculture Brezhnev announced guidelines in March 1965: no more reorganisation; no more grandiose 'campaigns' in the 'virgin lands' or anywhere else; and more money through higher subsidies, incomes and incentives. Production certainly rose to a considerable extent, but problems of organisation and distribution, machinery and personnel persisted and considerable quantities of the basic commodity, grain, continued to be imported. The blame for shortcomings was placed on the collective farm. But critics continued to argue that there could not be substantial progress until there was a more thorough overhaul of the whole system, with more incentives and more toleration, even encouragement, for the private plot.

(a) Compare Sources B and C and use your own knowledge. Comment on the usefulness of these Sources in assessing Stalin's policies towards agriculture. [12]

(b) Study sources A to D and use your own knowledge. 'Despite successive reforms, Russian agriculture remained inefficient and an obstacle to the modernisation of the economy.' How far do you agree with this assessment? [18]

2 Why did Russia, in the period 1855–1956, fail to develop a western-style democracy? [30]

3 'Poverty, war, revolutionary activity and the drive to industrialise created tensions which could only be contained by repressive government.' How valid is this assessment of Russia in the period 1855–1956? [30]

WJEC specimen

Chapter 7

Autocracy and reform in Germany and Russia

The following topics are covered in this chapter:

- Tsarist Russia and imperial Germany
- Opposition and reform before 1914
- The overthrow of the imperial regimes

- The Soviet Union and Nazi Germany
- Opposition to the Communist and Nazi dictatorships

7.1 Tsarist Russia and imperial Germany

After studying this section you should be able to:

- compare the system of power in tsarist Russia and imperial Germany

Autocratic power systems

AQA   M4 (synoptic)

Key points from AS

- **Tsarist Russia 1825–94**
  Revise AS pages 91–93
- **Nicholas II 1894–1917**
  Revise AS pages 93–96
- **The German Empire 1871–90**
  Revise AS pages 113–115
- **William II**
  Revise AS pages 115–118

Sections 4.4, 6.1, 6.2, 6.3 and 6.4 should be studied alongside this chapter.

The nobility maintained order in the provinces and provided government officials and army officers.

Both imperial Germany and tsarist Russia were governed by a form of **autocracy**. In Russia the Tsar's edicts were the sole source of law. All political authority came from him; ministers and officials were responsible to him alone and he was commander-in-chief of the army. In Germany the Kaiser was head of the executive and the army. The Chancellor was appointed by him and responsible to him.

Nevertheless there were important differences between the two autocracies. In Russia the Tsar presided over a system in which there were no rival institutions or even political parties, whereas in Germany the Kaiser's autocratic powers had to be exercised within a complicated system of institutions, parties and interest groups. This difference reflected the different histories of the two countries: the Tsars were heirs to a system with its roots in medieval Muscovy, whereas the Second Reich was established and its constitution drawn up in 1871.

Moreover, **Russian society** was very different from that of Germany. Until 1861 more than half the Russian people were serfs and even after the emancipation they were tied to the village commune by the collective responsibility for redemption payments. The middle class was tiny by western European standards; even in 1900, though industrialisation was under way, it was much smaller than in Germany. Thus the only class with political influence was the nobility. In Germany the middle class, both professional and commercial, was large and well educated. A wealthy and influential industrial elite had emerged, though it had not displaced the older land-based nobility and gentry, who were still powerful, particularly the Junkers in Prussia. Industrialisation had produced a large urban working class. All these factors affected the political balance.

There were other important differences between the two systems.

- In Russia there was no **parliament** until the establishment of the Duma in 1906. Even then the Dumas had very limited powers. The constitution of the German Empire provided for two houses of parliament. The upper house (the Bundesrat) consisted of representatives of the German states and was dominated by Prussia and thus ultimately by the Junkers, who controlled Prussia's government. The lower house (Reichstag) was elected by universal male suffrage. This conveyed the illusion of democracy, but in practice the Reichstag had little power. The limited power it did have, however, made it desirable for the Chancellor to try to gain the support of enough parties to approve his policies.

- Because there was no parliament there were no proper **political parties** in

It could veto legislation and controlled the non-military part of the imperial budget.

Russia until the beginning of the 20th century. In Germany the main political parties – the Socialists, the Catholic Centre Party, the Liberals and the Conservatives – were well developed, though their role in the system of government was limited.

- There was no equivalent in Russia to the Chancellor in Germany. From 1871 to 1890 Bismarck as **Chancellor** was the dominant figure. After the dismissal of Bismarck in 1890 the new Kaiser, William II, exercised much more direct personal control over the government.

- Imperial Germany was a **federal state**, in which the member states retained important local functions such as education and roads. There was no equivalent in Russia. Until 1864 the nobility and gentry controlled local government. The zemstva gave Russia a taste of elected local government but much of the power of the gentry was restored by Alexander III when he appointed Land Captains in 1889.

District councils set up in 1864.

- The **Orthodox Church** in Russia supported the autocracy by teaching the duty of unquestioning obedience to the Tsar. In Germany, which was divided between the Protestant north and the Catholic south, religion was a source of tension rather than strength, particularly during the Kulturkampf.

Bismarck's struggle with the Catholics in the 1870s.

- The tsarist autocracy was supported by a **secret police** to which there was no equivalent in Germany. Opposition was suppressed by executions or exile to Siberia.

- In Germany much political influence was wielded by powerful **interest groups**, especially landowners and industrialists. The agrarian interests were led by the Prussian Junkers. Industrialisation led to the emergence of a powerful and wealthy group of big industrialists. In Russia there was no real equivalent: the nobility were in decline because of increasing economic difficulties and industrialists were neither numerous nor powerful enough to exert significant political influence.

The Junkers had considerable political power through their control over the Prussian parliament.

- The **army** and the **bureaucracy** were politically powerful in imperial Germany. William II gave great weight to the advice of the generals.

> **KEY POINT**
>
> The system of power in imperial Germany was authoritarian but less autocratic than in tsarist Russia.

7.2 Opposition and reform before 1914

After studying this section you should be able to:

- *compare the concessions made to demands for reform in imperial Germany and tsarist Russia*
- *compare the ways in which they handled opposition*

LEARNING SUMMARY

The Second Reich

AQA   M4 (synoptic)

Opposition in Germany and Russia took very different forms. Although Germany had an authoritarian system of government, it had a constitution and opposition was organised through political parties.

Key points from AS

- **Bismarck and the Liberals**
  Revise AS page 113

The Liberals

In the first half of the 19th century liberalism and nationalism went together in Germany. The Liberals wanted a unified Germany governed by a liberal democracy.

The collapse of the Frankfurt Parliament in 1849 marked their failure to achieve unification by parliamentary methods.

With the establishment of the North German Confederation in 1867 and then the Second Reich in 1871, military strength and shrewd diplomacy succeeded where liberal methods had failed. The Liberals, who from 1862 to 1866 had been locked in dispute with Bismarck in Prussia over the military budget, changed their attitude towards him. The constitution of the Empire went some way to meeting their aspirations: the Reichstag was to be elected by universal male suffrage and to have some powers over both legislation and the imperial budget. In the 1870s therefore the National Liberals were Bismarck's main allies in the Reichstag, backing him in the Kulturkampf.

> The depression which began in 1873 led to pressure from industry and agriculture for protective tariffs.

During the 1870s this alliance broke down. A dispute about the military budget in 1874 was followed by a decisive break in 1879 when Bismarck decided to abandon free trade in favour of protection. From then on he relied on the Conservatives and the Catholic Centre Party in the Reichstag and the Liberals were politically marginalised.

Key points from AS

- **The socialists**
  Revise AS page 114

> Sickness and accident insurance and old age pensions – all introduced in the 1880s.

The socialists

In the view of both Bismarck and William II a more serious threat came from the socialists. In 1878 he introduced the anti-socialist laws, but he recognised that banning the party was not enough; it was necessary also to make concessions which would win the support of the working classes. This was the main purpose behind the introduction of 'state socialism'. William II tried to win over working-class opinion by withdrawing the anti-socialist laws and introducing further social reforms in the early 1890s, but he was disappointed that this did not reduce support for the Socialist Party. During the rest of his reign the Socialist Party was regarded as dangerous and no attempt was made to give even moderate socialists any share in political responsibility.

> In spite of the hostility of the Kaiser and the elites, the Socialist Party became the largest party in the Reichstag in the 1912 elections.
>
> **KEY POINT**

Tsarist Russia

AQA ▸ M4 (synoptic)

Key points from AS

- **Alexander II 1855–81**
  Revise AS pages 91–92

> See Chapter 6.4.

After Russia's defeat in the Crimean War, Alexander II introduced sweeping reforms: the emancipation of the serfs, the setting up of zemstva and reforms of the legal system, the army and education. These reforms were opposed by landowners and conservative forces around the court, but they also disappointed reformists. Moreover Alexander II refused to consider further political reform. He had no intention of sharing power with any sort of parliament.

Since the tsarist system provided no means for the expression of opposition, disappointed reformists turned to revolutionary activities. The two most important revolutionary movements were the 'populists', who wanted to educate the peasants to demand reforms, and the anarchists, who called for armed rebellion. Alexander II in response reverted to repression and under his successors, Alexander III and Nicholas II, the repression was intensified.

Despite this, new revolutionary movements arose.

- The Marxist **Social Democratic Party** was founded in 1898. In 1903 it divided into two wings – the **Bolsheviks**, led by Lenin, and the **Mensheviks**.
- **The Social Revolutionary Party** was formed in 1902 with the aim of uniting the intellectuals, workers and peasants.

- The **Liberals** set up the Union of Liberation, which demanded political reform, in 1904.

However, political reform came only as a result of revolution in 1905 and even then it was very limited. The Dumas represented a step towards a constitutional monarchy and led to the formation of legitimate political parties. However, the regime remained fundamentally autocratic. The Dumas had no control over ministers, who were still responsible solely to the Tsar, and they were only allowed to make reforms which the Tsar approved. Nevertheless, it is possible that a constitutional monarchy would have developed but for the First World War.

> The first two Dumas were dissolved after a few weeks because they demanded reforms of which Nicholas II did not approve.

> Russia had no constitution, no parliament until 1906 and no recognised political parties. Opposition, therefore, took revolutionary paths, whereas in Germany it was expressed through legitimate political parties.
>
> **KEY POINT**

7.3 The overthrow of the imperial regimes

After studying this section you should be able to:

- explain why the revolutions of 1917–18 in Russia and Germany had such different outcomes
- explain why democracy did not survive in Germany

LEARNING SUMMARY

The Russian and German revolutions of 1917–18

AQA ▶ M4 (synoptic)

The Russian revolution

> **Key points from AS**
>
> - **The 1917 Revolutions** *Revise AS pages 96–97*

> See also Chapter 10.1.

> Perhaps its biggest mistake was continuing the war.

Both tsarism in Russia and the Second Reich in Germany were destroyed by defeat in the First World War. In both cases the war ended in revolution and the establishment of democratic regimes. The outcomes were, however, very different.

In Russia revolution broke out in February 1917 (Russian calendar). The fourth Duma set up a Provisional Government composed largely of Liberals and the Tsar abdicated. Eight months later the Provisional Government was overthrown and the Bolsheviks led by Lenin seized power. This outcome was the result partly of the weakness of the Provisional Government, which never had a strong basis in popular support. By September the Bolsheviks had gained a majority in the Petrograd and Moscow Soviets.

> The tightly knit organisation of the Bolsheviks and the ruthless leadership of Lenin enabled them to take advantage of the failings of the Provisional Government and seize power in the October revolution.
>
> **KEY POINT**

The November revolution in Germany

> **Key points from AS**
>
> - **The establishment of the Weimar Republic** *Revise AS pages 135–136*

> The Kapp putsch was defeated by a general strike.

In Germany the November revolution of 1918 began in a similar way. Defeat in war led to the abdication of the Kaiser and the establishment of a provisional government under the Social Democrat Ebert. Unlike in Russia, the provisional government survived an attempt to seize power by the German Communists (**Spartacists**), though it had to call on the army and the freikorps to do so. It then went on to draw up the highly democratic Weimar constitution. In 1920 it defeated the Kapp putsch, an attempted right-wing coup, equivalent to the Kornilov affair in Russia.

Why was the outcome different in Germany than Russia?
- German political parties were much more firmly established than Russian ones.
- The imperial constitution provided the basis from which a democracy could evolve.
- Germany did not face a continuing war, nor did it have Russia's land problem.
- There was no equivalent to Lenin.

The Weimar Republic

AQA ▶ M4 (synoptic)

Key points from AS

- **The Weimar Republic**
  Revise AS pages 135–137 and 139–141

The Nationalists were not committed to democracy and the Communists and National Socialists were actively anti-democratic.

The breakdown of the Weimar constitution led increasing numbers of voters to turn to the extremists – the Communists and the Nazis.

The Weimar Republic failed to give Germany a lasting democracy. It was handicapped from the start because it was born of defeat in war and had to accept humiliating terms at Versailles. It had to rely on former servants of the Empire as civil servants, judges, teachers and, most importantly, army officers. The constitution embodied a system of proportional representation which made coalitions inevitable, but the mainstream parties, led by politicians who lacked experience of democratic government, were poorly suited for this. This opened the way for extremists.

Nevertheless it is quite possible that democracy would have survived but for the world economic crisis which began in 1929. Not all historians would agree about this. Some would point to the existence of significant sections of the population which were discontented even during the 'golden era' of Weimar between 1925 and 1928: industrialists, farmers and shopkeepers in particular. Others would argue that, even though the growth of democratic political institutions had been stunted by the authoritarianism of the Empire, the German liberal tradition stretched back to the early 19th century and the Weimar republic was therefore not an entirely alien growth. All agree, however, that the economic crisis posed problems that the Weimar politicians could not solve. With the breakdown of coalition government, Brüning resorted to government by presidential decree.

The Weimar Republic ceased to function as a genuine democracy three years before Hitler came to power.

7.4 The Soviet Union and Nazi Germany

After studying this section you should be able to:

- *compare the ideologies, political systems and economic policies of Nazi Germany and Communist Russia*

Communist and Nazi dictatorship

AQA ▶ M4 (synoptic)

Key points from AS

- **The National Socialist state**
  Revise AS pages 142–144
- **Stalin's dictatorship 1924–41**
  Revise AS pages 153–157

Similarities

- Both Communist Russia and Nazi Germany were **single-party** states based upon an all-embracing ideology and ruled by dictators who were the objects of a personality cult.
- Both were **police states**, enforcing conformity by terror. Enemies of the state were sought out by the secret police. In Russia Lenin set up the Cheka. This was replaced in 1922 by the OGPU, which in turn was merged with the NKVD

> Also the Nazi concentration camps were paralleled by the gulags.

(People's Commissariat for Internal Affairs) in 1934. The NKVD became notorious as the instrument by which Stalin carried out the purges. In Germany from 1936 Himmler controlled the SS, the police, the SD (the party's spy service headed by Heydrich) and the Gestapo.

- Both used **state control** over the media, the arts and education for the purposes of indoctrination.
- In both **the army was politicised**. The Red Army came under political control through a system of dual command, with political commissars working alongside military commanders. In Germany the loyalty of the army was secured by an oath of personal allegiance to the Führer and it was increasingly nazified by the influence of the Waffen SS.

Differences

The USSR and Nazi Germany embodied different **ideologies**. The USSR was based upon Marxism, a fully worked-out system of thought which embraced historical, political and economic theory and envisaged the ultimate emergence of a classless society. Nazi ideology was less systematic. It saw life as a perpetual struggle in which only the strongest would survive. In the view of the Nazis this should mean the victory of the Germans as the master race.

> These ideas originated in Social Darwinism.

Ideological differences produced different policies towards **political institutions**. In the USSR Lenin swept away existing institutions and replaced them by a system of Soviets. Real power, however, lay with the Communist Party, the only one allowed. The People's Commissars (ministers) were all members of the Politburo of the Communist Party. Stalin inherited this political system and developed it into the 'Stalinist' dictatorship – a police state based on terror. In Germany the Nazis kept the existing political structure but transformed it by giving Hitler **dictatorial powers** under the Enabling Act and by merging the offices of President and Chancellor. By the process of Gleichschaltung (co-ordination) all other political parties were dissolved and all other organisations were nazified.

A cartoon of Lenin cleaning up the world – sweeping away kings, priests and capitalists

The USSR was run by **a new elite** of officials who gained their influence from loyalty to the party. The system was, in theory at least, highly centralised but in practice it was not necessarily efficient, since central directives were often differently interpreted by local officials. The Nazis had no wish to displace the existing elites in industry, the bureaucracy or the army; rather they aimed to win their support by offering **an authoritarian regime** which would preserve Germany from Communism. The existing government departments and local authorities were retained but nazified. Alongside them, and competing with them for authority, were the institutions of the Nazi party. The powers of government and party authorities often overlapped.

> Thus for different reasons both regimes were less efficient than they seemed.

The role of **the army** was also different. In Russia the Red Army was newly created after the Revolution and was kept under control by political appointees alongside the officers. In Germany the army retained a degree of independence, despite the infiltration of the Waffen SS.

There was no parallel in Nazi Germany to Stalin's **purges**. The Night of the Long Knives served to destroy the radical wing of the Nazi Party and retain the support of the army, but thereafter Hitler did not need to follow it up.

Stalin's intervention in **the economy** was much more radical and far-reaching than Hitler's. His methods were collectivisation and the Five-Year Plans. In Germany peasant farmers were protected and private enterprise preserved. Economic policy worked within the existing capitalist framework, but used the power of the state to direct capital and labour. The aim was to strengthen the economy so that it would be able to support Hitler's expansionist policies. Nevertheless, the Second World War showed that Stalin's policies had made Russia better able to meet the demands of a prolonged war.

> Standards of living were much higher in Germany. Nazi economic policies seemed highly successful.

> **KEY POINT**
>
> The Communists tried to create an entirely new system in Russia, whereas the Nazis preserved much of the existing administrative and economic structure of Germany but superimposed their own system of political control.

7.5 Opposition to the Communist and Nazi dictatorships

After studying this section you should be able to:

- *compare the methods by which the Communists in Russia and the Nazis in Germany overcame opposition*

Communist Russia

AQA   M4 (synoptic)

Key points from AS

- **The purges**
  Revise AS pages 155–56

Having gained power for the Bolsheviks by revolution, **Lenin** used the power of the state to crush opposition. Nevertheless by 1921 the Kronstadt Mutiny brought him to the realisation that concessions were necessary. War Communism was replaced by the New Economic Policy. By sacrificing pure communist principles, Lenin enabled the Bolshevik regime to survive a crisis. Moreover, it is possible that Lenin would have abolished the secret police eventually if he had not been struck down by illness.

Stalin first had to overcome opposition to his claim to succeed Lenin. His victory in this was attributable not only to his own political skill, which his opponents

Rightists wished to continue the New Economic Policy, leftists wanted to overturn it.

underestimated, but also to the divisions among them. First he allied with Kamenev and Zinoviev against Trotsky. Then he exploited the divisions of his opponents over economic policy, aligning himself first with the rightists such as Bukharin against the leftists (Trotsky, Kamenev and Zinoviev) and then turning against the rightists.

There is some evidence that, in spite of his brutal methods, Stalin had much support.

Once he had established himself in power, he was ruthless in his handling of opposition. Political opponents were removed in the purges. To enable the collectivisation of agriculture to proceed the kulaks were simply destroyed. The power of the state was enlisted to enforce the Five-Year Plans despite the hardship they caused – though government propaganda seems to have had some success in putting over the message that the sacrifices were in a patriotic cause.

Nazi Germany

AQA   M4 (synoptic)

Key points from AS

- **The response of the German people to Nazism**
  Revise AS page 146

For a fuller analysis of support for the Nazis, see Chapter 11.2.

The Nazis had the power to crush opposition through the SS and the Gestapo, as was demonstrated in the Night of the Long Knives, but they also pursued policies designed to win popular support. The revival of the economy, the reduction in unemployment and the successes of Hitler's foreign policy won widespread support. Import controls, fixed farm prices and laws to give them security of tenure won the support of the peasants. Full employment and the Strength through Joy programme won working-class support. Opposition to Communism and the banning of trade unions won support from industrialists. The plebiscites organised by the Nazis showed substantial support, though of course intimidation inflated the pro-Nazi votes.

> **KEY POINT**
>
> Hitler's regime was based not only on terror but also on popular approval. In the 1930s his use of terror was more limited than Stalin's, but in the SS and the Gestapo he had created the organisations that carried out the Holocaust after 1941.

Sample question and model answer

Source A → Study Sources A to D and answer questions (a) and (b) which follow.
From _A History of Germany_, by W. Carr, 1991.
Undoubtedly Karl Liebknecht's celebrated description of the Reichstag as a 'fig leaf covering the nakedness of absolutism' contains a good deal of truth. But as the structure of politics changed with the transition to a more mature economic society, the Reichstag after 1890 became the focal point of German politics. And, limited though its powers were, it was able to exert more influence – even if only of a negative nature – on the government's policies than the Russian Duma. On the eve of the First World War there were some faint signs that Germany might be moving towards a more flexible form of government. That the outside world did not notice these tentative beginnings was due in no small measure to William II's frequent hysterical outbursts and exaggerated claims for the imperial dignity.

Source B → **From _A People's Tragedy_, by O. Figes, 1996.**
Nicholas had never accepted the October Manifesto as a necessary limitation upon his own autocratic prerogatives. He had reluctantly granted the manifesto under pressure from Witte in order to save his throne. But at no time had he sworn to act upon it as a 'constitution' (the crucial word had nowhere been mentioned) and therefore, at least in his own mind, his coronation oath to uphold the principles of autocracy remained in force. The Tsar's sovereignty was in his view still handed to him directly from God. The mystical basis of the Tsar's power – which put it beyond any challenge – remained intact.

Source C → **From _From Weimar to Hitler_, by E. Feuchtwanger, 1993.**
Article 48 of the [Weimar] constitution … empowered the president to restore public law and order in the Reich as a whole, if necessary by armed force. To this end he could temporarily suspend some of the basic rights guaranteed by the constitution. In 1919 article 48 did not occasion a great deal of discussion or uneasiness. It was felt that such emergency powers were necessary and that the safeguards against abuse were sufficient. It was only when the Reichstag became deadlocked in 1930 that article 48 came into use as a permanent extra-constitutional way of governing. It then acquired its quasi-dictatorial significance because it was used by Hindenburg in conjunction with the presidential power of dissolving the Reichstag.

Source D → **From _Stalin and the Soviet Union_, by S.J. Lee, 1999.**
The reality was that in [Stalin's] pursuit of power legitimacy was always a relative concept. The constitution was in many respects a façade, designed to justify Stalin's personalisation of power. It was also a gesture that was unimportant in practice since any increase in theoretical democracy within the Constitution was cancelled out by the reduction of democracy within the Party – which, of course, controlled the Constitution. Ultimately, there was nothing to stop the centre from pursuing any policy it considered appropriate. This was done, for example, in the economy through central planning which, from 1929, forced the pace of industrialisation and collective farming. It also made possible the terror and purges, sustained throughout Stalin's period in power.

(a) Study Sources A and B and use your own knowledge. Assess the usefulness of these sources in explaining the importance of the Reichstag and the Duma in imperial Germany and tsarist Russia respectively. [12]

(a) Source A (quoting Liebknecht) describes the Reichstag as a 'fig leaf covering the nakedness of absolutism', i.e. the Empire was autocratic but the Reichstag (elected by universal suffrage) gave it the appearance of a constitutional monarchy. The Reichstag's power was limited. Most

| Use of own knowledge to explain sources. |

Sample question and model answer *(continued)*

importantly, it had no control over the Chancellor, who was responsible solely to the Emperor. Its main power was negative – a veto over legislation and control over non-military parts of the budget. However, this did give it some influence: Chancellors needed to try to gain the support of enough groups to approve their policies. Source A argues, therefore, that it provided the basis for a gradual move to a less autocratic ('more flexible') system of government.

Source A compares the Reichstag with the Duma and source B confirms its judgement. Source B claims that Nicholas only accepted the October Manifesto (which set up the Dumas) under pressure and regarded it as placing no restrictions on his autocracy. The history of the Dumas supports this: in practice they could only make reforms of which the Tsar approved. Some historians, unlike Figes, believe that a constitutional monarchy could have emerged from them. This source is one interpretation of Nicholas's character, though by a distinguished historian.

> **Outline their history.**

(b) 'Constitutions counted for little. Despite changes in the forms of government, the regimes in Russia and Germany remained fundamentally authoritarian in the period 1825–1939.' Using Sources A–D and your own knowledge, consider the validity of this view. **[18]**

> **This question incorporates synoptic assessment.**

(b) There is no question that the tsarist regime from 1825 to 1905 was authoritarian. All power rested in the Tsar and there was no constitution. The October Manifesto of 1905 provided a sort of constitution, with the establishment of a Duma. But it was not called a constitution and Nicholas still regarded himself as an autocrat (source B). The Duma's powers were restricted – the Tsar had a power of veto over its proposals and the power to dissolve it at will. In all other ways the regime remained authoritarian – political arrests, secret police, press censorship, forcible dissolution of trade unions.

> **This is an outline answer, to which you should add more detail.**

> **Note that references to sources are woven into the argument.**

The power of the German Emperor, by contrast, was based on the imperial constitution of 1871. It may be argued that this counted for little: since the Kaiser appointed the Chancellor and controlled the army, he was effectively an autocrat and the Reichstag was comparatively powerless. Nevertheless, the regime was less authoritarian than Russia's, as source A suggests. The Kaiser's autocratic powers had to be exercised within a complicated system of institutions, parties and interest groups. The approval of the Reichstag was desirable for the smooth running of the government. There was a well developed system of political parties. Bismarck's anti-socialist law was mild by comparison with tsarist repression of opposition by the secret police, executions and exile to Siberia. And source A suggests that the Empire was developing 'a more flexible form of government'.

> **You can also refer to interest groups such as the Agrarian League.**

It certainly cannot be claimed that the constitution counted for nothing in Weimar Germany. Unfortunately Germany's political leaders had had no real experience of democracy under the Empire and proved unable to make a highly democratic constitution work effectively – though they were faced in the early 1930s with problems which established democracies would have found difficult to solve. Moreover many Germans on both the right and left were hostile to democracy. The constitution contained the seeds of its own downfall in the emergency powers granted to the President (source C). In the circumstances of the early 1930s Article 48 acquired a 'quasi-

> **Explain this carefully.**

Sample question and model answer *(continued)*

dictatorial significance'. The combination of economic difficulties and disillusionment with democracy brought Hitler to power. Hitler did not give Germany a new constitution: he simply suspended the Weimar constitution by the Enabling Act. Officially the constitution remained in existence; it was simply ignored. Instead Hitler set up a regime much more authoritarian than the Empire (dictatorial powers for the Führer, one-party state, secret police, concentration camps, censorship, control of opinion by propaganda).

> **You can develop these points.**

In Russia in 1917 the Provisional Government summoned a Constituent Assembly to draw up a constitution. By the time this met, the Bolsheviks had seized power and they dissolved it immediately after it met. Instead the constitution of Lenin's Russia was based on soviets, with supreme power nominally vested in the All-Russian Congress of Soviets. In practice power lay with the Politburo of the Communist Party, with Lenin at its head. No other parties were allowed and opposition was ruthlessly suppressed by the Cheka in the Red Terror. Stalin's rule, once he had defeated his rivals, was even more repressive. The 1936 Constitution provided for election of the Supreme Soviet by all citizens over 18 by secret ballot, and there were guarantees of personal liberty. The reality was that the Party controlled the government and through it Stalin imposed a totalitarian dictatorship on Russia (source D).

> **Purges, forced collectivisation.**

Thus, with the exception of the Weimar Republic, which failed, it is true that successive regimes in Germany and Russia were authoritarian.

Practice examination questions

1 Study Sources A to D and answer questions (a) and (b) that follow.

Source A ▶ **From *A History of Germany, 1815–1990*, by W. Carr, 1991.**
Under the [anti-socialist] law socialist and communist meetings, societies and publications were forbidden; the police were empowered to expel socialist agitators; and states could declare a state of siege in disaffected areas for periods of up to one year. Socialist electoral activity was not however forbidden; to its everlasting credit the Reichstag refused to interfere with the freedom of elections. The result was that Socialists could still stand for election and speak freely in both Reichstag and state legislatures, an anomaly unthinkable in the totalitarian state of the 20th century. … The anti-socialist law was enforced rigorously. The party simply went underground; it held congresses and published its journals as before but operated from outside Germany. By the beginning of the 20th century, it had become a well-disciplined and highly organised mass party, a model for all socialist parties. In short, Bismarck had completely failed to bring the socialists to heel.

Source B ▶ **From *A History of Russia*, by P. Dukes, 1998.**
If the crisis after the Crimean War called for concessions to the demands of the people, that after the assassination of Alexander II invited reaction. Alexander III responded to this challenge with enthusiasm, making no secret of his belief in autocracy... A 'Statute on reinforced and extraordinary security' of 14 August 1881 gave the government powers which according to the French observer A. Leroy-Beaulieu were appropriate for the commander-in-chief in an enemy country, and which according to Lenin formed 'the Russian constitution in fact'. Brought in originally for three years, the Statute was still in effect at the time of the fall of the monarchy. It allowed, for example, the arrest of suspects and the sequestration of their property in an extra-judicial manner, and the sentence of five years' exile without trial.

Source C ▶ **From *Russia in War and Revolution 1914–21*, by D. Orlovsky, 1997.**
In December 1917, faced with what seemed to be regime-threatening opposition, Lenin created a supreme political police – the 'Extraordinary Commission to Combat Counter-Revolution and Sabotage', known by its Russian acronym Cheka. At its head was a Polish Bolshevik, Feliks Dzerzhinskii, charged with becoming the 'sword of the revolution' against 'class' enemies, real and imagined. He rapidly made the Cheka a state within a state, arbitrarily meting out revolutionary justice and terror. His empire constructed a network of prisons and labour camps that later became the world's first concentration camp system.

Source D ▶ **From *Hitler, A Study in Tyranny*, by A. Bullock, 1952.**
Hitler had grasped as no one before him what could be done with a combination of propaganda and terrorism. For the complement to the attractive power of the great spectacles was the compulsive power of the Gestapo, the S.S. and the concentration camp, heightened once again by skilful propaganda. Hitler was helped in this not only by his own perception of the sources of power in a modern urbanized mass-society, but also by possession of the technical means to manipulate them.

(a) Explain how fully Sources C and D reveal the attitudes of Lenin and Hitler to the use of terror. [12]

(b) With reference to these sources and your own knowledge, consider the view that the characteristic response to opposition in Germany and Russia in the period 1825–1939 was repression. [18]

2 How far do you agree with the view that, in Russia and Germany during the period 1825–1939, genuine reform was only achieved by revolution? [30]

Chapter 8

Historical investigations: 19th-century Britain

The following topics are covered in this chapter:

- Chartism
- Gladstone and Disraeli 1846–80

8.1 Chartism

After studying this section you should be able to:

- discuss the causes of Chartism
- assess the contribution of O'Connor to the Chartist movement
- discuss interpretations of the reasons for the failure of Chartism

The causes of Chartism – economic or political?

AQA	M5 (synoptic)
EDEXCEL	M6
EDEXCEL	M6 (synoptic)

Key points from AS

- **Chartism**
  Revise AS page 22

The radical tradition.

Radical newspapers which were cheap enough to circulate among the working classes because they evaded the stamp duty.

Political causes

The main demand of the Chartists was political: parliamentary reform. The six points of the Charter were all directed towards making parliament a democratic institution. Many Chartists may have seen this as the means by which society could be reformed and social justice achieved for the working classes, but what gave the movement its distinctive character was its concentration on political reform. In this respect it differed from other movements which sought to improve conditions for the working classes, such as the Ten Hours Movement.

This demand for political reform had its roots in a radical tradition dating back to the late 18th century. Major **Cartwright's** *Take Your Choice*, published in 1776, argued for annual parliaments and 'equal representation'. Many Chartists consciously looked back to Cartwright and **Paine**, who was influential in publicising the ideas of the American and French revolutions in England. Francis **Place**, who helped to draw up the Charter, had been involved in radical politics since the 1790s. Other Chartists had been involved in the agitation for parliamentary reform after the end of the Napoleonic Wars.

There is a direct link between the 1832 Reform Act and the emergence of Chartism. Politically aware members of the working classes were disappointed by their exclusion from the reformed franchise, especially as they believed that working-class pressure had helped the Whigs to force the Act through. After 1832 the Whig governments created further political grievances:

- they passed the Poor Law Amendment Act in 1834
- they helped to bring about the collapse of the Grand National Consolidated Trades Union by encouraging magistrates to impose heavy penalties on trade unionists, culminating in the affair of the Tolpuddle Martyrs
- they tried to suppress the unstamped press by reducing the stamp duty but enforcing it more vigorously.

It was in these circumstances that **William Lovett** founded the London Working Men's Association in 1837. Its aim was 'equal political and social rights' for 'all classes of society'.

Working class disillusionment with the Whig governments was shared by middle-class radicals. The Birmingham Political Union, founded by Thomas **Attwood** in 1830 and prominent in the struggle for the Reform Act, was revived in 1838. It worked with the LWMA in drawing up the Charter. Attwood himself presented the first Chartist petition to parliament in 1839. However, the violence of the language used by some Chartists, especially O'Connor, and the development of the split between the advocates of moral force and physical force soon alienated many of the middle-class supporters. Chartism thus became an almost exclusively working-class movement.

> See pages 103–104 – 'The weaknesses of the Chartist movement'.

> **KEY POINT**
> The distinctive feature of Chartism was its focus on political demands.

Economic causes

The years of maximum Chartist activity coincided with economic hardship. After a period of relative prosperity, an economic depression began in 1837 and reached its lowest point in 1842. The economy revived after 1843 and support for Chartism declined. A further economic downturn in 1847–8, when there were two bad harvests and a financial crisis resulting from the bursting of the railway boom, coincided with the final outburst of Chartist activity.

> Relative prosperity between 1843 and 1846 coincided with Peel's free trade budgets and the 'railway mania'.

> **KEY POINT**
> For most of its supporters Chartism was a 'knife and fork question', even though its leaders saw their aims as political.

> It was particularly strong in Lancashire, Yorkshire and the East Midlands.

An examination of the geography of Chartist activity shows that it was primarily a phenomenon of the newly industrialised areas of the country. In that sense it was a product of the industrial revolution. Among its causes must be included poor conditions in factories and poor living conditions in industrial towns. But these were not in themselves sufficient to cause strong support for Chartism except in years of exceptional hardship or in association with particular local problems.

Support for Chartism

> There was also strong female involvement in the early years of the movement.

It is important in considering the causes of Chartism to note that it encompassed many groups with other aims beyond parliamentary reform, for example the Anti-Poor Law Movement. This diversity was a source both of strength (it drew together a variety of discontents in a single movement) and of weakness (it lacked unity of purpose).

> Historians have given much attention to this aspect since the publication of Asa Briggs' Chartist Studies (1959).

There was much local diversity. Support for Chartism was strongest where industrial change produced local grievances. For example, handloom weavers displaced by power looms were consistent supporters of Chartism in Lancashire and Yorkshire. Other groups which were prominent in the Chartist movement in their own areas included nail-makers in the Black Country, potters in Staffordshire, framework knitters in Nottingham and miners in South Wales and the north-east.

O'Connor – asset or liability?

AQA	M5 (synoptic)
EDEXCEL	M6 (synoptic)
WJEC	M6 (synoptic)

> The Complete Suffrage Union, founded by Joseph Sturge, aimed to mobilise middle-class support for a democratic electoral system.

Feargus O'Connor came from an Irish Protestant family with a history of involvement in radical activities. Traditionally historians regard him as a liability to the Chartist movement, alienating the middle classes by the violence of his language and by his refusal to co-operate with the Complete Suffrage Union or the Anti-Corn Law League. Some critics regard him as more interested in self-advertisement than in the aims of the Chartist movement. He is blamed for bringing the movement into ridicule in 1848 when his proposed procession to parliament to present a petition after a mass meeting at Kennington was banned. The petition was eventually delivered by O'Connor and a handful of supporters and was found to contain many forged signatures. His Chartist Land Society represented a diversion of the movement from its original political aims and in any case collapsed in a financial muddle after only three years.

Chartist demonstration at Kennington, London, 1848

James Epstein, however, regards his leadership as crucial to the considerable impact Chartism had. He was a brilliant orator and soon came to dominate the movement and to give it what unity it had. His paper, the *Northern Star*, became the main vehicle for Chartist propaganda. He was the only Chartist leader who achieved a genuine national standing.

> Was O'Connor, as Asa Briggs claims, 'probably more successful than any other leader would have been in maximising numbers'? **KEY ISSUE**

Why was Chartism unsuccessful?

AQA — M5 (synoptic)
EDEXCEL — M6 (synoptic)
WJEC — M6 (synoptic)

The weaknesses of the Chartist movement

Chartism suffered from leadership which was divided over aims and tactics. This was partly a matter of temperament and background.

Robert Owen, the New Lanark millowner, advocated producers' and consumers' co-operatives.

- William Lovett, who founded the London Working Men's Association, was a self-taught craftsman who had been involved in attempts to put into practice Owen's co-operative ideas. He was a moderate who believed that Chartism could attain its aims by **moral force**, i.e. by persuasion through meetings and pamphlets.
- Thomas Attwood was a Birmingham banker and Radical MP who had been prominent in the agitation for the Reform Bill in 1831–2. Like Lovett he believed in moral force. As leader of the Birmingham Political Union he was in a strong position at first, but later was alienated by the violent language of O'Connor.
- O'Connor, however, became the dominant figure. He alienated the other leaders by his advocacy of **physical force**.

The divisions within the movement are clearly illustrated by the story of the National Convention in 1839. Within a few weeks many of the delegates had withdrawn for one reason or another. Divisions over whether to use 'ulterior measures' were barely kept in check. The Convention decided on a 'sacred month'

I.e. a general strike.

and then went back on it.

Revisionists also draw attention to conflicts of interest between different groups within the working class.

The localism of much Chartist activity, on which more recent historians have laid much stress, accentuated the problem of divisions within the movement. Since the grievances which drew men to Chartism often arose from conditions in local industries, the level of Chartist activity varied from district to district. A further source of division was the existence within the movement of pressure groups with their own agendas. Attwood's advocacy of currency reform is an example of this. Others are the Temperance Chartists and the Christian Chartists, some of whom set up Chartist churches.

Another source of weakness was O'Connor's insistence on retaining the independence of the movement. For example he rejected the overtures of the Complete Suffrage Union. This ensured that Chartism would be almost exclusively a working-class movement, which suited O'Connor's appeal to the language of class struggle, but deprived it of invaluable middle-class support.

This is often seen as a reason why the Chartists failed but the Anti-Corn Law League succeeded.

External factors

The government took effective steps to deal with the Chartist threat. In 1839 it increased the size of the army in the north of England and appointed General Napier to command it. Napier was sympathetic to working-class grievances but made it clear that, if the Chartists used force, he would respond with force. The main outbreak of violence, the Newport Rising, was quickly suppressed by the magistrates, who knew in advance what was planned. In 1848 Wellington stationed troops at key points and 150 000 special constables were enrolled. The government made effective use of the newly invented electric telegraph and the newly constructed railways.

Because Chartism was a working-class movement, support for it depended on the depth of working-class discontent. Thus when economic prosperity increased, support for Chartism dropped. From about 1850 Britain entered on a long period of prosperity and Chartism lost much of its appeal.

Most historians, however, would agree that the fundamental reason for the failure of Chartism was that, in the words of Asa Briggs, 'It is difficult to see how, given the nature of English society and government in the Chartist period, the Chartists could have succeeded in the way that O'Connor's critics claim that it might have done. The cards were too heavily stacked against them.'

With the aristocracy and middle class united in opposing the demands of the Charter, only revolution could have achieved success, and there was no sign that the working class were in revolutionary mood.

KEY POINT

8.2 Gladstone and Disraeli 1846–80

LEARNING SUMMARY

After studying this section you should be able to:

- *explain how Gladstone and Disraeli became leaders of their respective parties*
- *discuss the political outlook and policies of Gladstone*
- *assess Disraeli's contribution to Conservatism*
- *compare the foreign and imperial policies of Gladstone and Disraeli*

Gladstone: from High Church Tory to Liberal leader

AQA → M5 (synoptic)
OCR → M4

Gladstone entered Parliament in 1833 as a High Church Tory. In 1868 he became the leader of the Liberal Party. How did this come about?

1846: the repeal of the Corn Laws

Gladstone supported Peel over the repeal of the Corn Laws, having been converted to free trade when he was President of the Board of Trade (1843–5). This marked the break with the Conservative Party, though it was not necessarily a final break as yet. Henceforth free trade was one of his guiding principles. As Chancellor of the Exchequer in the Aberdeen coalition (1852–55) and in the Liberal governments of 1859–66, he completed Peel's work in a series of **free trade budgets**, which made his reputation as a financier.

> Rivalry with Disraeli.

The repeal of the Corn Laws had another important effect on his career. His outrage at Disraeli's role in the ferocious attacks on Peel sowed the seeds of a lifelong antagonism. They clashed again in 1852, when Gladstone's brilliant speech attacking Disraeli's budget established his reputation as an orator. His dislike for Disraeli made it difficult for him to return to the Conservative Party, but he was also mistrustful of Palmerston's aggressive and expensive foreign policy. It was therefore difficult for him to join a Whig ministry. Consequently, between 1846 and 1859 he only held office for three years – as Chancellor of the Exchequer in Aberdeen's Peelite-Whig coalition (1852–55). By 1859 his political future was in doubt.

1859: Chancellor of the Exchequer in Palmerston's second ministry

> This is relevant to the charge of hypocrisy – see below, p. 106.

In 1859 Gladstone accepted office under Palmerston, whom he had previously opposed but who shared his sympathy for Italian liberalism. This brought him into a Liberal ministry – a combination of Whigs, Peelites and Radicals. Some historians suggest that his decision was not based only upon his passion for Italian liberalism but also on ambition: Palmerston and Russell were both old men and the Liberal Party would need a new leader before long. If he had joined the Conservatives, he would have had to challenge Disraeli for leadership when Derby retired.

> He said in 1864, 'Every man ... is entitled to come within the pale of the constitution'.

> He famously remarked, 'I am come among you unmuzzled'.

Gladstone's stature grew considerably during the 1860s. As Chancellor of the Exchequer he removed most remaining tariffs and reduced income tax to four pence in the pound. He won the approval of radicals by his endorsement of extension of the franchise in 1864. He began to use his talents as a public speaker to address mass audiences, earning the name **'the people's William'**. In 1865, after he had failed to secure re-election as MP for Oxford University because of his views about the Irish church, he turned instead to South Lancashire.

He also cultivated good relations with leaders of the Nonconformist churches. A devout High Church Anglican, his views about the role of the Church had changed greatly and by the 1860s he had adopted a tolerant outlook to both Nonconformists and Roman Catholics.

In 1868 he succeeded Russell as leader of the Liberal Party and went on to win the general election, in spite of the fact that Disraeli had been responsible for the Second Reform Act.

> **KEY POINT**
>
> Gladstone's acceptance of office under Palmerston in 1859 was the turning point in his career, leading to his emergence as leader of the Liberal Party and Prime Minister within ten years.

Gladstonian liberalism in practice

AQA	M5 (synoptic)
OCR	M4
NICCEA	M6

Gladstone believed in economic freedom. He derived from Peel his belief in **free trade**. He also believed in a minimalist state, which would lead to low taxation. He described 'excess in public expenditure' as 'a great moral evil'. In the 1860s he was able to reduce income tax to four pence in the pound, though he was not able to achieve his ambition of abolishing it.

Individualism.

He attached great importance to efficiency and economy in government. He believed that the role of the state was to provide the conditions in which the individual could flourish: **self-reliance** was an important element in Gladstonian Liberalism. The reforms of the great ministry of 1868–74 were therefore directed towards:

Key points from AS

- **Gladstonian Liberalism**
  Revise AS page 31
- **Gladstone's first ministry**
  Revise AS page 32

- administrative efficiency: the civil service and army reforms;
- equality of opportunity and abolition of privileges: the Education Act, the University Tests Act, the civil service and army reforms;
- removal of grievances: Irish reforms, University Tests Act, Trade Union Act.

> **KEY POINT**
>
> The principal weakness of the reforms of Gladstone's first ministry lay in the area of social reform, e.g. housing and public health. This resulted from his belief in a minimalist state.

Religion played an important part in Gladstone's political outlook; some historians would say it was fundamental. As a young man he believed that the Church of England, supported by the state, could be the means of bringing religious unity to the country. Later he came to accept that this was not practical and he came to a belief in religious tolerance, which made it possible for him to lead the party of nonconformity even though he was himself a devout Anglican. He shared with the

Moralistic outlook.

nonconformists a belief in the importance of morality in politics which was an essential element in both his foreign policy and domestic affairs. His approach to the Irish question, which he significantly termed a 'mission', reflected his belief that justice demanded disestablishment of the Irish Church and reform of the land laws.

It is this moralistic aspect of Gladstone's politics which attracted most hostility from Disraeli and the Conservatives and criticism from historians. Disraeli found his habit of claiming that he was doing the will of God hard to stomach. The charge of hypocrisy rests on the view that political advantage was always his top priority. Thus it is claimed that:

- the Irish policies of 1869–70 were in fulfilment of pledges made during the 1868 election campaign to win votes, not a concern for justice for the Irish
- the University Tests Act and the Licensing Act were to satisfy the nonconformist element in the Liberal Party (and to counteract their disappointment with the religious aspects of the Education Act)
- the Trade Union Act was intended to win working-class voters to the Liberals (though it backfired because of the Criminal Law Amendment Act).

Whether or not one accepts these criticisms it is important to note that the Liberal Party was an uneasy alliance of different factions which was liable to splinter. It comprised Whig landowners, middle-class industrialists and trade unionists, former Peelites and Benthamite radicals, Anglicans and nonconformists. One of Gladstone's main aims was to hold it together.

> Was Gladstone's moralistic outlook genuine or hypocritical? And was it compatible with the role of leader of a political party?

Disraeli: climbing the greasy pole, 1846–68

AQA	M5 (synoptic)
OCR	M4
NICCEA	M6

Disraeli's background was a handicap to an ambitious politician. Of Jewish descent and with no connections, he drew attention to himself by his extravagant dress and eccentric manner. Entering parliament in 1837 as a Tory, he was disappointed to be refused office by Peel in 1841. In 1842 he joined the Young England movement. In 1845 he published in his novel *Sybil* his view of England as '**two nations**'. In 1846 he took the lead in attacking Peel over the repeal of the Corn Laws. His attack was based not so much on belief in protection but on his view that Peel had betrayed his party.

> And possibly on personal antipathy to Peel.

> This is why he described his rise to the leadership as climbing 'to the top of the greasy pole'.

His brilliance as a debater marked him out as the outstanding figure among the Protectionist Tories. Nevertheless, because of his background and personality the Conservative Party would not accept him as their leader until 1868, preferring the aristocratic Derby. In the three Conservative ministries of 1852, 1858–9 and 1866–8 Disraeli was Chancellor of the Exchequer and leader in the House of Commons. He played a major role in the survival of the Conservative Party as a political force in this period. As Chancellor in 1852 he abandoned protection, thus making it possible for the Conservatives to broaden their appeal beyond the agricultural interest. In 1859 he introduced a parliamentary reform bill, again with the aim of broadening the electoral appeal of the Conservatives.

Key points from AS

- **The Second Reform Act 1867**
  Revise AS pages 30–31

The Second Reform Act, 1867

The third Derby-Disraeli Ministry came to office in 1866 because the Liberals were split over the terms of a reform bill. Disraeli then introduced a more moderate Conservative bill, which after considerable modifications became the Second Reform Act. Historians agree that it was one of Disraeli's most important achievements, but disagree about his motives.

> Was his aim to 'dish the Whigs'?

- Some believe his motive was political opportunism – to gain credit for the reform for the Conservatives. His desire to succeed where Gladstone had failed was certainly important.
- Some claim he was responding to mounting public pressure for reform and the threat of disorder (Hyde Park riots).
- He may have hoped to gain the support of the urban working class against the middle-class values of Gladstonian Liberalism.

Disraelian conservatism: 'Tory democracy'?

AQA	M5 (synoptic)
OCR	M4
NICCEA	M6

Between 1868 and 1874 Disraeli set about winning over the new electorate to the Conservatives. In his **Manchester and Crystal Palace speeches** in 1872 he set out the Conservative programme. He laid stress on the preservation of the power of the crown, the Church and the aristocracy, but insisted on the duty of the aristocracy and the government to help the working classes. This paternalist approach would unite the privileged and unprivileged and thus the Conservative

The phrase 'Tory democracy' was not used by Disraeli but was coined by Lord Randolph Churchill in 1886.

Key points from AS

- **'Tory democracy'**
  Revise AS page 35
- **Disraeli's second ministry 1874–80**
  Revise AS page 36

Party would be a national party drawing together all classes. He also stressed the idea of developing the empire. This programme has been labelled 'New Conservatism' or 'Tory democracy'. Some historians claim that what Disraeli actually said in these speeches was vaguer than was subsequently claimed. It has also been argued that he took up social reform simply to win votes. But it does seem to have won some working-class support: in 1874 the Conservatives won 18 out of 25 seats in Lancashire. Equally important in making the Conservatives a national party was the electoral organisation created by Gorst stretching from the Carlton Club at the centre to the constituencies.

> **KEY POINT**
>
> The appeal of 'new Conservatism' was based on social reform, preservation of old institutions and development of the empire.

Disraeli won the election of 1874 and his second ministry (1874–80) saw the 'new Conservatism' in action with the introduction of a number of important social reforms. These were mainly the work of the Home Secretary, Cross; Disraeli himself devoted his main attention to foreign and imperial affairs. The weakness of many of the reforms was that they were permissive, but they were sufficient to establish the appeal of 'New Conservatism' to working-class voters.

> **KEY POINT**
>
> The social reforms of Disraeli's second ministry contrasted with Gladstone's failure in this area. But unlike Gladstone, Disraeli showed little interest in Irish affairs.

Foreign and imperial policies

AQA	M5 (synoptic)
OCR	M4
NICCEA	M6

He described the rule of the Bourbons in Naples as 'the negation of God erected into a system of government'.

When Russia repudiated them he merely protested.

He demanded that the Turks should clear out of Bulgaria 'bag and baggage'.

He checked Russian ambitions by cutting the size of independent Bulgaria and gained Cyprus for Britain.

Gladstone's attitude to foreign affairs was based on his moralistic outlook. He sought to preserve peace through working with other powers. He believed in the right of small nations to govern themselves. He was a passionate supporter of Italian liberalism and wished to see the expulsion of the Austrians from northern Italy and the overthrow of the Bourbons in Naples. It was his support for the Italians which made him overcome his dislike of Palmerston's aggressive policies and join the Liberal ministry in 1859.

His handling of the problems he faced in the ministry of 1868–74 was unpopular. He was successful in getting France and Prussia to respect Belgian neutrality, but the public believed he had failed to uphold British interests over the Black Sea clauses of the Treaty of Paris. They also believed that he had been weak in agreeing to pay to the USA the compensation awarded by an arbitration conference for the Alabama affair. There was, however, little he could have done to enforce the Black Sea clauses, while in the Alabama affair he was pursuing what he believed to be the morally correct policy.

Disraeli's attitude to foreign affairs was much more in the Palmerstonian tradition. The Balkan crisis of 1875–8 highlighted the different approaches of Gladstone and Disraeli to European affairs. Disraeli took the traditional British line of opposing Russian expansion into the Mediterranean, even at the expense of propping up the inefficient and oppressive Turkish government. Gladstone took the moral view that such a brutal regime could not be supported and published an immensely successful pamphlet on the 'Bulgarian Horrors'. This further embittered relations between the two men as it prevented Disraeli pursuing his anti-Russian policy. Fortunately for Disraeli, public opinion swung round when the Russians declared war on Turkey and advanced towards Constantinople. The Congress of Berlin was regarded as a triumph for Disraeli.

Disraeli and Gladstone also clashed over imperialism. Disraeli wanted to expand the empire. Gladstone opposed this on moral and economic grounds: it involved interfering with the rights of native peoples and it was expensive.

Disraeli's proclamation of Queen Victoria as Empress of India and his purchase of the Suez Canal shares were both popular. The wars in South Africa and Afghanistan at the end of his ministry, however, involved military setbacks and were attacked by Gladstone as 'immoral' in his Midlothian campaign.

> A three-week campaign of speeches in northern England and southern Scotland. The first time a leading politician had campaigned in this way.

> **KEY POINT**
>
> Gladstone and Disraeli differed sharply over both foreign and imperial policies. Gladstone's attitude was moralistic while Disraeli was more forceful in pursuit of British interests.

Disraeli

Gladstone

Sample question and model answer

Study Sources A to D and answer questions (a) and (b) which follow.

Source A

From William Lovett's autobiography, published in1876.
I regard Feargus O'Connor as the chief spoiler of our movement – a man who, by his personal conduct joined to his malignant influence in the *Northern Star*, has been the blight of democracy from the first moment he opened his mouth as its professed advocate. Not possessing a nature to appreciate intellectual exertions, he began his career by ridiculing our 'moral force humbuggery'. By his constant appeals to the selfishness and vanity of man, he succeeded in calling up a spirit of hate, intolerance and brute feeling, previously unknown among Reformers.

Source B

From *The Making of Victorian England*, by G. Kitson Clark, 1962.
Feargus O'Connor, who had made himself the spokesman of the manufacturing districts, was unworthy of the trust which they so strangely reposed in him. He was an egoist who spent much of his time consolidating his own position and eliminating other leaders of whom he very early became jealous, and he was a braggart, a man who used rhetoric about force without clearly understanding what the words meant, and as a result under his inspiration the movement came to be conspicuously ill led. Probably this did not matter very much; however well led or however ill led, the Chartist agitation was without question doomed to failure. Their petitions were bound to be rejected, their half-hearted attempt at something like a general strike, ill prepared and ill supported, was a complete fiasco, and their threat of force such as could be contained by the Government with the greatest of ease.

Source C

From *The Lion of Freedom: Feargus O'Connor and the Chartist Movement*, by J. Epstein, 1982.
The central problem of national Chartist leadership was the maintenance of radical working-class unity. The magnitude of this task should not be forgotten. With remarkable forbearance, energy and enthusiasm O'Connor battled to overcome the divisions and sources of fragmentation within the working-class movement. Both from outside and within the Chartist ranks the movement was faced with a series of 'rival' or alternative agitations. In spring of 1841 O'Connor published his famous condemnation of 'Church Chartism, Teetotal Chartism, Knowledge Chartism and Household Suffrage Chartism'. His opposition was based on his fears that these various tendencies might become splinter groups, dissipating the movement's strength.

Source D

From *The Chartists: popular politics in the Industrial Revolution*, by D. Thompson, 1984.
O'Connor retained his unquestioned leadership of the Chartist movement above all because he kept the matter of the suffrage in the forefront of his arguments. His political stance was simple. But in the end, the qualities of leadership which keep a man at the head of a mass movement for ten years and more are not to be found in his political philosophy or his administrative ability alone. Too many historians have credited O'Connor with only the charismatic qualities of leadership, and it must be pointed out that he was a shrewd and capable politician and a not inconsiderable organiser and administrator in addition. No other leader or would-be leader in those days had the energy, ability, physique or charisma of Feargus O'Connor. For good or ill, he was the main inspiration and guiding force of the movement.

Both parts of this question incorporate synoptic assessment.

(a) Using your own knowledge and the evidence in Sources A, B and D, what do you consider to have been the main strengths and weaknesses of O'Connor as leader of the Chartist movement?

[10]

Sample question and model answer (continued)

Note references to provenance of the sources.

(a) Source A depicts O'Connor as stirring up hatred and intolerance among the Chartists by appealing to 'selfishness and vanity'. It is vague in content but emotive and abusive – not surprisingly since it is by Lovett. But it does point to one of O'Connor's great weaknesses – the hostility he aroused. But he also won an enormous following, as source B admits, perhaps rather reluctantly. This source, by a modern but pre-revisionist historian, denounces his character as a leader – 'an egoist', 'jealous', 'a braggart'. Source D (a revisionist) presents a completely different picture of a leader with energy, ability and charisma, a 'shrewd and capable politician' and a good organiser.

Note that the question requires own knowledge as well as use of the sources.

Undoubtedly he was a brilliant orator. The Northern Star was highly successful as Chartist propaganda. He was the only Chartist leader who achieved a genuine national standing. On the other hand he alienated the middle classes by the violence of his language and by his refusal to co-operate with the Complete Suffrage Union or the Anti-Corn Law League. The charge that he was more interested in self-advertisement than in the aims of the Chartist movement probably holds some truth. His handling of the 1848 petition brought the movement into ridicule. His Chartist Land Society collapsed in a financial muddle.

O'Connor was a brilliant but deeply flawed leader. There is some truth in all the views presented – they can be regarded as complementary.

(b) 'The main cause of the failure of the Chartist movement was its disunity'. Using your own knowledge and the evidence of all four Sources, explain how far you would agree with this view.

[20]

This is an outline answer, to which you should add more detail.

(b) Failure resulted from both internal weaknesses and external factors. Disunity was one of its weaknesses and is the main focus of source C, which particularly draws attention to diversity of aims and the existence of pressure groups with their own agendas. Source A hints at the moral force vs. physical force split, which was important, though it was not as simple a division as the phrases imply. Lovett's language in source A points up his hostility to O'Connor. The reference to jealousy in source B also shows disunity. The divisions within the movement are clearly illustrated by the story of the National Convention in 1839, which decided on a 'sacred month' and then went back on it (see in source B).

Sources A, B and C suggest that O'Connor was himself an important cause of failure, though Source D (the most recent interpretation) takes a different view. Another cause of disunity was the localism of much Chartist activity.

Explain this point, with examples if possible.

The discussion so far shows that it is difficult to disentangle disunity from the question of poor leadership. Leadership faults can also be seen in O'Connor's handling of the 1848 petition and his insistence on retaining the independence of the movement. This in turn deprived Chartism of invaluable middle-class support.

Explain this fully from your own knowledge.

External factors contributing to failure were:
- government counter-measures;
- economic upturn between 1842 and 1846 and after 1850.

All these factors were important but in the end marginal: the fundamental reason was that the governing classes were not prepared to meet their demands. Only revolution could have achieved that, and there was no sign of a revolutionary climate.

Practice examination questions

1 Study Sources A to E and answer questions (a) and (b) which follow.

Source A

From Disraeli's Crystal Palace Speech, 2 June 1872.

Gentlemen, I have referred to what I look upon as the first object of the Tory Party – namely, to maintain the institutions of the country. I think that the Tory party, or, as I will venture to call it, the National party, has everything to encourage it. I think that the nation has arrived at the conclusion which we have always maintained, that it is the first duty of England to maintain its institutions, because to them we principally ascribe the power and prosperity of the country. There is a second great object of the Tory party, to uphold the Empire of England. Another great object of the Tory party, and one not inferior to the maintenance of the Empire or the upholding of our institutions, is the elevation of the condition of the people.

Source B

From *England, 1870–1914*, by R.C.K. Ensor, 1936.

Disraeli could not skate so boldly in office as he had in opposition between his own reforming ideas and the property interests of those who had made him their champion. He had begun life as a radical, diagnosing England as 'two nations', rich and poor, and proclaiming the supreme need to make them one. He still cared sincerely for social reform; but few, if any, of his followers in parliament supported him for its sake. Leading the opposition to Gladstone he had taxed his rival's reforms with menacing 'every institution and every interest, every class and every calling in the country'. Such slogans are defensive, not progressive; they had made him the rallying point for the interests which were kicking at change. It was a legitimate position for a Conservative leader, but not one where he could take reform as his first motto, even when qualified as 'social' to distinguish it from the liberal brand. He needed others. And he chose two – the monarchy and the empire.

Source C

From *The Conservative Party from Peel to Churchill*, by R. Blake, 1970.

In 1872 and 1873 Disraeli was able to do something that no Conservative leader had done since Peel: to present his party as having not only a distinctive colour and style, but also a broad-based appeal on the one hand to the working class, on the other – and this was much more important – to the forces of property everywhere, not simply the landed interest, as a bulwark against the harassing, disturbing, restless legislation of the Liberals. At the same time – and perhaps this was even more significant – he boldly staked the claim of the Conservatives to be 'the patriotic party', something that could never be established while Palmerston lived.

Source D

From *Democracy and Empire*, by E.J. Feuchtwanger, 1985.

The personalities of Gladstone and Disraeli were central to the reform crisis of 1867, which in turn had a decisive impact upon their careers … Disraeli had a more difficult task, for he had to create the myth that what was a piece of shrewd tactics and 'dishing the Whigs' was, in fact, deliberate, long term policy, consistent with his own past principles and in the essential interests of the Conservative party. He started to claim that he had 'educated his party' and that what he had done with the Reform Bill was consistent with his lifelong convictions on the relationship of classes.

Source E

From *Benjamin Disraeli*, by M. Lynch, in *Modern British Statesmen 1867–1945*, ed R. Kelly and J. Cantrell, 1997.

Disraeli's remarkable coup in outmanoeuvring the Liberals and pushing through the Conservatives' own Reform Act in 1867 has often been cited as evidence of his genuine wish to extend democracy by enfranchising the working classes. Modern historians, however, tend to regard the Act as primarily a measure designed to safeguard the electoral interests of the Conservatives rather than a genuine broadening of the representative character of the parliament. … Ian Machin

Practice examination questions (continued)

suggests that in all that Disraeli did, 'the furthering of his party and of his political fortunes was paramount. He had a genuine wish to carry certain reforms but only if and when they assisted his political objectives'. But although doubts remain concerning Disraeli's motives in widening the franchise, there was one area where undoubtedly he did win over working class support to the side of Conservatism. His judgement that Imperialism would have special appeal for a large part of the electorate proved remarkably percipient.

(a) Examine the differences between the historians' views expressed in Source D and Source E concerning Disraeli's motives in the reform crisis of 1867.

[10]

(b) Using Sources A to E, explain how far, and why, they offer differing interpretations of the nature and appeal of Disraelian Conservatism.

[20]

2 To what extent were there significant differences of principle dividing Gladstone and Disraeli?

[30]

3 How far do you agree that the principal reason for the rise of the Chartist movement was social and economic distress?

[30]

Chapter 9

Historical investigations: 20th-century Britain

The following topics are covered in this chapter:

- *The decline of the Liberal Party, c.1900–1929*
- *Appeasement: Anglo-German relations 1918–39*
- *British politics 1918–51*

9.1 The decline of the Liberal Party, c.1900–1929

After studying this section you should be able to:

- *assess the strengths and weaknesses of the Liberals in the early 20th century*
- *outline the main developments in the Liberal Party from 1905 to 1929*
- *discuss historians' explanations for the decline of the Liberals*

LEARNING SUMMARY

The Liberal Party at the end of the 19th century

EDEXCEL ▸ M6 Synoptic

In 1886 the Gladstonian Liberal Party split over the issue of Home Rule. It lost most of the aristocratic Whigs along with Chamberlain and the Liberal Unionists. Between 1886 and 1900 it lost three out of four elections. Some historians argue that the seeds of its decline had already been sown.

In the late 1890s the Liberal Party was divided over two issues: imperialism and social reform. The party divided into pro-Boers and Liberal Imperialists during the Boer War. The Liberal Imperialists, led by Rosebery, Asquith and Grey, as well as supporting expansion of the empire, favoured social reform. New Liberalism developed out of Liberal Imperialism and this led to differences about the nature of liberalism and the relationship between the state and the individual.

- **Gladstonian Liberals** placed great emphasis on individual liberty and self-help and sought to limit the role of the state.
- **The New Liberals** argued that individual liberty had little meaning for the very poor, since their poverty restricted what they could do, and self-help could not lift them out of poverty. State intervention was necessary in the interests of both national efficiency and social justice. Their political outlook was thus collectivist rather than individualist.

> They were much influenced by the social surveys of Booth and Rowntree and the ideas of J.A. Hobson and L.T. Hobhouse (see p. 32).

The Liberal Party drew most of its support at the beginning of the 20th century from three different groups which were only loosely joined together:

- the working class, especially organised labour
- the nonconformists, traditional stalwarts of Gladstonian Liberalism – these formed the most important middle-class element
- the Celtic fringe – the Liberals offered Home Rule to Ireland and church disestablishment to Wales and Scotland.

> A few trade unionists were elected as Lib-Labs from the 1870s.

The effect of the 1884 Reform Act and the split in the Liberal Party in 1886 was to make the Liberals more dependent on the first of these, the working class. Yet they were only partially successful in winning working-class support. From the time of Disraeli, a substantial minority of working-class electors voted Conservative, especially in Lancashire. At the same time prominent working-class Liberals began to think in terms of the creation of a separate Labour group in parliament. This was partly because Liberal constituency associations, dominated by the middle classes, were reluctant to select working-class candidates. Keir Hardie, Ramsay MacDonald and Arthur Henderson were all rejected as Liberal candidates.

> The challenge from Labour.

The establishment of the Labour Representation Committee in 1900, which became the Labour Party in 1906, was a sign of the failure of the Liberals fully to respond to the aspirations of Labour. Nevertheless, at least until 1914 the threat posed by the Labour Party should not be exaggerated. The Lib-Lab outlook remained strong among trade unionists, though the decision of the mine workers to support Labour in 1909 was perhaps an ominous sign. In 1910 Labour won only 42 seats, 40 of them in constituencies where there was no Liberal candidate. The Labour Party in parliament behaved rather like a left-wing Liberal ginger group.

> **KEY POINT**
>
> There are many grounds for arguing that a long-term process of decline in the Liberal Party had set in by the end of the 19th century.

The 1906 election

EDEXCEL ▶ M6 (synoptic)

Key points from AS

- **The 1906 election**
  Revise AS page 52

> An electoral pact made in 1903 between the Liberals and the Labour Representation Committee.

The overwhelming Liberal victory in the 1906 election appears to contradict this view. It can be argued, however, that they only won because the policies of the Conservative government temporarily brought voters back to the Liberals.

- The Conservatives failed to meet the growing demand for social reform, in contrast to the ideas of the New Liberals.
- The Taff Vale case alienated trade unionists. The Gladstone–MacDonald pact consolidated working-class support for the Liberals at the price of giving Labour candidates a free run in selected constituencies.
- Nonconformists were angry about the 1902 Education Act. This brought back many middle-class voters whose support had been waning.
- Public indignation about conditions in the concentration camps in the latter years of the Boer War and about the Chinese labour scandal benefited the Liberals with their humanitarian traditions.
- Finally, and most importantly, Chamberlain's tariff reform campaign divided the Conservatives and provided an issue around which the Liberals could unite.

> **KEY POINT**
>
> The Liberal victory in 1906 can be seen in two opposing ways.
> - The Conservative domination between 1886–1906 was an aberration caused by Liberal abstentions. The 1906 election restored the normal pattern of Liberal power.
> - The Liberal victory in 1906 was an aberration from the emerging pattern of Liberal weakness, caused primarily by the renewal of Conservative divisions.

Key points from AS

- **The Liberal reforms**
  Revise AS pages 53–54

The debate about the nature of liberalism continued throughout the Liberal ministries of 1905–15. The enhanced role of the state implied in the New Liberal social reforms went against the Gladstonian Liberal tradition of minimal government. The National Insurance scheme, in particular, raised questions about the role of the state and the individual, since it forced workers to contribute part of their earnings to insurance.

> Uncomfortable because the Liberals stood for individual liberty.

The troubles of the years 1910–14 – militant suffragettes, serious industrial unrest and the threat of civil war in Ireland – posed serious problems for the Liberals. It seemed that government was breaking down. Some historians have claimed that the Liberals had lost the ability to govern. Certainly they were forced into an uncomfortable reliance on the coercive powers of the state. Nevertheless, historian Alan Sykes believes that the Liberals might well have won a general election in 1915 because the Conservatives had at least equal difficulties and Labour was still dependent for the success it had so far achieved upon the electoral pact of 1903.

The impact of the First World War

EDEXCEL ▶ M6 (synoptic)

Historian Trevor Wilson argues that the 'rampant omnibus' of the First World War destroyed the Liberal Party.

- The Liberals inherited a tradition of anti-war radicalism and they therefore accepted the war with reluctance (two Cabinet ministers resigned in August 1914).
- The demands of total war cut across liberal philosophy. The Liberal government was slow to accept the need for government intervention to mobilise the economy for war. This led to growing dissatisfaction with Asquith's conduct of the war.
- The issue of conscription, which meant the removal of individual liberty, was particularly difficult for Liberals. When it was introduced, the Home Secretary, Sir John Simon, resigned.
- Dissatisfaction with Asquith's conduct of the war led to his overthrow in December 1916 by Lloyd George, who was backed by the Conservative leader Bonar Law. Supporters of Asquith regarded Lloyd George as a traitor.
- Underlying this was a clash of philosophies. Lloyd George believed in the merits of government by coalition and an authoritarian state. He had thus moved away from traditional Liberal values.
- The Conservatives gained support as the 'patriotic' party. They came back into government in Asquith's coalition of 1915 and were the dominant group in Lloyd George's coalition. They thus gained the credit as the party which won the war.
- Labour was also strengthened. Under Henderson, it adopted a new constitution, drew up a programme and built up its constituency organisation.

This was crucial.

Lloyd George and Asquith, 1918–29

AQA ▶ M5 (synoptic)
EDEXCEL ▶ M6 (synoptic)

The Lloyd George coalition

The coalition won an overwhelming victory in the 'coupon' election of 1918 – but the majority of its supporters were Conservatives.

At the end of the war Lloyd George continued the coalition with the Conservatives. In doing so he was pursuing his own vision of a national or centre party dedicated to reconstruction and the pursuit of national efficiency – led, of course, by himself. But the post-war coalition failed to realise his vision. It suited the Conservatives because they benefited from Lloyd George's popularity as the man who won the war, but by 1922 they regarded him as a liability and ditched him.

The coalition contributed significantly to the decline of the Liberals because it perpetuated and deepened the division with the Asquithian Liberals. The result was that the Liberals failed to win the working-class support which they needed after the extension of the franchise in the 1918 Representation of the People Act. In the 1922 general election Coalition and Asquithian Liberals fought separately, sometimes against each other. With 117 MPs altogether (roughly half Coalition Liberals and half Asquithians) the Liberals had fewer seats than Labour.

> The continuation of the wartime coalition into peacetime by Lloyd George deprived the Liberals of the chance of reuniting. But Asquith was also to blame – he refused office in the post-war coalition.
>
> **KEY POINT**

The 1920s

Baldwin's decision to call an election on the issue of protection in 1923 provided the spur for the two factions to reunite under Asquith and the Liberals increased their representation to 159. Nevertheless, in an election fought on the classic

Liberal issue of free trade they remained the third largest party. Asquith decided to give tacit support to a minority Labour government, but laid down no conditions. Historian Chris Cook calls this a disastrous decision. It allowed Labour to demonstrate that it was capable of governing and at the same time it convinced middle-class Liberals that the only way to keep Labour out was to vote Conservative. In the 1924 election the Liberals were reduced to 40 MPs.

> The Zinoviev letter harmed the Liberals more than Labour.

In 1926 Asquith resigned the leadership and Lloyd George took over. The Liberals produced ideas in the late 1920s through the Summer Schools. Their policy statement *We can conquer unemployment* won some support in the 1929 election, but even so they were squeezed between the Conservatives and Labour and only won 59 seats.

> You should be able to explain the significance of each of these dates.

KEY DATES

1905–15	Last Liberal ministries led by Campbell-Bannerman and Asquith
1906	Election – massive Liberal majority
1916	Asquith succeeded by Lloyd George as Prime Minister
1918–22	Lloyd George coalition
1924	Election – Liberals reduced to 40 MPs

Explanations

AQA   M5 (synoptic)

EDEXCEL   M6 (synoptic)

> You need to decide which of these explanations you accept and which are the most important.

The historical debate about the decline of the Liberals has identified many possible explanations. These are some of the main ones.

- Long-term social changes such as industrialisation and urbanisation caused large numbers of the working class to turn to the Labour party.
- The growth of trade unionism also caused working-class voters to turn to Labour, which was the party of the unions.

> In other words the new voters would have behaved in the same way as those who already had the vote. So the increased support for Labour was not because of new voters.

- Labour emerged as the party of the people in response to the creation of a mass electorate by the 1918 Representation of the People Act. Some historians, however, question this, arguing that the 1918 Act did not enfranchise new classes of voter but simply extended the vote to women and younger men of classes that already had it.
- The Liberals failed to make themselves sufficiently attractive to the working classes, for example by failing to select working-class candidates. They were too elitist. Critics of this view point out that the Liberals were still able to attract working-class support after 1910.
- The First World War challenged Liberal ideas and divided them into two warring factions. Labour on the other hand emerged from it stronger than before.
- The Liberal leaders after the war were quarrelsome and ultimately ineffective.
- The British electoral system, which penalises third parties, hastened their decline.
- Liberal Party organisation was poor. The party lacked funds.
- This reflected the fact that they did not represent an interest group, unlike Labour (the trade unions) and the Conservatives (business).

> **KEY ISSUE**
>
> Was the rise of Labour inevitable? If so, the decline of the Liberals was equally inevitable.

9.2 Appeasement: Anglo-German relations 1918–39

After studying this section you should be able to:

- discuss Britain's role in the Versailles settlement and international relations in the 1920s
- outline the development of the policy of appeasement in the 1930s
- understand and explain the historical debate about appeasement

LEARNING SUMMARY

Aims and constraints

AQA	M5 (synoptic)
EDEXCEL	M4
OCR	M4
WJEC	M6 (synoptic)

The main factors underlying British foreign policy in the inter-war years were:

- the wish to avoid war
- the desire to maintain a balance of power
- the need to protect the empire
- economic problems, which led to cuts in defence spending.

The Versailles settlement

AQA	M5 (synoptic)
EDEXCEL	M4
OCR	M4

The Paris peace conference in 1919 was dominated by Lloyd George, Clemenceau and Woodrow Wilson. Clemenceau sought a peace which would punish Germany and destroy the threat of German militarism. Wilson wanted a peace based on national self-determination and the establishment of an international organisation to prevent war, the key ideas in his Fourteen Points.

Lloyd George's role was influenced by public opinion. He won the **'coupon election'** of December 1918 by a campaign in which he urged that Germany should be made to pay for the war 'to the limit of her capacity'. But he also realised that an excessively harsh settlement would leave Germany embittered and therefore opposed the more extreme French demands. The surrender of the German navy ensured Britain's security. Britain had no territorial claims in Europe, but Lloyd George aimed to secure Germany's colonies in Africa (as well as some Turkish territories in the Middle East). He shared Wilson's desire for an international organisation to preserve peace and the Covenant of the League was largely the work of the British Foreign Office.

> It scuttled itself at Scapa Flow in June 1919.

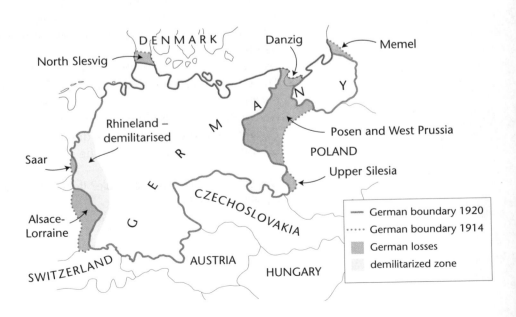

Germany's losses, 1919

How far the final settlement was the work of Lloyd George is a matter of debate. Some historians claim that he was its principal architect because he occupied a position midway between Clemenceau's demand for a punitive treaty and Wilson's opposition to such a treaty. Others argue that Lloyd George was the main opponent of French demands and so Wilson was the arbiter.

In the final settlement:

> Poland and Lithuania were states newly created by the peace settlement.

- Germany lost Alsace-Lorraine to France and other border areas to Belgium, Denmark, Poland and Lithuania. The Saar was placed under League of Nations administration for 15 years.
- The Rhineland was demilitarised and Germany was largely disarmed.
- By the War Guilt Clause Germany accepted full responsibility for the war and was therefore required to pay reparations. The figure was fixed at £6600 million in 1921.
- The League of Nations was set up.

> These former German and Turkish territories were governed by Britain on behalf of the League of Nations.

- Britain took control of 'mandated' territories in East Africa, Palestine, Transjordan and Iraq.

> **KEY POINT**
>
> Public opinion regarded the peace as very satisfactory, but criticisms soon emerged. Labour and some Liberals condemned it as too severe and unfair to Germany.

The 1920s

AQA	M5 (synoptic)
EDEXCEL	M4
OCR	M4

The German question

The Germans claimed that the reparations demanded were beyond their ability to pay, but the French insisted on strict enforcement of the Treaty. In 1922 Lloyd George called a conference at Genoa, hoping to settle the whole issue of reparations and war debts. It was a failure: the French refused to compromise and the Americans did not attend. In 1923 the French sent troops into the Ruhr after the Germans had defaulted on reparations. The German government responded by ordering passive resistance. The British Prime Minister, Ramsay MacDonald, played a key role in resolving the crisis by persuading the French and Germans to accept the Dawes Plan. This involved reducing Germany's reparations and thus amounted to a revision of the peace settlement.

This was followed by the most important attempt to resolve the German question, the Locarno Treaties of 1925.

> Unlike the Treaty of Versailles, which was dictated to the Germans, the Locarno Treaties were negotiated with them.

- Germany, France and Belgium accepted as final the boundaries laid down at Versailles. Britain and Italy guaranteed these boundaries.
- Germany agreed that its frontiers with Poland and Czechoslovakia could only be altered by arbitration.

These agreements were regarded as a triumph at the time and they were followed by a period of much greater harmony known as the 'Locarno honeymoon'. Germany was admitted to the League of Nations in 1926 and to the Kellogg-Briand Pact in 1928. In 1929 a further modification of reparations was agreed in the Young Plan. Relations between France and Germany were much more harmonious.

But many historians criticise Locarno.

> Hitler took advantage of this in the 1930s.

- No guarantees were given for Germany's eastern frontiers, thus suggesting that they were open to change.
- Britain had no plans to back the guarantees. No military talks were held with France because Locarno was as much a guarantee to Germany as to France.

The League of Nations

British public opinion, especially on the left, was enthusiastic about the League as a means of ensuring peace. It was in this spirit of enthusiasm for the League that MacDonald in 1924 proposed the Geneva Protocol which would have strengthened it by making arbitration compulsory. The Labour government fell from office, however, before it was ratified and the Conservatives, whose support for the League was more lukewarm, abandoned it. The Locarno Treaties signalled that the Conservatives preferred treaties between the powers to collective security.

Disarmament

The British and American navies were to have equal numbers of battleships.

Many people believed that one of the main causes of the First World War had been the arms race. One way of ensuring that such a war could never happen again, therefore, was to reduce armaments. British governments reduced armaments both because public opinion favoured it and because economic problems required cuts in public expenditure. In 1919 Lloyd George told the armed forces to assume there was no threat of war for at least ten years and this Ten Year Rule was applied until 1932. The army was cut back to a size sufficient to maintain control in the empire. The Washington Treaty (1922) made it possible to cut naval construction at the price of abandoning naval supremacy. Preparations were made for a World Disarmament Conference but progress was slow. It did not meet until 1932 and in 1933, with Hitler in power, Germany withdrew.

> At the end of the 1920s the 'Locarno honeymoon' raised hopes for international stability but there were signs that the League of Nations could not be relied upon and that general disarmament was unlikely.
>
> **KEY POINT**

Appeasement in the 1930s

AQA	M5 (synoptic)
EDEXCEL	M4
OCR	M4
WJEC	M6 (synoptic)

Key points from AS

- Appeasement
  Revise AS page 71

The episode seemed to show that the League's decisions could be ignored.

This implied that the Versailles settlement could be re-negotiated.

This confirmed the ineffectiveness of the League. Italy was left in possession of Ethiopia.

In the 1930s the world faced new and greater dangers from the aggressive nationalism of Japan, Italy and Germany. The response of British foreign policy was appeasement. This meant accepting the demands of the aggressors as reasonable and thus avoiding war. The most important incidents were as follows.

- The Japanese invasion of Manchuria (1931). The Lytton Commission, appointed by the League of Nations, criticised Japan's action and proposed that Manchuria should be self-governing under China. The League accepted this, but Japan rejected it. Britain and France, the leading members of the League, took no action and Japan established a puppet regime in Manchuria. At the time there was probably nothing else that Britain or France could do.
- German rearmament (March 1935): Hitler introduced conscription in defiance of the Versailles Treaty. Britain, France and Italy condemned this and agreed to resist any further breaches of the treaty (the Stresa Front). But the British government then undermined the Stresa Front by making the Anglo-German Naval Agreement, which it saw as a way of limiting German rearmament and preserving British naval superiority.
- The Italian invasion of Ethiopia (October 1935). The League declared Italy an aggressor and imposed sanctions, but coal, steel and – most importantly – oil were excluded. The sanctions therefore had little effect on Italy's war effort. The failure to impose effective sanctions was largely because Britain and France were not prepared for war and were anxious to maintain good relations with Italy. They even proposed, in the Hoare-Laval Pact, to allow Mussolini to keep two-thirds of Ethiopia, but public outrage in Britain and France forced the withdrawal of this plan.

- The reoccupation of the **Rhineland** (1936). Baldwin judged that public opinion would not support military action since the Rhineland was German territory.
- The **Anschluss** (March 1938). Britain and France accepted the incorporation of Austria into Germany on the grounds that Austria was German in nationality.
- **Munich** (September 1938). Hitler next demanded the Sudetenland, which was also German in nationality. Chamberlain flew to Germany three times to negotiate with him. Finally at the Munich Conference he agreed to the German demands.

He believed that Hitler was a man with whom he could do business.

The end of appeasement, 1939

Chamberlain's belief that Hitler had no more territorial demands was shattered in March 1939 when German troops occupied the rest of Czechoslovakia. For the first time Hitler had taken over a country which was not German-speaking. Chamberlain changed his policy and offered guarantees to Poland, which seemed likely to be Hitler's next victim. In April Hitler demanded Danzig and a road and railway across the Polish Corridor. The Poles, fearing that this was a prelude to a German invasion, as in Czechoslovakia, refused.

The key to the situation was the attitude of the USSR. Chamberlain began negotiations but progress was slow. Stalin decided that Russia's security would be better served by doing a deal with Hitler and signed **the Nazi-Soviet Pact** in August. Hitler believed that with Russia neutral the British government would revert to its policy of appeasement but he was wrong. He invaded Poland on 1 September. On 3 September Britain declared war.

You should be able to explain the significance of each of these dates.

1931	Japanese invasion of Manchuria	
1935	Hitler announces German rearmament. Stresa Front. Anglo-German Naval Agreement. Italian invasion of Ethiopia	
1936	Remilitarisation of the Rhineland	
1938	Anschluss between Germany and Austria. Munich Conference	
1939	German occupation of Bohemia and Moravia. Nazi-Soviet Pact. German invasion of Poland and outbreak of war	

KEY DATES

Appeasement: for and against

AQA	M5 (synoptic)
EDEXCEL	M4
OCR	M4
WJEC	M6 (synoptic)

It is important for the historian to understand how people saw things at the time – when they did not know what would happen later.

Arguments in favour

The policy of appeasement was very much in tune with public opinion. The British public wished above all to avoid war, as was demonstrated by the Peace Ballot in 1935. The slaughter of the First World War was a fresh memory and people were aware that a new war was likely to be even more devastating. The Spanish Civil War showed that in a new war the civilian population would be exposed to aerial bombing.

There was also a widespread feeling that Germany had genuine grievances. Hitler was able to play on this by claiming that Germans outside Germany had the right of self-determination. This justified the Anschluss and the annexation of the Sudetenland. Appeasement, it was believed, would remove grievances and thus promote Anglo-German friendship. Many people, especially Conservatives, thought this was particularly important because they saw Germany as a bulwark against Communist Russia, which they regarded as a greater threat than Nazi Germany.

There is a strong case for the view that there was no alternative to appeasement. Britain was militarily not prepared for full-scale war. Public opinion did not favour rearmament, as the Peace Ballot showed and governments were keen to keep public expenditure as low as possible because of the economic situation. The Ten Year Rule, which was only abandoned in 1932, meant that, even when Britain began to rearm in the late 1930s, it was trailing behind Germany. Moreover Britain had a world-wide Empire to defend and there was a risk that war with Germany would lead to war against Italy and Japan as well. In such a war Britain's main ally would probably be France, which was weak and divided. The USA was committed to isolation. It was likely, therefore, that Britain would find itself fighting alone, as indeed happened in 1940. The policy of appeasement did at least provide the opportunity for Britain to rearm from 1936 onwards.

> The three were linked in the Anti-Comintern Pact in 1937.

Arguments against

The fact remains, however, that Chamberlain's policies in the end failed to avert war. Consequently for many years he was blamed for pursuing a mistaken policy with disastrous consequences. Even at the time critics such as Churchill argued that Hitler's demands should be resisted and that concessions simply encouraged further demands. Hitler's aims – a great Germany embracing all German-speaking peoples and expansion to the east in the quest for Lebensraum – were no secret. Chamberlain has been criticised for allowing Hitler to dupe him by false promises, particularly at Munich. His detractors claim that he was weak, naïve and indecisive. They point out that he had little experience of foreign affairs. In the post-war era he was the obvious scapegoat for foreign policy failures which had resulted in a terrible war.

> This view, advanced in *Guilty Men* by Cato (1940) was generally accepted in the 1940s and 1950s.

The debate among historians

In '*The Origins of the Second World War*' (1961), A.J.P. Taylor challenged the view that Hitler had followed a set plan of conquest. This prompted revisionists to reconsider accepted views about appeasement. Martin Gilbert argued that Britain's limited resources and worldwide commitments left Chamberlain with little alternative. More recently historians have argued that while Chamberlain was undoubtedly constrained by Britain's lack of resources, he also under-estimated Britain's capacity to deter Hitler and failed to offer as much resistance as he could and should have done. Even so, it is doubtful, as D.C. Watt claims, 'whether any alternative course would have made any difference'.

> Does the fact that appeasement failed to prevent the outbreak of the Second World War prove that it was a wrong-headed policy to pursue at the time?
>
> **KEY ISSUE**

Conclusions

Much of the criticism is based on hindsight. As shown above, at the time public and political opinion was largely in favour of Chamberlain's policies. He was aware of Hitler's ambitions and did not trust him but he thought he had little alternative but to negotiate with him. He, more than anyone, was responsible for the acceleration in Britain's rearmament in 1938–9.

> There is no final verdict. You must weigh the arguments and reach your own conclusions.

Opinions are also divided about **Munich**. The established view is that it was a disaster, in which Britain sacrificed a potential ally in Czechoslovakia. Hitler himself, however, felt that he had been denied a military triumph and regretted making the agreement. Munich averted war and allowed Britain a year to rearm. It can be argued that Britain was better prepared for war in 1939, though of course Germany's armed strength also increased in the year after Munich.

> His claim to have secured 'peace with honour' proved wrong, but was greeted with relief by public opinion.

9.3 British Politics 1918–51

After studying this section you should be able to:

- *analyse the reasons for the political domination of the Conservatives between 1918 and 1945*
- *assess the achievements of Baldwin*
- *assess the achievements of the Labour governments of 1945–51*

LEARNING SUMMARY

> This section presupposes that you have studied *Revise AS History*, chapters 5 and 6.1. It provides supplementary information and ideas to help you cope with A2 questions on this period.
>
> **KEY POINT**

Why did the Conservatives dominate politics?

AQA   M5 (synoptic)

Between 1918 and 1945 the Conservatives, either on their own or as the dominant partner in a coalition, won every election except those of 1923 and 1929. Why?

- The Conservatives had a solid core of support from the upper and middle classes, who supplied money and leadership.
- Middle-class Liberals swung over to the Conservatives out of fear of socialism. The Conservatives benefited from the Communist scare in the 1924 election.

Arising from the Zinoviev letter.

- They benefited from a tradition of working-class Conservatism going back to Disraeli. Around a third of working class-voters voted Conservative.
- The skilful leadership of Baldwin won them the middle ground of politics. They accepted the social reforms introduced by the pre-war Liberals.
- They had the support of most of the press.
- Circumstances favoured them. The granting of dominion status to Ireland removed 80 anti-Conservative Irish Nationalists from the House of Commons. The financial crisis of 1931 destroyed the second Labour ministry and brought the Conservatives back to office (in the National Government) as the party which could be trusted.

> Probably the main reason was that the opposition was divided between Labour and the Liberals.
>
> **KEY POINT**

Baldwin

AQA   M5 (synoptic)

Key points from AS

- **The General Strike**
  Revise AS pages 66–67

Baldwin stood for stability and consensus. He was keen to prevent the Conservative Party from becoming an anti-working-class party. Unlike many Conservatives, he was prepared to accept the formation of a Labour government after he lost his overall majority in the 1923 election. He recognised that this would strengthen the 'responsible' elements in the Labour Party, led by MacDonald.

Especially Churchill.

His role in the General Strike is controversial. Some historians say he broke off negotiations with the TUC too soon and thus provoked the strike. They claim that he had given in to the more right-wing members of the cabinet who wanted a showdown and that he failed to restrain them during the strike itself. Others argue that he genuinely believed that the real issue was a constitutional one (the authority of the government) and that he was playing a waiting game, knowing that the TUC was not prepared to risk the revolutionary possibilities of a prolonged strike. It does seem, however, that he gave way to right-wing pressure in bringing forward the vindictive Trade Disputes Act of 1923.

Contributory old-age pensions, abolition of the Poor Law and reform of local government.

Despite the General Strike, his ministry of 1924–29 succeeded in preserving stability. Its main achievements in home affairs were the work not of Baldwin but of Neville Chamberlain. It failed, however, to come up with any new ideas for dealing with unemployment. Baldwin's election slogan in 1929, 'Safety First', summed up his outlook but failed to fire the electorate.

In 1931 he played a key role in the formation of the National Government. The financial crisis led to the introduction of tariffs – the issue on which Baldwin had lost the 1923 election. Voters associated the Conservatives with stability and this accounted for their success in the elections of 1931 and 1935, which they fought as the dominant partner in the National Governments.

After the resignation of MacDonald, Baldwin was Prime Minister between 1935 and 1937. In foreign policy he was involved in the appeasement of Hitler over the remilitarisation of the Rhineland. He was responsible for the decision to rearm, though he was accused of misleading the public about the scale of rearmament. He gained much credit for his handling of the abdication crisis of 1936.

> Despite his apparent laziness, Baldwin was an able politician, who played an important role in keeping class warfare out of British politics.
>
> **KEY POINT**

The record of the National Governments

AQA ▸ M5 (synoptic)

Key points from AS

- The National Government's economic policies
  Revise AS page 69

After the Second World War conventional wisdom held that the National Governments had failed to solve Britain's economic problems and had done too little to tackle the socially damaging problems of unemployment. This is not wholly fair. By 1937 economic recovery had been achieved and unemployment in most of the country had almost been eliminated. The problem was that in the older industrial areas unemployment was still high and therefore whole communities were dependent on benefits administered in accordance with a greatly resented means test.

The Labour governments of 1945–51

AQA ▸ M5 (synoptic)
WJEC ▸ M4

Key points from AS

- The Labour governments 1945–51
  Revise AS pages 76–79

Labour's achievements are a matter of debate. Many historians believe it was very successful. It set up a Welfare State, the main features of which have survived till today. Its economic planning put Britain on the way to recovery after the war. It played a valuable role in the formation of NATO, and it handled Indian independence well.

Some left-wing historians, however, argue that its policies were not sufficiently socialist. It nationalised only about 20 per cent of the nation's industries – mostly those that were badly run or unprofitable. Thus the whole idea of nationalisation was discredited. Moreover, the way nationalisation was carried out was disappointing to workers, who had no share in the running of their industries and merely exchanged one set of bosses for another. Left-wing historians also criticise the decision to develop the atomic bomb.

A different line of criticism was developed by Corelli Barnett in the 1980s. He argued that the welfare state was ruinously expensive, placed an unsustainable burden on the British economy and played a large part in Britain's post-war decline. The money should have been spent on modernising the economy. This view has, however, been criticised as giving too little weight to other causes of Britain's decline and ignoring the fact that other countries which did not experience the same decline also spent large sums on welfare.

Sample question and model answer

Study Sources A to D and answer questions (a) and (b) which follow.

Source A

From *English History 1914–45*, by A.J.P. Taylor, 1965.

Chamberlain's asset was his sharp rationalism. He beat down critics with the question: what is the alternative? Hardly anyone now believed that the League of Nations could be effective in its existing form, though many shrank from admitting it – Germany, Italy and Japan outside the League; sanctions shattered by the failure over Abyssinia. Churchill tended to talk as though Britain and France could still lay down the law to Europe. Some members of the foreign office thought that Hitler should be 'hit on the head'. Chamberlain had no faith in this policy. Though he regarded France as secure from invasion behind the Maginot Line and Great Britain as equally so behind the shield of sea-power, he believed that Germany was equally secure on her side. At least, she could only be tamed by a great war, lasting for years and tearing Europe in pieces. Such a war he and nearly all Englishmen wished to avoid.

Source B

From *The Twentieth Century 1880–1939: Modern British Foreign Policy*, by P. Hayes, 1978.

It was at this point (September 1938) that appeasement policy passed from having a moral content, however slight, and became instead one of bowing to German demands without regard to their nature. In effect, Britain ceased, temporarily, to have any foreign policy save that of avoiding war. If others had to pay the price in terms of territorial concessions or shattered alliances then that was regrettable but unavoidable.

Chamberlain and his supporters hardly realised the implications of their actions. They saw only that war had been avoided and not that for the first time in 250 years Britain had abandoned her policy of preventing by every means in her power the dominance of Europe by a single power.

Source C

From *Retreat from Power*, by D. Dilks, 1981.

In the years before the Second World War, the British found themselves forced by a growing threat from Germany, compounded in its seriousness by the aggressiveness of Japan and Italy, into a greater commitment to Europe than they would have wished. It may be that a more bold or deft policy would have enabled Britain to separate her potential enemies. However, nothing less than the defeat of Nazi Germany, or the ability to bargain on more than level terms with Hitler, would have resolved the essential problem facing the British governments of the 1930s. Germany was the only power which might not only dominate Europe but even conquer the British Isles and thus, by piercing the heart, put an end to the British empire.

Source D

From *The Realities behind Diplomacy*, by P. Kennedy, 1981.

Defence Weaknesses: this is a motive much seized on by historians and especially by Conservative apologists for Chamberlain eager to demonstrate the Prime Minister's wisdom in postponing a showdown until Britain's armed forces had been further strengthened. There is, to be sure, an enormous amount of documentary evidence for this, if only because the Chiefs of Staff had been cataloguing the nation's military deficiencies for some time.

However, no one asked the critical question, 'What will be left of the balance of power if Czechoslovakia is dismantled?' And no one, with the possible exception of Duff Cooper, appears before the Munich crisis to have been disturbed that the army had been *deliberately* kept small and thus incapable of carrying out a European field role. Whether or not the postponement of war for a year saved Britain, there is a strong case for arguing that it lost Europe.

Sample question and model answer *(continued)*

(a) To what extent do Sources C and D support the explanation in Source A of the considerations which influenced Chamberlain's policy in 1937–8? **[10]**

(a) Source A considers Chamberlain's rationale for appeasement: the weakness of the League, his wish to avoid war (supported by public opinion), his belief that Germany's defences ruled out a short war to curb its aggression. Source D agrees that he wished to avoid war, or rather postpone it, though the reason given is Britain's military weakness. Source C similarly implies that Britain was not strong enough to embark on war with Germany ('nothing less than the defeat of Nazi Germany ... would have resolved the problem' implies that this was not a realistic option). The sources are complementary rather than contradictory.

(b) Using Sources A to D, explain why Chamberlain's conduct in making the Munich Agreement is a subject of disagreement among historians. **[20]**

(b) There are essentially two views: (a) that appeasement was a reasonable policy in the circumstances; (b) that it was a policy of weakness which encouraged Hitler to further aggression and thus led to war.

For many years after the Second World War, the latter was generally accepted. Munich involved sacrificing Czechoslovakia, which meant abandoning the policy of upholding the balance of power (sources B and D). It meant 'bowing to German demands without regard to their nature' (source B) in order to avoid war at all costs. It meant sacrificing the most valuable potential ally in Eastern Europe – Czechoslovakia had probably the best army in Eastern Europe, as well as the Skoda armaments works. The Sudetenland proved not to be Hitler's last territorial demand. Munich did not prevent war – it simply postponed it for a year. Even at the time critics such as Churchill argued that Hitler's demands should be resisted and that concessions simply encouraged further demands. Hitler's aims were no secret.

But these criticisms largely derive from hindsight. Arguments for appeasement are stronger if viewed from the perspective of the 1930s. Public opinion supported it. There is a strong case for the view that there was no alternative (source A – ineffective League, likelihood that a war would be long and destructive). Britain was militarily not prepared for full-scale war (source D – though this source regards this as a poor defence of appeasement, pointing out that Britain's military unpreparedness was the result of deliberate policy). Moreover war with Germany might well involve Italy and Japan as well (source C). In such a war Britain's main ally would probably be France, which was weak and divided, while the USA was committed to isolation. Other reasons why many supported appeasement included guilt (the view that Germany had been badly treated in 1919 and had genuine grievances) and fear of Communist Russia (which many, especially Conservatives, saw as a greater threat than Nazi Germany).

There are good arguments for both views – hence the continuing debate.

Give examples of the League's failures, e.g. Ethiopia.

This is an outline answer, to which you should add more detail.

Use your own knowledge to set the ideas in the sources in context.

Explain his aims, especially Lebensraum.

A reference to the Ten Year Rule.

Practice examination questions

1 Study Sources A to D and answer questions (a) and (b) which follow.

Source A

From a letter from a 'New' Liberal J.A. Hobhouse to the editor of the *Manchester Guardian*, C.P. Scott, 7 November 1924.

I doubt if the Liberal Party any longer stands for anything distinctive. My reasons are on the one side that moderate Labour – Labour in office – has represented essential Liberalism better than the organised party since Campbell-Bannerman's death. On the other side the Liberal party never seems agreed within on essentials. Of the present fragment, part leans to the Tories, part to Labour, part has nothing distinctive. The deduction I draw is that the distinction between that kind of Labour man who does not go whole hog for nationalisation and the Liberal who wants social progress is obsolete.

Source B

From *A Short History of the Liberal Party*, by C. Cook, 1976.

The decision to install a Labour Government [in 1924] was both a vital and crucial decision for the Liberal Party. For such a decision to succeed, it was imperative for the Liberals, whilst the minority Labour government remained in power, to achieve several targets. To begin with, strong leadership was essential. And this meant a complete healing of the Asquith–Lloyd George split, as opposed to the hurried coming-together that Baldwin's Tariff election had brought about. Secondly, it was imperative to use the coming months to develop constructive policy proposals – in social reform, industry, unemployment and foreign affairs – so that in any subsequent general election the Liberals could offer a distinctive, constructive and wide-ranging manifesto. Further, so that the party could fight on as broad a front as possible, derelict constituencies would have to be revived, candidates recruited and finance made available. United and purposeful leadership was the prerequisite for new policies, revived organisation and sustained morale. ... Although, nominally, the party was united, in reality it remained as divided as ever.

Source C

From *The Decline of the Liberal Party, 1910–1931*, by P. Adelman, 1981.

Mass trade union power buttressed the Labour party and gave it an established and expanding electoral base among the industrial working classes. By contrast, in an age of increased class polarisation, the Liberal party lacked any definite class basis or class appeal, and this hampered it in a variety of ways. What social and economic policies had the Liberals to offer the country to rival the practical and emotional appeal of Labour? They passionately supported Free Trade – but that was a dying cause; they were not socialists – but they failed to evolve an industrial policy which could be regarded as a realistic and distinctive alternative to Labour's socialism. Nor, in the immediate post-war years, were the Liberal leaders in a position to counteract the class appeal of the Labour party on personal grounds. Asquith, always remote from working-class experience, was now a negligible figure; while Lloyd George, because of his leadership of a Conservative-dominated Coalition ... had now completely lost the confidence of the British labour movement.

Source D

From *The Great War and the Decline of the Liberal Party*, by M. Pugh, in *History Sixth*, October 1989.

Ultimately the impact of war may be crudely measured by the Liberals' dismal performance in the general election of 1918. Yet it is no easy matter to separate the effects of wartime politics from the effects of the new electorate or the redistribution of constituencies. ... Were the Liberals simply swamped by an influx of new voters?... [The huge growth in the electorate] led to a 25.6% share of the poll for Asquithian and Lloyd George Liberals combined in 1918, and only 22.2% for Labour. In the elections of 1922 and 1923 the two parties ran virtually level with 29–30% each. On the face of it Labour's performance was hardly good enough –

Practice examination questions (continued)

nor the Liberals' bad enough – to justify the claim that Labour had suddenly tapped a vast reservoir of support after 1918. ... One is driven back to the view that Liberal decline must be attributed less to structural changes than to wartime political changes which, by 1918, had begun to push existing Liberal supporters towards Labour and, indeed, towards Conservatives.

Ultimately what the war years did was to provide the opportunity which Ramsay MacDonald had always expected to arise eventually. By undermining Liberal credentials as the most effective party of reform, war allowed Labour to inherit the mantle of radicalism and to rally middle-class and working-class Progressives under its wing.

(a) Using your own knowledge and the evidence of Sources B and C, what do you consider to have been the main weaknesses of Liberal leadership during and after the First World War? [10]

(b) 'With the rise of a working class party it was inevitable that the Liberals would cease to matter as an electoral force.' Using your own knowledge, and these Sources, explain how far you agree with this interpretation of the decline of the Liberal Party. [20]

2 'Until 1936 appeasement was a sensible policy for Britain; after 1936 it was not.' How far do you agree with this view? [30]

3 Explain the dominance of the Conservative Party in British politics in the inter-war period. [30]

NICCEA GCE 1993 History Paper 1, Question 44

Chapter 10

Historical investigations: Lenin and Stalin

The following topics are covered in this chapter:

- Lenin 1903–24
- The Soviet Union under Stalin, 1924–41

10.1 Lenin 1903–24

After studying this section you should be able to:

- explain the role of Lenin and the Bolsheviks in Russian history from 1903 to 1917
- discuss historical interpretations of the establishment of the Communist state in Russia between 1917 and 1924
- understand and assess contrasting views of the significance of the career of Lenin

LEARNING SUMMARY

The origins and development of the Bolsheviks

OCR   M4
WJEC   M4

See Chapter 6.4.

The Marxist **Social Democratic Party**, founded in 1898, split into two factions, Bolsheviks and Mensheviks, in 1903. The **Bolsheviks** argued that the party should be a small body of professional revolutionaries, closely controlled by the leader – Lenin.

Orthodox Marxists expected the workers' revolution to take place in the advanced industrial countries of western Europe.

Lenin was in exile in Western Europe from 1903 to 1917, except for three months during the 1905 Revolution. Although the revolution failed, it played an important part in the development of his ideas. The orthodox Marxist view was that Russia would need to go through a 'bourgeois-democratic' revolution and a period of capitalist development before its proletarian revolution. Lenin held that the 1905 Revolution showed that the liberal parties had little revolutionary potential, but the peasants and the national minorities were revolutionary forces to be reckoned with. Thus a workers' revolution, in alliance with the peasants and national minorities, would enable Russia to miss out the capitalist phase and move straight to the dictatorship of the proletariat.

> Lenin adapted Marxism to conditions in Russia, a country only partly industrialised and with a large peasant population.
>
> **KEY POINT**

The Bolsheviks were reduced to a tiny underground group by repression after 1905. In 1912–14 they were involved in a series of strikes. By 1914 they controlled the biggest trade unions in Moscow and St Petersburg and their newspaper, *Pravda*, had the largest circulation of any socialist journal. In 1914, after a general strike in St Petersburg, *Pravda* was suppressed and many Bolsheviks arrested. The party within Russia was temporarily crippled but it regained support as the economic crisis deepened in 1916. Meanwhile Lenin, in exile, denounced the war and called on the workers of the world to use their arms against their own governments to end war.

The 1917 Revolutions

OCR   M4
WJEC   M4

Lenin returned to Russia in April 1917, two months after the overthrow of the Tsar. On his arrival in Petrograd (as St Petersburg was then named), Lenin issued the *April Theses*, in which he argued for an end to co-operation with the Provisional Government. Instead power must be transferred to the soviets, and within the

Key points from AS

- **The 1917 revolutions**
  Revise AS pages 96–97

soviets to the Bolsheviks, who at this stage were in a minority even in the Petrograd Soviet. Capitalism must be overthrown and the land and banks nationalised. These ideas were the practical application of Lenin's view that Russia could move straight from tsarism to the dictatorship of the proletariat.

The *April Theses* aroused much opposition and debate in the party. It is wrong to regard it as a monolithic organisation controlled by Lenin at this stage. The **Mensheviks** supported the Provisional Government as the necessary capitalist stage in a process leading eventually to socialism and some Bolsheviks moved over to join them. Lenin had to display considerable political skill to get his way and gain the support of the All-Russian Party Conference.

Orlando Figes comments, 'It must have seemed to Lenin that the Bolshevik cause was finished'.

In July a rising in Petrograd appeared to offer a chance to overthrow the Provisional Government. Soviet historians portray **the July Days** as a spontaneous rising, but most western historians claim that the Bolsheviks planned to seize power and then lost their nerve. Whichever view is correct, the rising was poorly organised and lacked clear aims. It soon collapsed and the involvement of the Bolsheviks gave the government the opportunity to arrest a number of their leaders. Lenin himself fled to Finland to escape arrest.

Kornilov, the newly appointed commander-in-chief, headed an attempted coup in September.

The crucial factor in the revival of the Bolsheviks after this setback was **the Kornilov affair**. They played the leading role in organising resistance by the soviets and as a result soon afterwards gained control of the Petrograd and Moscow Soviets. The membership of the Party rose to 200 000. Soviet historians subsequently alleged that Kornilov aimed to overthrow the Provisional Government and establish a military dictatorship. It may be, however, that he was trying to save it by uniting the army and the Provisional Government against the Soviet.

With the growth of Bolshevik support in the autumn of 1917 Lenin saw the opportunity for the Bolsheviks to seize power. The Central Committee of the Party decided to organise an armed coup. Lenin was supported by Trotsky, Stalin and seven others. Only Zinoviev and Kamenev voted against.

What explains the October Revolution?

OCR ▸ M4

Trotsky argued in 1918 that the support of the Russian workers would have brought the Bolsheviks to power but counter-revolutionary forces headed by Kerensky and Kornilov tried to prevent this. Thus the October Revolution simply ensured that the will of the workers was fulfilled. A later Soviet version stressed the logic of the class struggle and argued that the role of the Bolsheviks, and Lenin in particular, was to mould events to bring about the inevitable triumph of the proletarian revolution.

Western historians e.g. E.H. Carr, tend to stress the role of Lenin, stamping his personality on events, and to portray the October revolution as a coup rather than a popular revolution with mass support. Others such as L. Shapiro and H. Seton-Watson emphasise the importance of the war, which they claim halted Russia's progress towards liberal institutions and gave extremists the opportunity to seize power.

The failings of the Provisional Government (see Chapter 6.3) were also important.

> Was the success of the Bolsheviks in seizing power solely the result of Lenin's leadership and organisation of the party? **KEY ISSUE**

How did the Bolsheviks secure their hold on power?

OCR ▸ M4

Several important aspects of Lenin's rule between 1917 and 1924 require explanation.

Key points from AS

- **Lenin 1917–24**
  Revise AS pages 150–153

The debate on the causes of the Terror.

This was Lenin's explanation – but it was one that he advanced after the event.

What was its significance in the development of Russian Communism?

Why was the NEP controversial?

The **Treaty of Brest-Litovsk** was extremely harsh. Russia lost 34 per cent of its population. Why did Lenin accept it? He insisted that he was prepared to make any sacrifice to keep the Bolsheviks in power. In any case the territory lost was largely in German hands at the time and there was no prospect of reconquering it.

The **Red Terror** was organised by the Cheka (secret police), which was set up in December 1917. Between then and 1922 several hundred thousand victims were executed, murdered, imprisoned or tortured. Lenin regarded it as necessary to defend the Revolution. Some historians have explained the terror as an intrinsic part of Bolshevik rule, employed to build up their power. Others see it as a response to the dangers of the civil war. Orlando Figes argues that it was really rooted in the hatred of the people for the rich, which had produced a 'war on privilege'. The Bolsheviks, he claims, simply took this over and institutionalised it. Perhaps it was an inevitable consequence of the fact that the Bolsheviks had seized power by force.

War Communism, according to Soviet historians, was simply an emergency measure to deal with the crisis in the economy caused by war, revolution and then civil war. On this view the New Economic Policy was a return to the policy Lenin originally wished to pursue. The alternative view is that it was an attempt to put into practice Communist ideology – an attempt which failed and had to be modified in the NEP.

Why did the Whites lose the **Civil War**? One view is that the odds were stacked against them. The Reds controlled the main cities and the railways, which gave them the advantage of internal communications. They had a united command, headed by Trotsky, and a disciplined army of five million men, giving them overwhelming superiority of numbers. The Whites, on the other hand, faced difficulties of communication and co-ordination between different fronts. Other historians, while accepting the validity of all these points, argue that the fundamental reason for the defeat of the Whites was political: the Russian people believed that they would try to turn the clock back. Thus the peasants would lose the land they had seized and the urban workers would see the revolution reversed. Some Whites wanted a tsarist restoration. Figes concludes that the problem was that the Whites were 'too counter-revolutionary'.

The **Kronstadt Rising** was the catalyst for the introduction of the New Economic Policy. It also led Lenin to introduce the ban on factions in the Communist Party. This was to be a major factor in the rise to power of Stalin, who was appointed as General Secretary of the Party to enforce it. The rising was suppressed with great brutality and was seen by socialists throughout the world as proof that the Bolsheviks were tyrants.

The **New Economic Policy** was introduced in 1921 when it became clear that War Communism was failing and causing massive discontent. Another factor was the realisation that there was no immediate hope of a socialist revolution throughout Europe. Russia must therefore rely on building up its own resources, which for Lenin meant a retreat from the ideological purity of War Communism. He saw the NEP as a temporary retreat from pure communism, though 'temporary' might mean many years. It was 'a partial surrender to the peasants' – a recognition that their co-operation would have to be won. But it disappointed many Communists, who saw it as a surrender of the principles of the revolution.

> **KEY POINT**
>
> The NEP produced a mixture of a market economy in food and the retail trade and a command economy in finance and large-scale industry. This was inherently unstable and produced much argument among the Communists.

Assessment of Lenin

OCR ▸ M4

Lenin played a crucial role in 1917 in the overthrow of the Provisional Government. The Decrees on the Land and on Peace enabled the Bolsheviks to hold on to power. With the help of Trotsky, he held the new Communist state together through the Civil War.

He was a major contributor to the theory of communism, producing a revised interpretation, suited to Russian conditions, of Marxist ideas about the course of history and the means by which socialism would be achieved. At the same time, he could be pragmatic in his approach. His decision to replace War Communism by the New Economic Policy was realistic, even though it involved compromising the basic principles of Marxism.

See p. 136 for discussion of how far Lenin laid the foundations for Stalinism.

Nevertheless, the Russian state which he established was a totalitarian police state, based on a system of terror. His belief that Russia could leap from tsarism to the dictatorship of the proletariat through the militant action of the party involved sweeping aside democracy. He left Russia with unresolved tensions, especially the relationship between the state and the peasantry.

Lenin addresses the crowd in Red Square, Moscow, on the first anniversary of the Revolution, October/November 1918

> Most historians accept the greatness of Lenin in the sense that without him the course of Russian history would have been different.
>
> **KEY POINT**

10.2 The Soviet Union under Stalin, 1924–41

After studying this section you should be able to:

- explain Stalin's rise to power
- analyse the main features of Stalinism
- assess how far Stalinism was a development of Leninism

LEARNING SUMMARY

The struggle for the succession to Lenin

AQA	M4 (synoptic)
EDEXCEL	M6 (synoptic)

Key points from AS

- **Rise to power**
  Revise AS pages 153–154

> Rightists wished to continue the New Economic Policy, leftists wanted to overturn it.

Josef Stalin, 1879–1953

Why did Stalin win the leadership battle?

Stalin was a skilful, resourceful and ruthless politician. He used his position as General Secretary of the Communist Party to appoint his supporters to key posts throughout the party at local and national level. Shrewdly, he encouraged the cult of Lenin and portrayed himself as his natural heir, in contrast to Trotsky who made the mistake of attacking the New Economic Policy. He exploited the debate over economic policy in the late 1920s between the 'rightists', who advocated the continuation of the NEP, and the 'leftists', who opposed further concessions to the peasantry. Stalin first allied himself with the 'rightists'. Between 1925 and 1927 the leading 'leftists', Trotsky, Kamenev and Zinoviev, were expelled from the party. Then, when the procurement crisis of 1927–8 (the peasants' refusal to produce enough grain at the prices offered by the state) convinced him that the NEP was failing, he turned against Bukharin and the 'rightists'. In 1929 they in their turn were expelled from the Politburo.

Trotsky's failings also contributed to Stalin's victory. He was mistrusted by other Communist leaders, who regarded him as too clever, too western in his ways and too arrogant. He failed to build up a power base. But it would be a mistake to regard the struggle as purely a matter of differences of personality and political skill. Underlying the struggle was a debate about the future path of the Communist regime – 'permanent revolution' or 'socialism in one country'. 'Permanent revolution', which Trotsky advocated, was undermined by the failure of revolutions elsewhere in Europe, especially in Germany in 1919, and was deeply unattractive to Russians after the First World War and the Civil War.

Stalinism

AQA	M4 (synoptic)
EDEXCEL	M6 (synoptic)

Key points from AS

- **Stalin's Dictatorship**
  Revise AS pages 153–157

> This basically meant glorifying the Soviet state and Stalin.

The Communist Party and the government of the USSR

Stalin made the Party the instrument of his personal will. Although under the **Constitution of 1936** the democratically elected Supreme Soviet was nominally the supreme authority in Russia, in practice power lay with the Party, since no other parties were allowed. Within the Party promotion depended entirely on unquestioning loyalty to Stalin.

Stalin's policies were enforced by terror and all opposition, real or imaginary, was suppressed by the **NKVD**. Guarantees of personal liberty under the constitution were meaningless. At the same time Stalin became the focus of an extraordinary personality cult. Russian children were taught to look up to him as the 'brilliant leader'. Statues of him appeared everywhere. The arts were made to conform to Stalin's ideas of 'socialist realism'.

Revisionist historians, who challenge traditional interpretations, have questioned how efficient this totalitarian system was. Central directives were differently interpreted by local officials, who were often vying with each other for influence.

The purges

You need to be able to explain the main arguments in the debate on the causes and significance of the purges...

Stalin's terror reached its height in the purges. In trying to explain the reasons for them, historians have generally focused on Stalin's personality. He is alleged to have been paranoid and to have wished to eliminate all possible sources of opposition and even potential opponents who at the time had not shown any disloyalty. It is claimed that he wanted to make sure there would be no internal rivals in a position to profit from any external disaster such as defeat in war. The timing of the purges suggests that they were a reaction to the upheaval of collectivisation and the resulting tensions within the Communist Party.

Revisionist historians accept these arguments about the show trials and the purges at the centre, but claim that the purges also demonstrated a breakdown of central control in the provinces. Local factors such as conflicts between managers and workers, or personal quarrels, played an important part. In a sense the purges in the provinces were a continuation of the terror in the countryside unleashed by collectivisation. Thus while the purges strengthened Stalin's hold at the centre, they weakened the control of the central government over the localities.

Industrialisation

...and also the debate on the effectiveness of the Five-Year Plans.

The implementation of the Five-Year Plans raises similar questions about the effectiveness of central control. Undoubtedly the growth of Russia's industrial capacity was impressive, but it was achieved at a high price in hardship for the workers – harsh discipline, poor housing and low standards of living. Historians disagree about whether Stalin's policies helped or hindered the process.

- Some claim that implementation at local level was inconsistent and inefficient. Local managers often hoarded materials to ensure they could meet their targets, thus creating imbalances elsewhere. If this was so, then it can be questioned whether Stalin's methods were necessary or helpful.
- Others claim that much of the credit for Russia's industrial progress should go to the tsarist regime, which laid the foundations.
- Others again argue that over-ambitious targets and coercion of the workforce were necessary to achieve such results.

Were Stalin's methods necessary – or even helpful – to achieve the industrialisation of Russia?

Collectivisation

This has traditionally been regarded as the prime justification for the brutality of the collectivisation policy.

Was collectivisation a 'war against the peasants' or a 'war between peasants', i.e. poorer peasants and kulaks?

Collectivisation has been generally condemned by historians as a disaster. The cost in human suffering was enormous. Agricultural production was severely dislocated and took years to recover. Even the argument that it enabled Russia to raise the capital needed for industrialisation by selling grain abroad seems dubious. Much of the capital generated by agriculture stayed within the agricultural sector and the Motor Tractor Stations represented investment by industry in agriculture, rather than the reverse. In Stalin's defence it can be said that the policy received considerable backing from Party members at both local and national level. Moreover the peasant base of Russian society and the backwardness of agriculture were major obstacles to the modernisation of the economy. The fault lay in the means adopted to change Russian agriculture.

Collectivisation had enormous social consequences. Millions of displaced peasants moved to the towns, providing the labour force for industrialisation. In due course their families became urbanised and better educated.

> **KEY POINT**
>
> The judgement of E.H. Carr on Stalin is: 'Seldom perhaps in history has so monstrous a price been paid for so monumental an achievement.'

A demonstration by peasants against the kulaks, 1930. The banner reads 'We demand collectivisation and the extermination of the kulaks as a class'

Was Stalinism a continuation of Leninism?

EDEXCEL   M6 (synoptic)

Solzhenitsyn asserted that Stalinism was the inevitable consequence of Leninism. Other critics point out that Lenin was ruthless in eliminating enemies in the Red Terror and argue that the Cheka led to Stalin's NKVD. Lenin created a one-party state and set up the Party apparatus by which Stalin came to power. When he died a personality cult was already in place.

Other historians claim that Lenin's terror was not as savage as Stalin's and that he would have abolished the secret police eventually. E.H. Carr claimed that for Lenin terror was a necessary but temporary measure and that he would have had the moral authority to mitigate it. Although he introduced the ban on factions, there was still debate within the Party, as is shown by the ideological arguments which accompanied the struggle for power between Stalin and Trotsky. He recognised the danger presented by Stalin's intolerance and tried to prevent his succession – but was incapacitated by illness. Historians favourable to Lenin, such as the Russian historian Roy Medvedev, claim that he was moved by a genuine idealism – the aim of removing social and material inequalities.

> This is the interpretation put forward by Robert Conquest in *The Great Terror.*

It is generally agreed that Stalin moulded the system he inherited from Lenin with a unique degree of ruthlessness. By his purges he changed its nature, making it a bureaucracy for the execution of his will. The growth of the personality cult of Stalin symbolised the change from government by the Party to government by Stalin's personal will.

Another view, advanced by David Lane and Alec Nove, is that both Lenin and Stalin were borne along by forces greater than themselves – a Russia so backward economically that only by drastic action could they achieve political success, and so imbued with authoritarian traditions that only coercion would work.

> **KEY ISSUE**
>
> Was Stalinism, as Schapiro argues, 'not a necessary consequence of Leninism, but a possible result'?

Sample question and model answer

Study Sources A to D and answer questions (a) and (b) which follow.

Source A

From *The Russian Revolution*, by P.S. O'Connor, 1968.
At least until the return of Lenin to Russia there was no single Bolshevik view. Some talked fire about immediate negotiations for peace, fraternisation between the soldiers of Russia and Germany at the front, and turning the war everywhere against capitalists and imperialists. Others, almost certainly the majority, held opinions close to those of the Mensheviks. They expected a long period of bourgeois parliamentary rule during which the soviets must be vigilant on behalf of the people but would not themselves try to seize power. As for the war, they simply wanted the Provisional Government to seek the kind of peace which would also satisfy the Mensheviks. Only a day or so before Lenin's arrival, an All-Russian Conference of the Bolsheviks agreed to hold discussions to see if the two factions into which the Social Democratic Party had been split for so long could find a basis for unity. This was not at all what Lenin had in mind.

Source B

From *The Russian Revolution*, by A. Wood, 1986.
The key to Lenin's success did not lie primarily in a different interpretation of Marxism, although his was certainly different; nor on the sureness of his political instinct, although this too was outstanding. What distinguished him from the other Socialist leaders was his conception of the party which he had outlined in his pamphlet *What is to be done?* and which had led to the Bolshevik-Menshevik split at the Russian Social Democrat congress in 1903 in Brussels. However radical the attitude of the non-Bolshevik Socialists, they all believed in a free exchange of debate in which compromise with the minority groups might eventually lead to a majority decision – in fact, the parliamentary processes for which Lenin had supreme contempt. In contrast to them, Lenin believed that the opportunity offered by the revolution could be grasped by a small dedicated 'elite whose discipline would enable them to act decisively when the moment came'.

Source C

From *Interpreting the Russian Revolution*, by C. Read, in *History Sixth*, October 1989.
Why did the Bolsheviks succeed? Perhaps the most important, and frequently overlooked, explanation arises from Lenin's injunction on his arrival in Petrograd in April, that the party should give no support to the Provisional Government. This policy reaped rich rewards. All the other major parties of the left – notably the Social Revolutionaries and the Mensheviks – decided it was necessary to shore up the Provisional Government in order to prevent a right-wing backlash against the democratic gains of the February revolution. Their increasing identification with the Provisional Government was fatal. As the Provisional Government sank, so did they. This left the Bolsheviks as the only receptacle for the waves of disillusioned militants and voters looking for an alternative.

Source D

From *The Russian Revolution 1900–27*, by R. Service, 1999.
The success of the Bolsheviks was intimately connected with the fact that they were the only main party unconditionally hostile to the Provisional Government. Their standpoint was clear by April. They wanted the government to be overthrown and replaced by an administrative structure based upon the soviets. They wavered a little; they dropped the slogan 'All power to the Soviets' in late summer when their prospects of enhancing their position in the soviets seemed poor. But the abandonment was temporary. On the war, moreover, Bolshevik policy was constant. They aimed at an immediate general peace. ... Until 1917, Bolsheviks had expected autocracy's demise to be followed by a lengthy epoch of rule by bourgeoisie. Now they wanted to commence the transition to socialism without delay. The party leader Vladimir Lenin expressed these ideas in his *April Theses*.

(a) Compare Sources A and D as accounts of the state of the Bolshevik party in 1917. [15]

(a) At first sight they differ on three points: how united the party was, its attitude towards the Provisional Government and its view about peace.

Sample question and model answer (continued)

Note that points from the two sources are set alongside each other.

Source A emphasises divisions within the party. Many wanted to co-operate with the Mensheviks. Source D makes no mention of divisions. Source A claims the Bolsheviks did not wish to overthrow the Provisional Government, while source D describes unconditional hostility to it: the Bolsheviks wished to replace it by a government based on the soviets. Source A says they wanted the Provisional Government to make 'the kind of peace which would also satisfy the Mensheviks', Source D 'an immediate general peace'. However, the two accounts are complementary rather than contradictory: the key to the relationship between them is the last sentence in Source A, referring to the role of Lenin. Source A refers mainly to the period before his return in April, source D mainly to the period after. There is some difference about when the Bolsheviks' position hardened into that described in source D.

(b) Using Sources A to D, explain how far, and why, they offer differing interpretations of the role of Lenin in 1917. [30]

This is an outline answer, to which you should add more detail.

(b) Source A does not directly address this issue until the last sentence but it accurately describes the state of the party in the few weeks between the overthrow of the Tsar and Lenin's return. The last sentence draws attention to his crucial role in unifying the party and directing it away from compromise with the Mensheviks. It is hard to imagine the party as described in source A carrying out the October Revolution. Source D takes up the idea that Lenin gave the Bolsheviks a new sense of direction. It stresses the importance of the Bolsheviks' hostility to the Provisional Government – which is also the key point in source C – and goes on to explain the ideas put forward by Lenin in the *April Theses* for a government based on soviets, an immediate general peace and an immediate 'transition to socialism'.

This idea should be explained from your own knowledge and contrasted with Marx's own ideas.

This is one of the points made by source B (a 'different interpretation of Marxism'). This source identifies three qualities which distinguished Lenin: his interpretation of Marxism, his political instinct and his idea of the party as a small elite of determined revolutionaries. It argues that the last of these was the key to his success. Unlike other socialist leaders, he rejected the idea of debate and compromise. Therefore, as source C points out, under his leadership the Bolsheviks were the only party which was not associated with the failings of the Provisional Government.

Note use of own knowledge to set the sources in context.

Lenin imposed on the Bolsheviks what can be seen with hindsight as a high-risk strategy. Source D draws attention to the temporary abandonment of the slogan 'All power to the Soviets' in the late summer. Lenin himself had to flee after the failure of the premature attempt at revolution in July. In the autumn he forced his belief that the moment had come for the dedicated 'elite ... to act decisively' (source B) through the Bolshevik Central Committee against the opposition of Kamenev and Zinoviev. The October Revolution proved that his judgement was correct; by then the Provisional Government had little support. Even so, most historians, except Soviet ones, regard the revolution as a coup by a determined minority such as Lenin had argued for since 1903 (source B).

Practice examination questions

1 How far is terror an adequate explanation for Stalin's pre-eminence in Russia between 1929 and 1941? [30]

2 How successful were Stalin's economic policies in the Soviet Union in the years 1928–41? [30]

3 Why did the tsarist regime survive in Russia in 1905, but not in 1917? [30]

The following topics are covered in this chapter:

- *Bismarck and the unification of Germany*
- *Hitler and the origins of the Second World War*
- *Hitler and the Nazi State 1933–39*

11.1 Bismarck and the unification of Germany

After studying this section you should be able to:

- *explain the obstacles to German unification before 1862 and the factors that favoured it*
- *discuss historians' interpretations of Bismarck's aims and methods in bringing about the unification of Germany*

LEARNING SUMMARY

Germany in the 1850s

| OCR | M4 |
| NICCEA | M4 |

I.e. the principle that the legitimate rulers were the hereditary princes.

Or would the other parts of the empire wish to become nation-states?

Key points from AS

- **Germany 1815–62**
  Revise AS pages 108–109

By creating a Prussian-dominated free trade area covering most of Germany except Austria.

Austria dominated the German Confederation, which it regarded as a means of upholding the principle of **legitimacy** and suppressing the forces of liberalism and nationalism throughout Germany. Because the Austrian empire was multinational, its very existence was threatened by these forces.

- It had no wish to see a German nation-state emerge because this would raise the question of whether Austria was to be part of it. If it was, what would be the relation of a unified Germany to the non-German parts of the Austrian empire?
- Liberalism, which stood for constitutional government, could lead to demands for national independence by the peoples of the empire.

The revival of the Confederation after the failure of the revolutions of 1848 therefore suited Austrian interests. Austria, however, had a number of weaknesses.

- The multinational nature of the empire created great problems, particularly the relationship between Austria and Hungary.
- The army, widely thought to be one of the greatest in Europe, was actually less efficient than Prussia's, as was shown in 1866.
- In the 1850s it became increasingly isolated. It alienated Russia, which had been a key ally during the 1848 revolutions, by its attitude in the Crimean War. It fought – and lost – a war against France in northern Italy in 1859.

Prussia had some important sources of strength.

- It was far the biggest state in northern Germany, with territories stretching from the Rhineland to East Prussia. Unlike Austria, it was largely German in population, with only one significant national minority (Poles in the east).
- Its economy was strong, with valuable natural resources, including the Ruhr coalfields, and good river communications (the Elbe, Oder and Rhine). From the 1850s it benefited from rapid development of the railway system and growing industrial strength.
- The Zollverein consolidated its economic predominance.
- From the late 1850s the army was enlarged and reorganised by Roon, backed by William I (regent in 1858 and king from 1861). The infantry was re-equipped with the breech-loading rifle. Moltke (Chief of the General Staff from 1857) was the first general to recognise the strategic importance of railways.

The rulers of the **smaller German states**, who were concerned above all to preserve their independence, regarded Prussia as a threat. For this reason they supported the Confederation and looked to Austria for protection.

Liberalism and **nationalism** attracted much support. German liberals aimed to achieve unification by constitutional means. Despite the failure of the Frankfurt Parliament of 1848, however, nationalism remained strong. 1859 saw the foundation of the National League, a largely middle-class movement which advocated a *kleindeutsch* solution to the German problem. A rival organisation, the Reform League, was set up in 1862 in support of a *Grossdeutschland*.

See Chapter 4.1.

> **KEY POINT**
> The problem for Liberals was that a *Kleindeutschland* would be dominated by Prussia, which was a bastion of authoritarian government.

International considerations

The unification of Germany was bound to affect international relations profoundly. Thus the attitude of neighbouring states was critical. This is what Bismarck meant by talking of the primacy of foreign relations. The most obvious opponent of German unification was France, which had a strong interest in keeping Germany divided.

Bismarck

OCR   M4
NICCEA   M4

Bismarck came from a family of **Junkers** (Prussian aristocracy). His main aim, many historians would argue, was to preserve the social and political power of the Junkers. For this reason he was anti-liberal in 1848. Another important aim was to expand Prussia's power within Germany and end Austria's predominance. From 1851 to 1859 he was the leader of the Prussian delegation to the Diet of the German Confederation, where he took every opportunity to challenge Austria's predominance.

The Liberals also wished to preserve the militia, which was a sort of citizen army.

You need to be able to discuss this issue.

W.E. Mosse argued that he was an opportunist who exploited the growing weakness of Austria and the isolation of France.

Bismarck was appointed Minister President of Prussia in 1862 because of his known hostility to liberalism. William I had appointed Roon as Minister of War to build up Prussia's military strength. Roon proposed to expand the infantry, reduce the size of the militia and re-equip the army with breech-loading rifles. The Liberals, who had a majority in the Prussian parliament, opposed the cost of these reforms. William therefore called in Bismarck, who proceeded to collect the necessary taxes without parliamentary approval.

Bismarck himself later claimed that the process of German unification between 1864 and 1871 had been planned from the beginning. This has been challenged, notably by A.J.P. Taylor in 1952, and most historians now believe that he took advantage of events as they happened, profiting from the mistakes of others.

> **KEY POINT**
> Bismarck may well have planned for a war against Austria, but it is more debatable whether he planned, or even foresaw, the eventual establishment of the German Empire in 1871.

Key points from AS

- **Bismarck and the wars against Denmark and Austria, 1864–66**
  Revise AS pages 110–111

The wars against Denmark and Austria

The Danish and Austrian Wars of 1864 and 1866 demonstrated Bismarck's opportunism in pursuing his aim of overthrowing Austria's predominance in Germany. **The Schleswig-Holstein question** gave him the opportunity to portray himself as the protector of German interests against the King of Denmark and the Convention of Gastein (1865), which brought it to an end, gave him the chance to pick a quarrel with Austria whenever he liked. He then aimed to isolate Austria.

Bismarck, 1815–1898

Prussia also annexed Schleswig-Holstein, Hanover and several other North German states.

Firstly, he gained the support of the Tsar by supporting Russia in the suppression of the Polish Revolt of 1863. He then neutralised France in his meeting with Napoleon III at Biarritz, and went on make an agreement with Italy in April 1866 which virtually committed him to go to war by July.

Almost all the other German states sided with Austria, but even with their support Austria was no match for Prussia's military strength (though the Prussian victory at Sadowa was not as inevitable as it seems in retrospect). Bismarck's success in the war was not entirely due to Prussia's strength and his own diplomatic skill. Circumstances favoured him: the Austrian Emperor and his ministers were men of lesser ability and Austria was a state with serious weaknesses.

The Seven Weeks' War had several important consequences:

- Austria was pushed out of Germany by the abolition of the German Confederation and turned its attention to the Balkans
- the Prussian-dominated North German Confederation was set up
- the Prussian Liberals abandoned their battle with Bismarck over the army and passed the 'iron budget' in 1866
- French opinion was alarmed by the sudden emergence of a powerful new state to its east.

> Did the North German Confederation represent a Prussian takeover of northern Germany to serve Prussian ends rather than the aims of the German nationalists? Many historians, e.g. Otto Pflanze, claim that Bismarck's aim was to protect the Junker domination of Prussia against Liberals and nationalists. Unification achieved by a Liberal revolution would threaten the Junkers.
>
> Was the North German Confederation all that Bismarck wanted? A.J.P. Taylor thought so and argued that the war with France and the creation of the second Reich were not part of his plans.

KEY ISSUES

Key points from AS

- The Franco-Prussian war
Revise AS pages 111–112

He kept Britain neutral by revealing Napoleon III's designs on Belgium and Luxemburg and he encouraged Russia to repudiate the Black Sea clauses.

Erich Eyck demonstrated that he engineered the candidature, but whether he intended to provoke war is more debatable.

Did Bismarck provoke the Franco-Prussian War?

There is little doubt that Bismarck thought a war against France was very likely after 1866 and that he prepared for one. This does not mean that such a war was a necessary part of his plans, but simply that he realised that it might be forced upon him. French opinion was alarmed by the growth of Prussian power and Napoleon's position in France was increasingly unstable. Bismarck could not possibly agree to Napoleon's demands for territory in Belgium, Luxemburg or the Rhineland. Consequently it became increasingly likely that Napoleon would be forced to seek a way out of his difficulties by winning a diplomatic or military victory at Prussia's expense. In these circumstances it was typical of Bismarck that he prepared for war by isolating France and that he brought it about at a time when it suited him.

An alternative interpretation, however, is that Bismarck recognised that German unification could not be complete and secure without the defeat of France and that he therefore planned for a war he regarded as necessary and inevitable.

A key issue in deciding whether the Franco-Prussian War was planned by Bismarck is his role in the Hohenzollern candidature for the Spanish throne. It seems likely that he instigated it, perhaps with the aim of provoking a war which by 1870 he regarded as inevitable. Alternatively he may have seriously hoped for a Hohenzollern on the Spanish throne, raising Prussian prestige and gaining a useful ally. That the episode led to war, however, was as much due to French mistakes as to Bismarck. When it became apparent that Napoleon was bent on either humiliating Prussia or war, Bismarck opted for war but used the Ems telegram to shift the blame onto Napoleon.

A.J.P. Taylor would argue that it was another example of Bismarck's opportunism.

It is also debatable whether Bismarck intended from the outset that the war should lead to the establishment of the Empire or whether he simply took advantage of the widespread support for Prussia in the south German states to bring it about. It may even have been that the upsurge of national feeling left him with little choice.

> - Did Bismarck plan a war against France from the beginning?
> - Did he intend the Hohenzollern candidature to lead to war?
> - Did he intend the war to lead to the establishment of the Empire?

The German Empire

The constitution of the Second Reich, which was basically the same as that of the North German Confederation of 1867, gives some clues as to Bismarck's essentially conservative aims. The illusion of democracy was provided by a Reichstag elected by universal male suffrage, but its powers were limited. It had no control over the Chancellor or ministers. The Bundesrat, which was composed of representatives of the states, was dominated by Prussia and thus gave Prussia a veto over constitutional change. Furthermore, the Prussian contribution to imperial finances, which was far larger than that of any other state, was controlled by the Prussian Diet (assembly). This in turn was dominated by the Junkers because of the three class electoral system.

The Junkers had far more members in proportion to their numbers than the other classes.

> The constitution effectively set up a Prussian dominated Reich, with Prussia itself controlled by the Junkers.

11.2 Hitler and the Nazi state 1933–39

After studying this section you should be able to:

- *explain why the Nazis had widespread support in Germany*
- *assess the role of propaganda and terror in the Nazi state*
- *explain the relationship between the Führer, the party and the state*
- *discuss the view that Hitler was a 'weak dictator'*

How popular was Nazi rule?

AQA	M4 (synoptic)
EDEXCEL	M6 (synoptic)
WJEC	M6 (synoptic)

Germany in the early 1930s faced political, social and economic collapse. The Nazis offered the hope of economic recovery and firm government. This explains the rapid growth in support for them. Between 1933 and 1939 they enjoyed genuine popularity with much of the German population. This was primarily because of the success of their economic and foreign policies but also because of their appeal to many different classes of society.

The middle classes had suffered particularly badly from the 1923 inflation.

- The core of their support from the mid-1920s onwards lay in the lower middle and skilled working classes – people who feared that economic breakdown would undermine the modest prosperity and status they had achieved. The Nazi 'economic miracle' in the 1930s consolidated this support.
- Almost equally important was the support of the peasants. The Nazis' share of the rural vote rose from 22 per cent in 1930 to 52 per cent in 1933. Falling farm prices in the late 1920s and early 1930s accounted for this. The Nazis promised to reduce the burdens on small farmers and honoured this by

Key points from AS

- **Hitler's belief and policies**
  Revise AS pages 138–139
- **The response of the German people to Nazism**
  Revise AS page 146

introducing import controls, fixed farm prices and laws to give them security of tenure.

- **Industrialists** saw in Hitler a bulwark against the threat of Communism. The Nazis received substantial financial support from industrialists such as the steel magnate Thyssen.
- Although the majority of the **industrial working class** before 1933 supported the Socialists or Communists, it is clear that many voted for the Nazis. The economic gains of Nazi rule, particularly full employment, won working-class support after 1933, even though trade unions were banned.

The Nazis also appealed to **German nationalism**. In the Harzberg Agreement (1930) they allied with the Nationalist Party. This not only gave them the support of nationalist opinion but also the backing of the industrialist and press magnate, Hugenberg, and the president of the Reichsbank, Dr Schacht, who was later to play a major role in the Nazi 'economic miracle'.

Finally, the Nazis gained support by their appeal to the streak of **anti-semitism** in German society, which they exploited in the Nuremberg Laws and Kristallnacht.

> All the evidence suggests that the Nazis were genuinely popular in Germany in the 1930s.
>
> **KEY POINT**

Propaganda and terror

AQA	M4 (synoptic)
EDEXCEL	M6 (synoptic)
WJEC	M6 (synoptic)

The Nazis gained overwhelming approval for their policies in plebiscites during the 1930s. How far was this the result of propaganda and terror? Undoubtedly these were effective and played a part, but it is unlikely that they did more than exaggerate results which the Nazis would have achieved without them. Goebbels as Minister of Propaganda controlled the arts and the media. He made particularly effective use of the new media of film and radio. There was also, of course, strict censorship.

The first concentration camp was set up at Dachau in 1933. It housed mainly political enemies such as Socialists and Communists.

The main instrument of terror was **the SS**, an elite paramilitary body under the command of Himmler. From 1933 it controlled the concentration camps and from 1934 the police. In 1936 Himmler became police chief for the whole of Germany and also took control of **the Gestapo** (secret police). The SS also had its own security service, the SD, under Heydrich. Through this network of police organisations the Nazis suppressed almost all opposition. Nevertheless, some historians argue that the extent of the terror should not be exaggerated. The regime in the concentration camps was brutal but they were not extermination camps in the 1930s and the number of inmates was relatively small, though it increased to 25 000 in 1939. The influence of the SS was more limited than it became during the Second World War and Himmler's power was challenged by other powerful figures outside the SS such as Goering and Bormann.

Resistance

AQA	M4 (synoptic)
EDEXCEL	M6 (synoptic)
WJEC	M6 (synoptic)

Key points from AS

- **The churches**
  Revise AS pages 143–144
- **The army**
  Revise AS page 144

Such opposition as survived was largely underground. About 200 000 members of the Communist and Socialist parties were imprisoned or went into exile, leaving no organised political opposition. There was some opposition from within **the churches**. In 1937 the pope issued an encyclical criticising the regime, particularly its acceptance of euthanasia, and some 400 Catholic bishops and priests were sent to concentration camps. The same fate awaited those Protestants who spoke out, such as Niemöller and Bonhoeffer. For the most part, however, members of the churches accepted the regime, often with as much enthusiasm as other Germans.

On the other hand they approved strongly of rearmament.

The only other potential source of opposition was **the army**. The general staff became increasingly worried by the trend of Hitler's foreign policy and opposed his plans for the expansion of Germany, as set out in the Hossbach memorandum in 1937. Hitler's response was to dismiss the War Minister, Blomberg, and the Commander-in-Chief of the Army, Fritsch, and put the army under his direct command through the OKW. When General Beck in 1938 tried to persuade the General Staff to remove Hitler, he received no support and resigned.

The structure of the Nazi state

AQA	M4 (synoptic)
EDEXCEL	M6 (synoptic)
WJEC	M6 (synoptic)

Ein Volk, ein Reich, ein Führer!

A poster of 1938–39 with the rallying cry, 'One People, One Country, One Leader!'

In theory the government of Nazi Germany was highly centralised. There was only one political party and so, according to the Law to Ensure the Unity of the Party and State, the party was the state. Through the process of Gleichschaltung all other organisations were subordinated to the Nazi party. Both party and state expressed the will of one man, Hitler, the Führer or Leader. According to Nazi theory the unifying principle of the Nazi state was the **Führerprinzip** or 'leader principle'. Through unquestioning obedience to their great leader the German people would achieve their destiny. Many Germans warmed to this idea in reaction against the failure of the Weimar democracy.

In practice power was diffused through conflicting authorities. Government was still organised through the old ministries and the provincial governments and local authorities also survived. Alongside them, and competing with them for authority, were the institutions of the Nazi party. The powers of government and party authorities often overlapped. Thus the work of the Party Chancellery under Martin Bormann overlapped with that of the Ministry of the Interior, as did that of the Nazi Bureau for Foreign Affairs with the Foreign Office. Alongside the provincial governments were the Nazi Gauleiters, though sometimes the same person was both Gauleiter and provincial minister-president or governor. Another complicating feature was Hitler's tendency to create special commissions for specific tasks: Todt, for instance, was given the job of building the autobahns. Himmler as head of the SS was made directly answerable to Hitler, which led to conflict with both the Ministry of the Interior and the Party Chancellery.

> Although Nazi government was highly centralised, in practice there was a good deal of administrative confusion.

KEY POINT

You need to be familiar with this debate.

This has led some historians to describe Hitler as a **'weak dictator'**. He was lazy, frequently getting up late and doing little work. He was bored by administrative detail, seeing himself as the visionary leader who made the big decisions and left their implementation to subordinates. The Cabinet rarely met. The Führerprinzip, however, meant that if Hitler was not involved decisions were not made. Thus the system has been described as 'authoritarian anarchy'. Martin Broszat describes Hitler's government as 'a shambles of constantly shifting power-bases and warring factions'.

There was also much corruption.

An alternative interpretation is that Hitler was content to leave his subordinates competing with each other on the principle of 'divide and rule'. Ian Kershaw argues that distancing himself from day-to-day political conflict enabled Hitler to 'represent the image of national unity'. Certainly the system meant that ultimately the influence of subordinates depended on which of them had the ear of the Führer. Moreover, Hitler did make decisions on matters which he considered vital such as foreign policy. The special agencies he set up did get things done. The success of Nazi foreign and economic policies in the 1930s suggests that the 'authoritarian anarchy' view is rather exaggerated. The 'intentionalist' school of historians claims that Hitler's vision or 'intentions' were at the heart of Nazi government even if the details were left to others.

E.g. Andreas Hillgruber and Klaus Hildebrand.

KEY
ISSUE

Was Hitler a 'weak dictator'?

Hitler's lieutenants

AQA ▶ M4
EDEXCEL ▶ M6

He held all these posts simultaneously.

The effect of this system was to give some of Hitler's lieutenants considerable power.

- **Goering** was appointed President of the Reichstag in 1932, and Minister President of Prussia and Air Minister in 1933. He was responsible for building up the Luftwaffe and took charge of the Four Year Plan which was introduced in 1936.
- **Goebbels** was put in charge of Nazi party propaganda in 1929. His appointment as Minister for Information and Propaganda followed naturally when the Nazis came to power in 1933. He was also Gauleiter of Berlin.
- **Himmler** was appointed head of the SS in 1929. The role of the SS in the Night of the Long Knives in 1934 left him in a powerful position. In 1936 he became chief of the unified German police forces. His power was enormous: he controlled the police, the SS, the SD (the party's spy service headed by Heydrich), the Gestapo and the Death's Head Unit, which ran the concentration camps – in effect, a 'state within a state'.

This set of institutions became so powerful that some historians claim that by 1941 the Nazi state had become the SS state.

KEY POINT

Josef Goebbels

Heinrich Himmler

11.3 Hitler and the origins of the Second World War

After studying this section you should be able to:

- *discuss the importance of Nazi ideology in shaping Hitler's foreign policy*
- *explain how Hitler freed Germany from the restrictions imposed at Versailles*
- *discuss the changing relationship between Hitler and Mussolini*
- *explain how Hitler's foreign policy led to the Second World War*

The aims of Nazi foreign policy

AQA ▶ M6
EDEXCEL ▶ M4
NICCEA ▶ M4
WJEC ▶ M4

Hitler set out his foreign policy aims in *Mein Kampf*: he wanted to overturn the hated Versailles settlement, to reunite all German peoples in a Greater Germany and to acquire 'lebensraum' – living space for the Germans. The notion of struggle was central to his view of the world and he therefore believed that it was the duty of the German state to acquire 'land and soil', which could only be won at the expense of 'Russia and the border states subject to her'.

The Taylor view...

Historical debate focuses on how far these ideas actually shaped Hitler's foreign policy when he came to power. **A.J.P. Taylor** argued in *The Origins of the Second World War* (1961) that his foreign policy aims were in the tradition of previous German statesmen. He was not pursuing a predetermined strategy of aggression but merely responding to opportunities as they arose. His success between 1933 and 1939 was due to the failings of other European leaders, especially those of Britain and France, and the outbreak of war in 1939 was the unintended outcome of a miscalculation of the response of Britain and France to his demands for Danzig and the Polish corridor.

...and the views of his critics.

Critics of this view argue that Nazi ideology, as set out in *Mein Kampf*, added a potent new element to German foreign policy. Alan Bullock, for example, argues that his aims did not change but he pursued them with 'enormous flexibility of method'. Thus, although he recognised that Lebensraum could only be acquired at the expense of Russia, he was prepared to make a pact with Stalin in 1939 to partition Poland. Similarly his attitude towards Britain changed from regarding it as a possible ally to an enemy.

Most historians now regard Hitler's foreign policy as differing from traditional German foreign policy in several ways.

- He abandoned the aim of acquiring an overseas empire, concentrating instead on control over Eastern Europe and self-sufficiency.
- His attitude towards Eastern Europe introduced a distinctive racial element – the belief in the destiny of the Aryan races to rule over the Slav races.

When Germany joined the League of Nations and the Kellogg-Briand pact.

- His attitude to Russia was coloured by his hatred of Communism. Russia was therefore not just a strategic threat but an ideological enemy.
- He wished to break up the system of international co-operation in which Germany had participated in the 1920s. He preferred bilateral agreements.

> Was Hitler's ultimate aim domination of Europe or, as Andreas Hillgruber and Klaus Hildebrand would argue, domination of the world?
>
> **KEY ISSUE**

The challenge to the Versailles settlement, 1933–36

AQA	M6
EDEXCEL	M4
NICCEA	M4
WJEC	M4

Hitler's first moves were cautious. He continued for a while to participate in the Geneva **Disarmament Conference**, but in October 1933 withdrew on the grounds that Germany was not being given equal treatment. At the same time he withdrew from the League of Nations. He balanced these moves with a ten-year Non-Aggression Pact with Poland in 1934. The purpose of this was to break up the French system of alliances in Eastern Europe.

See also Chapter 9.2, p. 120.

By March 1935 he felt confident enough to issue a direct challenge to the Versailles settlement by announcing that Germany now had an air force and by reintroducing conscription. This prompted Britain, France and Italy to make an agreement (the **Stresa Front**, April 1935) to resist by force any future attempt to change the settlement. This soon broke down as a result of the Anglo-German Naval Agreement (June 1935) and Mussolini's invasion of Ethiopia.

This was a gamble on Hitler's part, but its success encouraged him to make further aggressive moves.

This encouraged Hitler to gamble on the next major breach of Versailles, the **remilitarisation of the Rhineland** in March 1936. This was a crucial step. It allowed Hitler to fortify Germany's western frontier, thus protecting it against France and making it easier to concentrate on expansion to the east. France was unwilling to oppose Hitler without British assistance and Britain was unwilling to intervene. British opinion regarded Hitler's action as redressing a legitimate grievance.

The remilitarisation of the Rhineland completed the destruction of the Versailles settlement so far as it applied to Germany itself and opened the way for the expansion of Germany to unite all Germans in a Greater Germany.

Hitler and Mussolini: the forging of the Axis

AQA	M6
EDEXCEL	M4
NICCEA	M4
WJEC	M4

This would mean a powerful new state on Italy's northern borders.

Despite similarities between Nazism and Fascism, relations between Hitler and Mussolini were at first poor. Hitler viewed Mussolini as a potential ally against the Versailles settlement but Mussolini was alarmed by the revival of German power. When the Austrian Nazis assassinated Chancellor Dollfuss in 1934 and attempted to seize power, Mussolini feared that this could lead to a union between Austria and Germany. He moved troops to the Austrian frontier as a warning and Hitler quickly disowned the Austrian Nazis. In response to this episode and to German rearmament Mussolini joined Britain and France in the Stresa Front in 1935.

The invasion of Ethiopia changed everything. Mussolini, angered by the imposition of sanctions by Britain and France, turned to Germany. In October 1936 Germany and Italy signed an agreement which became known as the **Rome-Berlin Axis**. When the Spanish Civil War broke out, both Italy and Germany gave military assistance to Franco. Italian involvement widened the breach with Britain and France and increased Mussolini's dependence on Germany. In 1937 Italy joined Germany and Japan in the Anti-Comintern Pact. When Germany took over Austria in the Anschluss (March 1938), Mussolini accepted it without question – a complete reversal of the policy he had pursued in 1934.

From 1936 Mussolini was increasingly in the shadow of Hitler.

Hitler in Rome with Mussolini

The road to war, 1936–39

AQA	M6
EDEXCEL	M4
NICCEA	M4
WJEC	M4, M5

Hitler consolidated his position in 1936–7. Rearmament proceeded apace and the Four Year Plan was put into effect with the aim of making Germany ready for war, if necessary, in that time. At the end of 1937, according to the **Hossbach memorandum**, he informed his military commanders of his intention to acquire Lebensraum, beginning with the takeover of Austria and Czechoslovakia. This would have to be completed by 1943–5 at the latest, because by then Germany would have lost its military superiority. This appeared to suggest that Hitler had a timetable for his expansionist policies, though A.J.P. Taylor thought he was simply daydreaming.

The expansion of Germany, 1935–39

In 1938 the creation of an enlarged Reich got under way.

- The **Anschluss** with Austria (March 1938). The Austrian Nazis, led by Seyss-Inquart, caused growing disorder. Schuschnigg, the Chancellor, tried to defuse the situation by holding a referendum on the question of union with Germany. This provided an excuse for Hitler to intervene and take over Austria. It was another triumph for Hitler in the eyes of German nationalists.
- The **Sudetenland** (September 1938). Hitler used the excuse of discontent, stirred up by the Sudeten German Nazis, to demand that the Sudetenland be handed over from Czechoslovakia to Germany. At the **Munich Conference** Britain and France gave way to this demand. The USSR was not consulted.
- In March 1939 German troops occupied the rest of Czechoslovakia. Bohemia and Moravia became German protectorates; Slovakia was nominally independent. For the first time Hitler had taken over a country which was not German-speaking – a development which played a crucial role in changing British policy towards Germany.
- Memel was handed over by Lithuania (March 1939).
- In April 1939 Hitler demanded Danzig and a road and railway across the Polish Corridor. The Poles, fearing that this was a prelude to a German invasion, refused.
- The **Nazi-Soviet Pact** (August). Hitler believed that with Russia neutral the British government would revert to its policy of appeasement.
- Germany invaded Poland on September 1. On September 3 Britain declared war.

Donald Watt argues that Hitler wanted a war with Poland, anticipated a subsequent war against Russia but did not expect a general European war with Britain and France.

> **KEY POINT**
> Hitler calculated that Britain and France would either back down or offer only token support to Poland. He was wrong.

Sample question and model answer

Study Sources A to E and answer questions (a) and (b) which follow.

Source A

From *Twelve Years with Hitler*, by O. Dietrich, 1955. Dietrich was Hitler's Press Officer.

In the 12 years of his rule in Germany, Hitler produced the biggest confusion in government that has ever existed in a civilised state. ... It was not laziness or an excessive degree of tolerance which led the otherwise so energetic and forceful Hitler to tolerate this real witch's cauldron of struggles for position and conflicts over competence. It was intentional. With this technique he systematically disorganised the upper echelons of the Reich leaders in order to develop and further the authority of his own will until it became a despotic tyranny.

Source B

From *Hitler, A Study in Tyranny*, by A. Bullock, 1952.

Hitler bore the final responsibility for whatever was done by the regime, but he hated the routine work of government, and, once he had stabilized his power, he showed comparatively little interest in what was done by his departmental Ministers except to lay down general lines of policy. In the Third Reich each of the Party bosses, Goering, Goebbels, Himmler and Ley, created a private empire for himself. ... Hitler deliberately allowed this to happen; the rivalries which resulted only increased his power as the supreme arbiter. Nobody ever had any doubt where the final authority lay – the examples of Röhm and Gregor Strasser were there, if anyone needed reminding.

Source C

From *Explaining Hitler's Germany*, by J. Hiden and J. Farquharson, 1983.

Whilst newer research has destroyed the concept of a monolith it equally suggests that the idea of 'weak dictatorship' is unsatisfactory as an overall explicatory model of the Third Reich. The Röhm affair illustrates how Hitler could run the entire gamut of the exercise of power. When the SA leader complained in October 1933 that too many people in the Party thought the real revolution was over when in fact it was not, Hitler allowed him to set up SA Commissars in Prussia inside Goering's own domain, and these also competed with the Party in general. This apparently shows Hitler as weak and indecisive, but the point has been made that he was probably riding with events until an opportune moment arrived to settle the problem. As we now know this came on the night of 30 June 1934, when the SA leadership, including Röhm, was annihilated on Hitler's orders. Clearly then, the Führer could and did intervene decisively at key moments.

Source D

From *The Nazi Dictatorship*, by I. Kershaw, 1993.

Distant rather than immediate leadership in everyday affairs, and hesitancy about deciding before the situation had all but resolved itself were not simply a reflection of Hitler's style of rule, but were necessary components of his 'charismatic' Führer-authority, helping to maintain both in the ruling circle and among the people themselves the myth of Hitler's unerringly correct judgement and his independence from factional disputes – from 'normal politics'.

Source E

From *Hitler and Nazi Germany*, by F. McDonough, 1999.

Hitler frequently by-passed formal government departments to set up rival institutions and specialist agencies. It has been estimated that there were 42 separate agencies with executive power to implement policy within the central government machine of Nazi Germany. Hitler was quite aware of this confusion, but he consistently blocked initiatives designed to make the governmental structure more efficient and co-ordinated. In essence, the political system in Nazi Germany was a complex maze of personal rivalries and overlapping party and state institutions, which resulted in chaos and confusion.

Sample question and model answer *(continued)*

Both parts of this question incorporate synoptic assessment.

(a) Using your own knowledge and the evidence of Sources A, B and E, what do you consider to be the main features of the organisation of government in Nazi Germany? **[10]**

E.g. an agency under Todt to supervise building of autobahns.

(a) Hitler did not reform the system of government in Germany. The existing ministries and local authorities of Weimar Germany continued to work normally. Alongside them were Nazi Party organisations and special agencies created by Hitler. Source E refers to 42 separate agencies. Key figures in the Nazi establishment were allowed to build up private empires in competition with each other (source B). E.g. Schacht, Goering and Ley were all involved in economic policy. There was little co-ordination between these ministries and agencies. All were responsible to Hitler, but he was often uninterested in what they were doing. The Cabinet rarely met (not at all after 1938). Ultimately, all initiatives depended on Hitler as Führer, i.e. on who had his ear at any time. The result was the 'confusion' described in source A.

(b) Using your own knowledge and all five sources, how far do you agree with Dietrich (Source A) that the 'confusion in government' in Hitler's Germany was 'intentional'? **[20]**

This is an outline answer, to which you should add more detail.

Structuralists are also known as functionalists.

(b) Underlying this question is the debate among historians between 'intentionalists' and 'structuralists'. Intentionalists claim that Hitler's 'intentions' were at the heart of all Nazi policies and the key to understanding them. Structuralists see Hitler as a 'weak dictator', never in complete control of Nazi Germany and acting as an umpire in disputes between rival power blocks.

Sources A and B support the intentionalist view. Source A claims that Hitler deliberately created confusion in order to increase his own authority and make it a 'despotic tyranny'. Dietrich cannot believe that the 'energetic and forceful' Hitler could have allowed the confusion to arise unintentionally. Source B also sees Hitler as 'deliberately' allowing rivalries to develop in order to increase his own power.

Source E also implicitly supports the intentionalist view, arguing that Hitler was aware of the confusion and blocked attempts to remedy it. Source D only hints at confusion in government ('hesitancy about deciding') but supports the view that Hitler deliberately kept aloof from factional struggles to enhance his 'charismatic' power as Führer. The evidence of source C is more indirect. It rejects the idea of 'weak dictatorship', using the example of the Night of the Long Knives to show that Hitler could be decisive. The remark that 'he was probably riding with events' is revealing: it suggests that Hitler was in control even when he appeared not to be. As a set, therefore, the sources support the intentionalist view.

Use own knowledge as well as sources.

If you can, explain the arguments of structuralists such as Broszat, who claim he was a weak dictator.

Nevertheless it remains debatable whether Hitler was pursuing a deliberate policy of 'divide and rule' which explains the chaotic nature of Nazi government. Hitler <u>was</u> lazy. He avoided the routine work of government because he simply did not like it. Decisions were often taken in response to the last advice received. Creation of specialist agencies was a way of cutting through bureaucracy but often simply created more rivalries. It seems that his 'intentions' were important in spheres which interested him, e.g. foreign affairs; but organisation of government was not one of them. It may be that he had no particular plan in mind but simply responded to problems as they arose and in the process created an organisational jungle in which he could be no more than an arbiter between rivals.

Practice examination questions

1 Study Sources A to D and answer questions (a) and (b) which follow.

Source A

From the *Memoirs* of Frederick von Holstein, Prussian diplomat, published in 1906.

My impression of the respective attitudes of Bismarck and the Emperor Napoleon to the question of war is this. Bismarck handled the Hohenzollern candidature rather as one waves a lighted match over a gas tap to see whether it is turned on. The Emperor was free to make the candidature seem acceptable or unacceptable to the French. The provocative speech of Gramont on 6 July showed, in Bismarck's opinion, that France had decided on war, since Prussia could not possibly tolerate such language. So from then on Bismarck took a hand in things. From July onwards Bismarck wanted war, but Napoleon had wanted it before then.

Source B

From *Europe since Napoleon*, by D. Thomson, 1957.

There is no doubt that Bismarck, backed by Moltke and Roon in charge of the Prussian army, wanted and planned for war against Austria as the next step in Prussian domination of Germany. Bismarck might have preferred to gain his ends without war, but he came to regard war as indispensable. Despite the complexities of the Schleswig-Holstein question, it was only a pretext for war; despite the strenuous diplomatic manoeuvres throughout Europe in 1865 and 1866, and the series of proposals to preserve peace, neither had any chance of preventing Prussia from attacking Austria whenever she chose.

Source C

From *Years of Nationalism*, by L. Cowie and R. Wolfson, 1985.

It was traditionally held that Bismarck achieved the unification of Germany by embarking on a set plan of war and diplomacy that deliberately set out to hoodwink or subdue the other powers. In this scheme, he created a war with Denmark in 1864 in order to provide the excuse for a subsequent war with Austria, he made Napoleon III believe France would benefit from Prussia's defeat of Austria, won Austria to his side by the generous terms of the Treaty of Prague and then connived with the Spanish to bring about a war in which he could humiliate France. In this scheme of things, Bismarck was the master diplomat, manipulating the other powers of Europe with consummate ease.

This view, created at least in part by Bismarck himself, is now regarded more as a pattern imposed on events after they took place than before. Instead Bismarck is seen as a talented politician and expert opportunist, who took advantage of situations as they arose and who was in a number of cases, downright lucky in the way in which others behaved and events turned out.

Source D

From *The Origins of the Wars of German Unification*, by W. Carr, 1991.

It is abundantly clear that Bismarck played a major role in promoting the Hohenzollern candidacy from February 1870 onwards. This does not of course, explain his motives for seeking to put a Hohenzollern prince on a Spanish throne. Because he concealed his part in the affair and re-edited the Ems Telegram, it does not follow that his objective from the outset was war. Broadly speaking, there are three possible interpretations of his actions in 1870. First, that he was without blame, did not seek war but had it forced on him by the trigger-happy French. Secondly, that he deliberately sought war, believing this to be the only way to achieve final unification, i.e. to extend the boundaries of Prussia down to the Bodensee. And thirdly, that he made use of the candidacy to try to out-manoeuvre the French, his intention was to score a diplomatic victory, throwing them into disarray, and to absorb the southern states when a favourable opportunity presented itself. Only when the manoeuvre misfired did Bismarck opt for war to escape an impasse.

Practice examination questions (continued)

(a) Compare the value of Sources A and D as explanations of Bismarck's motives in promoting the Hohenzollern candidature. [10]

(b) How far, and why, do Sources A to D offer different views as to whether Bismarck deliberately planned wars in order to achieve German unification? [20]

2 Why was Bismarck more successful than the revolutionaries of 1848–1849 in ending Austria's influence in Germany? [30]

OCR 1999

3 How successfully did the Nazis gain and retain the loyalty of the German people in the years 1933 to 1939? [30]

Assessment and Qualifications Alliance 1999

4 'Hitler's foreign policy successes between 1933 and 1939 rested on his remarkable tactical skills and ability to exploit his opponents' weaknesses.' How far do you agree with this view? [30]

Practice examination answers

Chapter 1 The development of democracy in Britain, 1832–1992

1 (a) Forces promoting reform:
- Underlying forces – social change (rise of industrial middle class, changes in population distribution, growth of a politically aware working class – Chartists, trade unions).
- Radical tradition from 18th century – 19th century radicals such as Bright and Chamberlain. Ideal of 'one man (and later one woman), one vote'.
- Pressure for reform from those without the vote: 1832 middle classes (Birmingham Political Union) and working classes (reform riots); 1838–48 Chartists (unsuccessful but gave issue high profile); 1867 working-class agitation (Hyde Park riots). Women's suffrage movement – suffragettes.
- Pressure from above. 1832 Whigs saw limited reform as politically advantageous and necessary to avert revolution and attach the middle classes to the constitution. 1867 Disraeli – political advantage for Conservatives ('dishing the Whigs'). Gladstone had already become an advocate ('pale of the constitution' speech).

(b) Factors hindering reform.
- Obstruction from above, most obviously in 1832 (Tories). Reform was only possible if those who already had political power were willing to share it.
- Fear that reform would lead to revolution (reform riots, Chartism). Mistrust of working classes (e.g. Adullamites in 1867).
- Traditional ideas about the role of women.
- Party political calculation, e.g. Liberals reluctant to grant vote to women for fear they would vote Conservative.

2 The key theme is the replacement of the Liberals by Labour.
- The Gladstonian **Liberal** Party (a coalition of Whigs, Peelites and Radicals) won first election after 1867 Reform Act. In power 1868–74 and 1880–5, but split over Home Rule in 1886; Liberal Unionists eventually joined Conservatives.
- 1906 Liberal election victory. In power until 1915 – Liberal reforms. But there were underlying differences between Gladstonian and 'New' Liberals and Liberals also faced challenge from infant Labour Party.
- 1916 Asquith–Lloyd George split. 1922 election – Liberals won fewer seats than Labour. Remained third party thereafter, reaching lowest point in 1950s.
- Underlying reasons for decline include rise of working-class electorate and of trade unionism, divided leadership, lack of organisation and funds, the impact of the electoral system on third parties. They were not identified with any interest group or class, unlike Labour.
- **Labour** emerged from growth of trade unions and socialist societies, which came together in Labour Representation Committee (1900). Twenty-nine MPs in 1906 as result of Gladstone–MacDonald Electoral Pact. 1922 emerged as main opposition party. 1924 and 1929–31 Labour minority governments, but overtaken by 1931 financial crisis.

- 1945 election – first Labour majority government (until 1951). 1964–70 and 1974–9 Wilson and Callaghan governments. Increasingly weakened by economic difficulties and association with trade unions. 1979 election, followed by bitter internal disputes which kept Labour out of office.

3 Outline role of trade unions in 1868: New Model unions, with industrial rather than political aims. Then explain the main turning points:
- 'New' Unions in the 1890s – more political in outlook.
- Formation of Labour Representation Committee in 1900; importance of Taff Vale Case (1901).
- Liberals, Labour and trade unions: Trade Disputes Act (1906) and Trade Union Act (1913).
- Wave of strikes, 1910–13 – syndicalism.
- Industrial disputes of 1920–1 – collapse of Triple Alliance.
- General Strike (1926) – impact of failure on trade unions and Labour movement.
- Rise of Labour Party in the 1920s – two Labour ministries – collapse in 1931 – weakness of trade unions and Labour in 1930s.
- Labour victory in 1945. Trade unions at height of their influence 1945–79, under both Labour and Conservative governments.
- Growing unease at effect of trade union power on economy – 'winter of discontent' 1978–9.
- Thatcher reforms of trade union law in 1980s.

4 Outline situation in 1868: no popular press, London and provincial papers catered for middle class. Then explain main developments:
- 1867 Reform Act – working-class electorate in boroughs, followed by 1870 Education Act – beginning of (almost) universal elementary education.
- 1896 foundation of the *Daily Mail* by Alfred Harmsworth, later Lord Northcliffe – the first mass circulation newspaper. Designed to appeal to people with limited education. Followed by *Daily Express* (1900), *Daily Mirror* (1904) and *Daily Herald* (1912).
- 1918 Representation of the People Act – mass electorate. Role of popular press as opinion formers became even more important. Most of the mass circulation newspapers throughout the 20th century supported Conservatives.
- Radio: 1922 formation of British Broadcasting Company (became the BBC, in 1926). By 1939 90 per cent of households had a 'wireless'. The BBC became an important source of news but not a direct influence on voters like the popular press. But radio changed relationship between politicians and voters because it was a direct means of communication. Baldwin proved particularly adept at using it. Churchill used it to great effect to boost national morale during the Second World War.
- Spread of television in 1950s – an even more powerful vehicle of mass communication. First major politician to make effective use of it was Macmillan. From the 1960s the ability to perform effectively on television was a vital attribute for the successful politician.

Chapter 2 Poor Law to Welfare State 1830–1948

1
- Provision for the poor in 1830; the Speenhamland system.
- Poor Law Commission recommended reform on grounds of cost, administrative efficiency and belief that outdoor relief encouraged dependency: workhouse test would promote self-reliance. Needs of the poor were only recognised in narrowly defined cases of unavoidable poverty (e.g. sickness). No account taken of cyclical unemployment in industrial areas.
- Some mitigation of harshness of workhouse system in mid-century because of awareness of need.
- Increasing awareness of need at turn of century with Booth and Rowntree surveys and effects of working-class electorate on political opinion. Views of 'New Liberals' led to Liberal reforms – old age pensions, meals for needy children, 1911 National Insurance. But opponents objected to non-contributory pensions and state subsidy for National Insurance. The Poor Law remained.
- Inter-war years: basic principles of Liberal reforms accepted and extended by unemployment insurance schemes, an improved pension scheme, abolition of the Poor Law and establishment of the Unemployment Assistance Board.
- Though the balance between awareness of need and cost had changed markedly since the mid 19th century, the tension remained. Unemployment was high, so to cut costs the unpopular Means Test was introduced.

2
- Poor Law Amendment Act (a social reform even though in many ways it made matters worse for the poor) was primarily a response to ratepayers' alarm at the rising cost of the Poor Law and the ideas of the Utilitarians.
- Factory reform was a response to campaigns by humanitarians and the Ten Hours Movement. Ministers, influenced by laissez faire and opposition of factory owners, sought compromises which delayed reforms.
- The 1848 Public Health Act resulted mainly from Chadwick's 1842 Report and ideas of doctors such as Snow. Chadwick's aim was efficiency – sickness led to poverty. Subsequent piecemeal improvements were drawn together in the great Act of 1875, the work of Cross. An important factor was Disraelian Conservatism (social reform to win support of working-class electors). Cross was also responsible for the Artisans' Dwellings Act

and other public health reforms of Disraeli's Ministry.
- Liberal reforms were the result of 'New Liberalism', which was partly a response to a working-class electorate, the challenge of the Labour Party, increased public awareness of the need for social reform after the Booth and Rowntree surveys. Social reforms in the inter-war years built on the 'social service' state created by the Liberals.
- Further 'significant' social reform took place after 1945: the creation of the welfare state by Labour. This was not the result of being 'pressurised' by outside factors but the electorate turning to Labour to create a better post-war world in the light of the Beveridge Report.

3
- 1840 – laissez faire attitudes prevailed – the state took virtually no responsibility for public health.
- 1848 – first major Public Health Act. Resulted from Chadwick's 1842 Report. Based on utilitarian principles: sickness caused poverty, which led to increased cost for the Poor Law. But the Act did not make local boards of health compulsory.
- Awareness of the problems of public health in an urban society increased in 1850s and 1860s through developments in medical knowledge (especially causes of illnesses such as cholera and typhus). The work of sanitary engineers showed the way forward.
- The pressure for social reform was increased by 1867 Reform Act: to win the support of working-class voters, Disraeli embarked on social reform. In his 1874–80 ministry, Cross introduced the great Public Health Act of 1875, which laid down clear and extensive duties for local boards of health. Also the Artisans' Dwellings Act: this gave local authorities powers, but not the duty, to clear slums and was used to great effect by Chamberlain in Birmingham. Since poor housing was clearly a cause of disease, subsequent Acts in 1890 and 1900 made clearance of insanitary housing a duty.
- In the 20th century public opinion swung increasingly away from laissez faire towards state intervention to tackle social problems, as can be seen in 'New Liberalism' and the rise of the Labour Party. This led to provision of housing for the working class by the state, working through local authorities (Addison, Wheatley and Greenwood Acts, 1919–30). The state also took powers to regulate housing and other developments through planning laws.

Chapter 3 Britain and Ireland 1798–1921

1 Grievances: religion, the land question, relationship with Westminster.
- Catholic emancipation: promised at the time of the Act of Union; not conceded until 1829 under pressure from O'Connell's Catholic Association.
- Church of Ireland – resented by Catholic majority – grievance not tackled until 1869, when it was no longer the main problem.
- The land question. First serious attempt to tackle the problem the 1870 Land Act – unsuccessful – overtaken by agricultural depression, evictions, formation of Land League. 1881 Act tackled major grievances of three Fs. Resulted from pressure of Land War, so seemed to convey message that pressure would bring concessions. Violence continued. Land question finally resolved through land purchase schemes, culminating in Wyndham's Act (1903) – by which time Home Rule had

been the main Irish demand for over 20 years.
- Home Rule proposed by Gladstone (1886 and 1893) but rejected first by the Commons, then the Lords. Finally passed in 1914 as result of Parliament Act, but suspended because of the war. Debatable whether it would have succeeded if passed in 1886 – perhaps Unionists in Ulster would not have been prepared to go as far as in 1914, when civil war seemed certain. The solution of combining partition with Home Rule might have worked but Asquith hesitated.
- After 1916 Home Rule was no longer acceptable to the majority in southern Ireland. Self-government for the south along with partition was the only practicable solution, and then only after the Anglo-Irish War.

2 Obstacles in Ireland.
- The Protestant Ascendancy controlled the land and the church. Had close links with the ruling elite in England.

Chapter 3 Britain and Ireland 1798–1921

Open voting enabled them to control parliamentary elections; when challenged by the Catholic Association in the 1820s, the franchise was restricted. After 1870 Ascendancy power diminished. The Irish Church was disestablished (1869). The Ballot Act (1872) led to the rise of the Nationalist Party. The Land and Land Purchase Acts undermined landlordism.

- Divisions among the Irish. O'Connell v. Young Ireland in 1840s. Divisions in Irish Nationalist Party after fall of Parnell. Most importantly, Catholic south v. Protestant Ulster.
- The major obstacle after 1885 was Ulster Unionism. In 1886, at the time of the First Home Rule Bill, Lord Randolph Churchill 'played the Orange card'. The Third Home Rule Bill led to the Covenant, the Ulster

Volunteers, the Larne gun-running and the probability of civil war in 1914.

Obstacles at Westminster.

- Ignorance of Irish problems. British governments saw the problem as one of law and order (hence coercion) rather than Irish grievances.
- Religion. Tories were the party of the Church and opposed Catholic emancipation.
- English support for unionism. Chamberlain and Liberal Unionists – split Liberal Party over First Home Rule Bill, joined Conservatives in 1895. Bonar Law and Ulster Unionists in 1912–14.
- The House of Lords – Conservative, landowning majority, with close links with the Ascendancy. Rejection of Second Home Rule Bill, 1893.

Chapter 4 German nationalism 1815–1919

1
- Zollverein. Prussian-dominated customs union from 1834 which corresponded closely with the eventual German empire. Excluded Austria. Provided Prussia with internal market of 25 million.
- Development of Prussian economy. Railways (from 1840s) opened up German market and stimulated economic growth, especially in Prussia, which had good natural resources (e.g. coal in Ruhr). By 1860 producing more coal than France. Prussia had capital to finance industrial development and railway building.
- Industrial development and Zollverein underlay Prussian power in 1860s and were basis for unification of Germany under Prussia. But this does not mean they were the cause of unification. Process of unification was political and military, the work of Bismarck.
- Rapid industrial development after unification. Unification provided stimulus – common currency and uniform commercial law introduced – but Germany's natural resources and well-developed transport and banking systems were also important. Coal, iron and steel, electrical engineering and chemicals all highly developed. By 1914 Germany was greatest industrial power in continental Europe.
- This provided basis for, and made possible, William II's aggressive nationalism (Weltpolitik), but was only part of the explanation for it. Political factors (e.g. the character of William, the power of the emperor under the constitution, the role of the army in imperial Germany) must also be taken into account.
- Industrial growth produced an elite of industrial magnates who encouraged nationalistic policies, e.g. building of the navy as it provided industrial contracts.

2
- Liberalism in 1815 had limited appeal, mainly in intellectual circles. Linked with nationalism. Seen as a threat by Metternich, who used Confederation to defend legitimism – Carlsbad Decrees. But some states had constitutions.
- 1848 revolutions – Metternich overthrown, constitutions granted in many states. Frankfurt parliament: aimed to create unified Germany with a liberal constitution but while it debated the definition of Germany ('Grossdeutschland' or 'Kleindeutschland'),

counter-revolutionary forces regained control in Austria and Prussia. The Liberals – intellectuals rather than politicians – had failed.

- Liberals gained a majority in Prussian Parliament in 1858. Clash with William II over taxes for reorganisation of army – appointment of Bismarck (1862), who collected the taxes in defiance of the Assembly.
- Bismarck's wars against Denmark and Austria, leading to North German Confederation, won over Liberals who settled the quarrel over taxes. He succeeded where Liberals had failed: nationalism, previously associated with the Liberals, had been taken over by a Prussian conservative and linked with military strength rather than constitutionalism.
- The imperial constitution, which provided for a Reichstag elected by universal suffrage, pleased Liberals. But it was not a liberal constitution because it gave the Reichstag little power.
- In the 1870s Bismarck allied with National Liberals against Catholics, but quarrelled with them over the size of the army (1874) and broke finally with them over protection in 1879 (free trade was a major Liberal issue). Thereafter he relied on Conservatives and Catholic Centre.
- 1879–1914: Liberals divided into National Liberals and Radicals and lost ground to Conservatives and Socialists. Liberals a declining political force.

3
- For the Liberals, the material used in the previous answer is appropriate.
- Socialists: won half a million votes in Reichstag elections in 1877. Bismarck introduced anti-socialist laws in 1878, but tried to win working-class support by state socialism. Nevertheless socialists gained increasing votes in Reichstag elections – 35 per cent in 1912. Anti-socialist laws lapsed in 1890, but socialists were not allowed any share of power.
- Conclusion: rulers were successful in resisting demands, partly by making concessions on some issues but not others. Liberals were pleased by unification and some aspects of imperial constitution, but did not get a liberal Germany. Socialists were given state socialism but no share in power.

Chapter 5 Economic modernisation in Germany, c.1880–c.1980

1 (a) Both sources point to failings of Nazi 'economic miracle'. Source C: a foreign observer in 1936 notes that reduction of unemployment is partly artificial. Source B: economic growth did occur but was diverted to rearmament, not to improved living standards. Most historians agree with these sources and add that Nazi economic policies, especially Four Year Plan, would have led to inflation if war had not intervened.

(b) • Before 1914 rapid growth of industrial economy mainly due to natural resources, transport, banking, growing population, but government's protectionist policies also helped.

• Government policies 1919–23 disastrous. Led to French occupation of Ruhr, passive resistance and hyper-inflation. Recovery brought about by Stresemann (source A). His policies were attacked, but they brought a fragile prosperity in late 1920s.

Unfortunately this depended on American loans, hence economic crisis in Germany after Wall Street crash. Massive unemployment.

• Nazis virtually eliminated unemployment, partly by artificial means (source C), but also aided by revival of world trade. But their economic policies were directed toward preparation for war (source B) and by 1939 threatened inflation, which could only be prevented by conquest of territories in Eastern Europe to supply food at low prices.

• Post-war: 'economic miracle' in Western Germany – partly result of Erhard's free market policies, but also other factors – Marshall Plan, modern machinery, good labour relations, Korean War. In East Germany government followed Communist path. This made it strongest economy in Eastern Europe but by comparison with West Germany very inefficient (source D).

Chapter 6 Dictatorship in Russia, 1855–1956

1 (a) Source B – Stalin himself sets out his aims: more-efficient agriculture is essential, sees problem as too many small farms and collectivisation as the solution. But B does not tell us how he went about it – by force. Source C reveals the cost. Own knowledge supports this. There was famine in 1932–3. Grain production recovered by the late 1930s but collectivisation did not produce agricultural efficiency.

(b) • In the late 19th century, despite emancipation of the serfs, agriculture was very backward, using traditional methods (source A). There were frequent famines, much rural unrest and poverty.

• Stolypin tried to modernise it (1906–10): peasants were allowed to consolidate strips into privately owned farms. Some progress by 1914, but it was a long-term process, overtaken by war and revolution.

• 1917 revolutions led to redistribution of land from landlords to peasants. Under War Communism agricultural production fell. Famine led to introduction of New Economic Policy – peasants allowed to sell their surplus. Kulaks prospered, but even so most kulaks' farms were relatively small and inefficient.

• Stalin's diagnosis (source B) was probably correct, but his solution, forced collectivisation, produced enormous hardship for kulaks, famine in 1932–3 and a dramatic drop in production (source C). Production only slowly recovered – grain by late 1930s, livestock by 1950s – though collectivisation did make possible some modernisation (motor tractor stations).

• After Second World War agricultural productivity was still low. Hence Khrushchev's Virgin Lands policy: food production increased, but there were problems of poor management and soil erosion. Brezhnev abandoned this policy (source D) and tried to improve things by giving collective farms more freedom. Even so agriculture remained a problem.

2 Three main reasons: strength of tsarist autocracy; failures of Dumas and Provisional Government; seizure of power by Bolsheviks.

• Tsars believed in autocracy and had army and secret police to repress opposition. Nobility and gentry controlled the countryside, even after emancipation.

• Demands for constitutional government confined to intellectuals. Populists tried to arouse peasantry to support demands for reform but failed.

• 1905 revolution: failure in war v. Japan enabled reformist opposition to combine with growing urban proletariat in revolution. Constitution granted (October Manifesto), but loyalty of army and divisions among opposition enabled Tsar to regain control. Concessions whittled down, Dumas only a small step towards constitutional government. Might have led to democracy eventually but for war.

• 1917 Tsar overthrown, Provisional Government established. Summoned a Constituent Assembly to draw up a democratic constitution. But failings of Provisional Government (give details) and ruthlessness of Bolsheviks led to October revolution.

• Lenin dissolved Constituent Assembly as soon as it met. Instead drew up a constitution based on soviets. Defeat of Whites in Civil War left Communists firmly in power.

• USSR was nominally a democracy, especially after introduction of 1936 constitution, but based on a hierarchy of soviets, with ultimate power vested in the Supreme Soviet. In practice power lay in the Communist Party, which embodied the dictatorship of the proletariat and was the only one allowed. Thus liberal democracy was impossible under communist theory.

3 • Tsarist rule was autocratic and repressive. Russia was economically backward. Alexander II tackled this by reforms, especially emancipation. Despite this, agriculture remained inefficient – frequent famines and rural unrest, met by repression. But poverty was not the only reason for discontent – Alexander's reforms disappointed liberals. Faced by reformist movements and terrorism by anarchists, Alexander II reverted to repression. After his assassination Alexander III intensified repression, which Nicholas II continued.

• Failure in war led to revolution in 1905. Tsar forced to make concessions but limited and quickly whittled down (Dumas). Repression returned under Stolypin, but he also introduced agrarian reforms.

• First World War brought end of tsarist rule in 1917 and overthrow of the Provisional Government by Bolsheviks.

• Lenin dissolved the Constituent Assembly at its first meeting and went on to revise the Russian

Chapter 6 Dictatorship in Russia, 1855–1956

constitution, setting up the All-Union Congress of Soviets and the Politburo. Faced by civil war, established the Cheka, i.e. repression.
- Under Stalin, regime became even more repressive. Rapid industrialisation (Five-Year Plans) and

collectivisation forced through by power of the state. Opposition eliminated by purges. 1936 Constitution theoretically democratic but in reality USSR ruled by the Communist Party.

Chapter 7 Autocracy and reform in Germany and Russia

1 (a) Lenin (source C) instituted 'Red Terror' to preserve the regime in civil war: Cheka, concentration camps, arbitrary 'justice'. Regime was genuinely threatened. Source implies that Lenin regarded terror as a means to an end but does not discuss whether he would have relaxed it if he had lived. Hitler (source D) saw terror as a means of controlling opinion, with propaganda as its counterpart. Used same means as Lenin – secret police and concentration camps – but Nazi terror had fewer victims than Lenin's because regime not threatened.

(b)
- Tsarist Russia: Nicholas I consistently repressive. Alexander II listened to advice of westernisers after Crimean War but when opposition developed (populists, anarchists) reverted to repression. Assassination of Alexander II confirmed Alexander III in repression (source B), which continued under Nicholas II until 1917. Even after 1905, although some concessions were made (Dumas), there was repression (Stolypin).
- Imperial Germany, by contrast, had a well-developed party system in Reichstag. Thus anti-socialist law (source A) was an exception – and even so did not keep socialists out of Reichstag or stop growth of support. But it indicates an authoritarian tendency.
- After 1917 Lenin faced 'regime-threatening opposition' (source C) – responded with Cheka and Red Terror. But opposition to War Communism led to concession (NEP). Possibly Lenin would have relaxed repression later. Stalin responded to opposition with extreme repression – forcible collectivisation, purges.
- Weimar Germany was far the most liberal regime. Arguably too much freedom was given to anti-democratic opposition (Nazis, communists).
- Nazis repressed opposition. All other parties dissolved; socialist and communist leaders imprisoned; SS, Gestapo and concentration camps (source D). But the source points out this was accompanied by propaganda to win support.
- Repression was normal response in tsarist and communist Russia: opposition seen as a threat to regime. In Germany it was not the norm, except under

Hitler – and even then opposition could not be completely suppressed (e.g. from religious leaders).

2 Russia
- No significant political reform until the 1905 revolution, but a very important social/economic reform – emancipation. This was achieved not by revolution but in response to the need to modernise Russia after defeat in the Crimean War.
- First important political reform – October Manifesto and establishment of Dumas – was result of 1905 revolution. But was this 'genuine reform'? Dumas had little power and franchise was restricted after failure of 1906 and 1907 Dumas.
- First World War led to revolution, overthrow of Tsar and Provisional Government, i.e. genuine reform. But mistakes of Provisional Government and ruthlessness of Lenin and Bolsheviks led to October Revolution.
- Lenin dissolved Constituent Assembly as soon as it met and set up a constitution based on soviets, with real power in the hands of the Politburo. On the basis of Lenin's state Stalin made himself dictator. So revolution led not to democracy but to communist dictatorship. But it also led to massive social and economic reform – collectivisation and industrialisation.

Germany
- 1848 Revolutions – failed to achieve unification or significant liberalisation of constitutions of main states.
- 1862–71 – Bismarck achieved unification, i.e. political change, by military and diplomatic means, not by revolution. Constitution of imperial Germany, though it incorporated a Reichstag elected by universal suffrage, made the Emperor the real source of authority, i.e. not political reform in the liberal sense. 1871–1918 no genuine political reform. Empire remained autocratic.
- 1918 November revolution – establishment of Weimar Republic – a genuine democracy. But Weimar failed in face of economic crisis. Hitler appointed under Weimar constitution – not a revolution. Established dictatorship by Enabling Act. I.e. not political reform in the liberal sense, but reaction.

Chapter 8 Historical investigations: 19th-century Britain

1 (a) The 1867 Act was more radical than the original Whig bill. Both sources suggest that Disraeli's motive was party advantage rather than democratic principle. Source D claims he employed 'shrewd tactics', but he had to create the 'myth' that they were based on 'lifelong convictions'. Conservatives mistrusted him, so he needed to convince them he was a man of principle, not a mere political opportunist. In any case it was difficult to get them to agree to a working-class franchise. Source E agrees about his true motives but acknowledges that it is debatable. Interpretations depend on assessment of Disraeli's character and career.

(b)
- Source A identifies three aims: maintaining the institutions of the country, upholding the empire and social reform. It is a speech by Disraeli and the basis of his victory in the 1874 election. But we cannot tell how far Disraeli genuinely believed in these ideas.
- Source B: social reform could not be the main priority for a Conservative leader, especially one who had attacked Gladstone's reforms for their assault on privilege. So he took as his 'mottoes' monarchy (upholding institutions) and the empire.
- Source C identifies three factors: appeal to the working classes (presumably by social reform); appeal to the

Chapter 8 Historical investigations: 19th-century Britain

'forces of property' (middle class as well as landowners); and the claim to be the 'patriotic party' (i.e. imperialism and a Palmerstonian foreign policy). The source gives the greatest weight to the last.

- Source D suggests that Disraeli's conduct in 1867 was essentially opportunist but began the process of making the Conservatives attractive to the working classes.
- Source E provides a similar interpretation of 1867 but links it to an assessment of the relative importance of reform and party advantage. It judges that Disraeli's greatest contribution to winning working-class support for Conservatives was imperialism.
- Overall the differences between the sources are matters of emphasis and priority. They are complementary. As a set they demonstrate how elusive both Disraeli's ideas and his contribution to Conservatism are.

2 There were differences of principle, but personal antagonism sharpened the rivalry.
- Both were involved in extension of franchise in 1867, though Disraeli's motives may have been more opportunistic than Gladstone's.
- Gladstone's domestic policies based on 'Gladstonian liberalism' (explain). Reforms of 1868–74 ministry directed towards removing privilege, providing equality of opportunity and increasing individual freedom. Reforms can be cited to support these points.
- Disraeli believed in a paternalist government protecting the poor through social reform (Crystal Palace and Manchester speeches). This led to social reforms in 1874–80 ministry (give examples) – unlike Gladstone's reforms which were administrative and legal.
- But perhaps differences not all that great. Gladstone believed in 'the aristocratic principle'. Disraeli's social reforms were more the work of Cross than Disraeli.
- They did differ on Ireland. Gladstone, with his religious convictions, believed he had a 'mission' to pacify it, while Disraeli had little interest.
- Also differed on foreign and imperial affairs. Gladstone's approach based on morality – hence paid

up over Alabama affair, condemned Turks for Bulgarian atrocities. Disraeli opposed him on these and other issues, basing his policies on British interests, patriotism and imperialism.
- Arguably, Disraeli had no principles – purely opportunistic. But Gladstone's 'principled' approach seemed to some hypocritical.

3
- Peak years of Chartist activity coincided with periods of economic depression: first and second Chartist petitions, Newport Rising, Plug Plot all during depression of 1837–43. Chartist activity subsided with prosperity after 1843 but revived with economic difficulties of 1847–8.
- Studies of local nature of Chartist activity also link it with distress – declining industries, e.g. handloom weavers in Lancashire and Yorkshire.
- Chartist activity was most marked in the newly industrialised areas, where living and working conditions caused unrest, e.g. the Plug Plots in Lancashire and the Black Country. This again shows social and economic distress as a major cause.
- Political factors were also important. At its core Chartism was a political movement making political demands which had a pedigree stretching back to the 18th-century radicals. For many Chartists the demand for the Charter was a phase in a lifetime of radical activity – Lovett is an example. Thus disappointment with the Reform Act was a key factor.
- Chartism drew on other sources of unrest, especially the failure of trade unionism (collapse of GNCTU, Tolpuddle Martyrs) and hostility to the new Poor Law. The building of workhouses in the industrial areas coincided with the depression of 1837–43. Chartism drew some of its support from taking over the anti-Poor Law movement: political, social and economic factors came together.
- Thus social and economic distress was only one among many causes of support for Chartism – but it was the one which turned it into a mass movement.

Chapter 9 Historical investigations: 20th-century Britain

1 (a) Asquith was a poor leader in war, lacked dynamism – overthrown by Lloyd George (with Conservative help). Lacked rapport with working class (source C). Lloyd George: good war leader but then carried on as PM of Conservative-dominated post-war coalition – hence lost confidence of working-class voters (source C). Saw himself as leader of a 'national' party. Used by Conservatives for own ends, then ditched – by which time Liberals were in terminal decline. The two came together in 1923 in support of free trade, but divisions papered over rather than healed (source B) Failed to develop distinctive policies (source C) or to rebuild party organisation.
(b) • Some historians interpret decline of Liberals as result of long-term social and political changes – growth of industrial working class, trade unions, Labour Party and extension of franchise. Emergence of a mass electorate in 1918 coincides suspiciously with decline of Liberals.
- Source C accepts this view and contrasts Liberals' lack of class appeal with Labour. But source D, discussing impact of the new electorate, disputes this.
- Source A provides a slightly different interpretation of

the link between rise of Labour and Liberal decline: moderate Labour was little different from 'essential' (progressive) Liberalism, i.e. Liberalism was not distinctive – but it was divided. Source D also claims that Labour had inherited 'the mantle of radicalism' and attributes this to the war.
- Some historians regard the war as the major factor – challenged Liberal ideas (increased role of government contrary to ideas of freedom) and divided them into two warring factions.
- Liberals contributed significantly to their own decline: divided leadership; failed to make themselves sufficiently attractive to the working classes, e.g. did not select working-class candidates; neglected organisation.
- Source B points to 1923 as turning point: Liberals allowed a Labour minority government but failed to take steps to prove themselves a credible alternative.
- Decline of Liberals not inevitable – many factors involved – different interpretations a matter of prioritising them. But rise of a working-class party made it very likely. Once they lost ground, electoral system worked against them.

Chapter 9 Historical investigations: 20th-century Britain

2
- At the time there was a strong case for appeasement: public opinion (horror of war); guilt over Versailles settlement; Britain's comparative military weakness; fear of USSR as an even greater threat than Germany.
- Appeasement (in effect) of Italy over Ethiopia was understandable because Italy a potential ally against Hitler (Stresa Front). Doubtful whether sanctions on oil would have worked or whether public opinion would have allowed military action. But sent out wrong message to Hitler, so doubtful if it was sensible.
- Rhineland. Many in Britain thought Hitler's action reasonable. Baldwin thought risk of war too great to intervene – but probably this was last point at which Hitler's aggression could have been checked.
- Anschluss: appeasement inevitable – little Britain could do.
- Munich. The case for appeasement: public opinion approved; Britain not prepared for war – appeasement gave time for rearmament; Sudetenland was Hitler's 'last territorial demand' – and a reasonable one, since people were German.
- Case against Munich: encouraged Hitler's belief that Britain would back down under pressure – hence occupation of Prague (March 1939) and demand for Polish Corridor; betrayed a potential ally with a strong army; alienated USSR.
- Conclusion: 1936 dividing line not helpful – with hindsight, least sensible act of appeasement was over Rhineland. But there is a case to be made for appeasement in 1938.

3
- Baldwin – shrewd politician – reassuring. Won middle ground. Portrayed Conservatives as moderates. Avoided danger of becoming an anti-working-class party.
- Conservatives had a solid core of support from the upper and middle classes. Won support of middle-class Liberals who feared socialism and benefited from the tradition of working-class Conservatism going back to Disraeli.
- Conservatives had money and support of most of the press.
- Decline of Liberals. But they were still strong enough to split the anti-Conservative vote.
- Labour – new and untried. Lacked experience. Had solid base of working-class support but frightened middle classes because of socialism. Collapse of Labour ministry in financial crisis of 1931 convinced many voters it was not fit for government. Conservatives returned to office (in the National Government) as the party which could be trusted.
- They were lucky: Zinoviev letter frightened many middle-class voters; defeat in 1929 election left Labour to face 1931 crisis.
- Conclusion: explanation is a combination of Conservatives' strengths and weakness of opposition.

Chapter 10 Historical investigations: Lenin and Stalin

1
- Terror was a major explanation but not the only one.
- Lenin established a one-party state – opponents dealt with by terror (Cheka).
- Stalin inherited this state but used terror on a different scale. Collectivisation enforced by terror. Kulak class destroyed. Industrialisation also involved use of force, as well as incentives. Failure to meet production targets was regarded as sabotage.
- Purges: removed all elements which Stalin believed were not absolutely reliable. (Refer to show trials, execution of army generals, terror at all levels in party and army.)
- But the basis of Stalin's power was control of the party organisation as General Secretary – the means by which he rose to power and removed Trotsky and other rivals in the 1920s.
- Propaganda, films and the arts were used to build up an extraordinary personality cult of Stalin as the father of his people. He seems not to have been held responsible for the hardship of the Russian people but looked up to.

2
- Russian economy before Stalin. Industrialisation under way before 1914, but still behind Western Europe; agriculture backward. Economy battered by war and civil war. Some recovery under Lenin's NEP, but at price of reintroduction of a measure of private trading.
- Agriculture – problems were: low productivity (too many small farms); jealousies between kulaks and poorer peasants; kulaks were an offence to communist ideology and able to hold Russia to ransom by reducing production.
- Stalin's solution – collectivisation. Began 1929, carried out by force, virtually complete by 1939. Result: huge loss of production (famine 1932–3), but by late 1930s grain production had recovered (but loss of livestock not made good until 1950s). Productivity remained low. But social aims were achieved – elimination of kulaks as a class (at huge cost in life).
- Industry: Five-Year Plans aimed to achieve rapid industrialisation. Planned economy – direction of labour, targets, rewards and punishments. Result: considerable growth in industry – especially capital goods, which were given priority in first and third plans. But workers saw little benefit: low wages, harsh conditions, shortages of consumer goods.
- Could it have been achieved by other means? Tsars had laid foundations for industrialisation. Need to meet impossible targets led to inefficiencies – managers competing for scarce resources.
- On balance Stalin's policies were successful, though less than used to be thought – agriculture and industry both still inefficient. Human cost was enormous.

3
- 1905 revolution sparked off by defeat in Russo-Japanese War – a humiliation but remote and with no direct effects on people in European Russia. 1917 revolution resulted from failures in First World War, which had much more serious effects – food shortages, transport breakdown, loss of life (husbands and brothers). Unrest in 1905 was confined to a few major centres, especially St Petersburg and Moscow – rural areas little affected. More widespread in 1917 – by the summer peasants were seizing land throughout Russia. Crucially, army remained loyal in 1905 – in 1917 it joined the revolution, mainly because of defeat in war.
- Why the difference? (a) War demonstrated incompetence of regime. (b) Tsarist regime failed to take advantage of recovery after 1905. Dumas allowed very little power, Nicholas ruled as autocrat, repression stepped up (Stolypin's terror). (c) Loss of respect for Tsar – Bloody Sunday, role as commander in war, Rasputin.

Chapter 11 Historical investigations: Bismarck and Hitler

1 (a) Source A argues Bismarck did not want war until he thought France had decided on war; the Hohenzollern candidature was designed to test French intentions. Source D offers three possible explanations, pointing out that the Ems Telegram affair does not prove that he wanted war from the outset. Source A is valuable because it comes from a Prussian diplomat. Source D is valuable because it shows that the matter is still debatable. Modern historians tend to favour the third interpretation in source D – Bismarck was prepared for war but was seeking to gain maximum advantage from the situation by diplomacy if possible, by war if necessary. This fits with source A.

(b) • Bismarck later claimed that he had followed 'a set plan of war and diplomacy'. But source C doubts this – it is an interpretation 'imposed on events after they took place'. Instead it sees him as an opportunist.

• Even if he did not plan the whole sequence of events, source B claims that Bismarck deliberately planned war with Austria, with the aim of 'Prussian domination of Germany', not unification. This would accord with his attitude towards Austria in the 1850s as ambassador to the Diet of the Confederation.

• Source D argues that one possible interpretation of 1870 is that he deliberately sought war to achieve final unification. But two other possibilities are advanced: (a) that war was forced on him, and (b) that he sought a diplomatic victory with the aim of taking over the southern states (i.e. final unification), but opted for war when he failed to achieve his object.

• Source A claims Bismarck did not plan war but decided on it when he regarded it as inevitable. This supports C's view of him as an opportunist. The fact that it is by a Prussian diplomat adds weight.

• The matter remains controversial. Germany's 20th-century history directed attention to the manner of its unification but the evidence does not exist for a final conclusion. French and German historians naturally took different views.

2 • Main reason is that revolutionaries in 1848–9 were divided about their aims: some advocated Greater Germany, others supported Little Germany, excluding Austria. I.e. ambivalent about Austria. Main aim was unification – ending Austria's influence simply as by-product of setting up a Little Germany. Religion also a divisive factor – Greater Germany would be predominantly Catholic, Little Germany predominantly Protestant.

• Bismarck, by contrast, was single-minded in his determination to assert Prussian predominance in Germany at the expense of Austria – unification was almost a by-product. Refer to his conduct in 1850s as Prussian ambassador to Diet of Confederation.

• Frankfurt parliament lacked means to enforce constitution of Little Germany against the princes – no army. Bismarck had well-equipped Prussian army.

• 1849: Frederick William IV of Prussia in 1848 refused to accept crown from a liberal assembly. Bismarck had

confidence of William II.

• Bismarck's diplomacy was crucial to success. Used Schleswig-Holstein dispute to win support of German nationalist opinion and provide excuse to pick a quarrel with Austria. Then isolated Austria – allied with Italy, kept Russia and France neutral. Aim achieved by victory in Seven Weeks War.

3 • Nazis came to power because they seemed to offer economic stability, restoration of national pride, strong leadership and end of Communist threat. Ability to win support depended on success in these.

• Elimination of unemployment and revival of economy won much support. Policies appealed to many groups in German society. Core support came from lower middle and skilled working classes, but also supported by peasants (benefited from import controls and fixed farm prices), industrialists (Nazis a bulwark against Communism), and even much of industrial working class (full employment). Weaknesses of economic policy, especially probability of inflation, not apparent by 1939.

• Foreign policy restored national pride (selected details).

• Hitler projected image of strong leadership – Führer principle.

• Propaganda reinforced loyalty. Skill of Goebbels.

• True extent of support hard to determine because of suppression of opposition. Some overt criticism from Churches. Probably many Germans ignored aspects they disliked because of (a) Nazi successes, (b) risks involved in open dissent. But overall Nazis seem to have had widespread genuine support.

4 Main examples of tactical skill and ability to exploit opponents' weaknesses:

• Reoccupation of Rhineland (timed to exploit breakdown of Stresa Front as result of Italian invasion of Ethiopia)

• Rome–Berlin Axis – also exploited breakdown of Stresa Front

• Anschluss – exploited unfairness of Versailles to Germans. Since Austria was German, there were no grounds for opposition.

• Sudetenland – based on same tactics. Successful tactics in pressurising Chamberlain, exploiting British reluctance to contemplate war.

• Nazi-Soviet Pact: exploited mutual mistrust between western powers and USSR. Purely tactical, as shown by invasion of Russia in 1941 – purpose was to enable Hitler to invade Poland.

Overall Hitler exploited general fear of another war, British guilt feelings over harshness of Versailles and slowness to rearm. His demands were often difficult to oppose because he had a case (Rhineland, Austria, Sudetenland, even Polish Corridor). But his successes were also the result of mistakes by British and French: Anglo-German Naval Agreement (suggested Versailles could be revised); failure to oppose reoccupation of Rhineland; Chamberlain's belief at Munich that Hitler could be trusted; failure to seek Russian support.

Index

abdication crisis 124
Act of Union 46
Alexander II 75–6, 82, 91
Alexander III 76, 82, 84, 90, 91
anarchists 81, 91
Anglo-Irish war 49
Anschluss 121, 146–7
anti-semitism 76, 142
appeasement 120–2, 124
Asquith 26, 116–17
Attlee 24
Austria 55–8, 59, 121, 139–40, 146–7
Austrian wars 57–8, 139
autocracy 89–90
Baldwin 23, 116, 123
BBC 28
Berlin Wall 70
Beveridge Report 36
Bismarck 56, 57–8, 59–60, 90, 91, 138–41
Bloody Sunday 77
Bolsheviks 82, 83, 84, 91, 92, 95, 129–32
Brezhnev 85
Bundesbank 69
Bundesrat 89, 141
Bundestag 55–6
Cadet Party 82
Catholic emancipation 51
Catholics 46–7, 59
Chamberlain 121–2, 124
Chartists 19–20, 34, 101–4
church 40, 105–6, 142
Churchill 26
coal mines 39
collectivisation 83, 85, 95, 96, 134–5
communes 76, 84
communist dictatorship 79–81
Communist Party 83, 94, 133–4
communists 69, 93–6, 131–2
concentration camps 142, 144
conscription 116, 120, 145
Conservatives 21, 23, 25, 27–8, 33, 105, 107–8, 115–17, 123
Corn Laws 19, 105
Czechoslovakia 118, 121, 122, 147
Danish wars 57–8, 139
Dawes Plan 66
Deutschmark 68
disarmament 120, 145
Disraeli 22, 105, 106, 107–9
Dumas 77–8, 82, 89, 92
East Germany 69–70
Easter Rising 48–9, 51
education 40–2
Education Acts 27, 41, 42, 106, 115
Edwardian age 35
electoral reform 17–20

Ethiopia 120, 146
European Economic Community 69
factory legislation 39–40
Fenians 47, 48, 53
First World War 61, 65–6, 84, 92, 116, 117
Five-Year Plans 85, 95–6, 134
foreign policy 108
France 58, 59, 60, 140
Franco-Prussian War 58, 140
Frankfurt Parliament 56
free trade 60, 105–6
Gaitskell 24
General Strike 27, 77, 123
Geneva Protocol 120
German Confederation 55–6, 58, 138–40
German Democratic Republic 69–70
German economy 57, 60, 64–6, 68–9
German Empire 58, 59–61
German industrialisation 64
German military 60
German nationalism 55–6, 59–61, 142
German politics 90–1
German rearmament 120
German revolutions 56, 92
German unification 138–41
Germany – post-war 68–9, 118
Gestapo 96, 142, 144
Gladstone 22, 48, 51, 105–7, 108–9, 114
Goebbels 142, 144
Goering 144
Great Depression 66
Great Reform Act 19–20
Heath 25, 26
Himmler 142–4
Hitler 67, 95, 96, 120, 121–2, 141–7
Home Rule 48, 50, 51, 114
House of Commons 20–1
House of Lords 22
housing 38
humanitarians 32
imperial Germany 89–90
Irish economy 52–3
Irish Free State 49
Irish nationalism 46–9
Irish parliament 46, 49
Irish reforms 51
Irish religion 46
Irish Republican Army 49
Italy 120, 140
Japanese 120
Junkers 139–41
Kaiser 89, 92
Khrushchev 85
Kornilov affair 130
Labour 23, 24–5, 26–7, 32, 33, 115, 117, 124
laissez faire 32
Land Purchase Acts 53

land tenure 52
League of Nations 119, 120, 145
Lenin 79–80, 82–5, 91–5, 129–32, 135
Liberal Democrats 26
Liberals 21–2, 23, 26, 32–3, 35, 105–7, 114–17
Lloyd George 22, 23, 49, 116, 118–20
Locarno Treaties 119–20
MacDonald 23, 26, 119–20, 123–4
Manchuria 120
Marxism 94, 129, 132
media 27–8
Mensheviks 82, 91, 129–30
Metternich 55–6
Munich Conference 121, 122, 147
Mussolini 146
Napoleonic period 55
National Government 26, 124
National Health Service 36
nationalisation 124
NATO 124
Navy League 60
Nazis 66–70, 93–5, 96, 141–5
Nazi-Soviet Pact 121
New Economic Policy 80, 83, 84, 95, 131–3
Nicholas II 76, 78, 82, 91
North German Confederation 58, 59, 91, 140
O'Connell 47
O'Connor 102–4
Octobrists 82
Orange Order 49–50
Orthodox Church 75, 90
Palmerston 105
Pan-German League 60
parliamentary reform 17–20, 101–2
partition 51
peasants 83
Peel 47, 51, 105–6, 107
Poland 118, 121, 145, 147
police states 93
Politburo 79, 80, 81, 94
Poor Law 33–7, 102
populists 81, 91
potato famine 47, 52–3
protection 60
Protestants 46, 49–50
Provisional Government 79, 130, 132
Prussia 55–60, 69, 138–41
public health 37–8
purges 83, 94, 95, 96, 134
radio 28
Red Army 80, 81, 83, 94, 95
Red Terror 131
Reform Acts 17–18, 101, 107, 114
Reich 59–60

Reichstag 89, 91, 141, 144
reparations 65–6, 69, 119
repression 76–7, 79–81, 91
Russia and Second World War 81
Russia 59, 145
Russian dictatorships 75–85
Russian economy 80, 84–5
Russian industrialisation 134
Russian Liberals 82
Russian nuclear industry 85
Russian parliament 77
Russian revolutions 77, 78–9, 92, 129–30
Russo-Japanese War 77
Second Reform Act 20
Second Reich 90, 91, 92, 141
Second World War 68, 85, 121, 147
secret police 79–81, 90, 93–4, 131, 142
serfdom 75
Sinn Fein 48–9
Social Democratic Party 26, 82, 91, 129
social reform 32–3, 106
Social Revolutionaries 82, 91
socialists 91
Soviet Union 93–5
Soviets 79
SS 96, 142, 144
Stalin 80–1, 83, 84–5, 94–6, 131, 133–5
Stolypin 78, 84
television 28
textile mills 39
Thatcher 25–6, 27
Tories 18–19
trade unions 26–7, 101, 123
Trotsky 82, 83, 131–3
tsarist autocracy 75–8, 88–90, 91–2
Ulster Unionism 49–50, 51
Ulster Volunteer Force 50
Union of Soviet Socialist Republics 80, 83, 95, 121, 133
United Irishmen 46
utilitarians 32
Versailles settlement 118–19, 120, 144, 145, 146
War Communism 80, 84, 95, 131–2
Weimar constitution 92–3
welfare state 24, 33, 35, 36–7, 124
Weltpolitik 60, 61
West Germany 68–9
Whigs 18–19, 101, 105, 114
Whites 82–3
William II 60, 61, 90, 91
Wilson 24–5, 26
Witte 84
women's suffrage 22
workhouse 34
Young Ireland 47
Zollverein 57, 64